THE JESUS PUSHER

COLLECTION 2

THE
JESUS
PUSHER #2

a 365 day exploration of Jesus

Stephen Manley

CROSS
STYLE
PRESS

The Jesus Pusher: Collection 2
a 365 day exploration of Jesus

© 2022 by Stephen Manley

Paperback ISBN: 978-1-957219-98-1
eBook ISBN: 978-1-957219-99-8

CrossStyle.org

Introduction

I am a Jesus pusher!!! The root of the Greek word "doulos," translated "slave" or "servant," is used one hundred eight-two times in the New Testament. Some uses refer to an addiction. Peter wrote, "While they promise them liberty, they themselves are slaves of corruption; for by whom a person is overcome, by him also he is brought into bondage," (2 Peter 2:19). This is an emphasis of addiction and is highlighted many times with the word "doulos."

We must be addicted to Jesus. We were created by Him and for Him (Colossians 1:16). The absence of His presence creates a living hunger, which only Jesus can fill (Matthew 5:6). I am addicted to Jesus. One moment without Him and I have withdrawal pains. He is not a fix that wears off and I must seek Him again. His presence consistently fulfills my life. I must be aware of Him every moment. If He were removed from my life death would be immediate. Without Jesus I have no resource. Without Him I am a glove without a hand, an engine without fuel, a book without letters, supper without food, a car without a driver, or a job without a worker. Nothing happens without Him. I cannot get by without Him. He does not just make life better; He is life.

I am addicted to Jesus. I seek nothing but Him. I have no other desire in life. Join me in seeking Jesus. I am a Jesus pusher!!!

– Stephen Manley

Jesus PUSHER | 1

I am a Jesus pusher!!!

"Blessed are the meek," (Matthew 5:5). We must clarify the definition of meekness. What is the exact quality we are discussing? The Greek word "prautes," translated **meek**, bespeaks a quiet and gentle spirit. This is contrasted with the proud and arrogant Scribes and Pharisees. In years gone by the English word for "gentleman" expressed the clear meaning of **meek**, but has long since lost its meaning. Our English word "meek" comes from the old Anglo-Saxon word "meca." It means a companion or equal. The one who is meek or gentle will associate with all mankind. He has no feelings of superiority; he knows what he has spiritually or temporally he has received from the goodness of God.

The focus of the Greek word "prautes," translated **meek** is God. Primarily it means inward grace of the soul, not outward expression of feeling. It is calmness toward God. It is the atmosphere of the heart accepting God's dealings, seeing them as good in that they enhance closeness in relationship with Him. It is the ability to see all the circumstances of life through the lens of Jesus. This person does no dispute or resist but accepts and embraces. You and I are lifted to a new level of confidence and security in Christ. This level of living expresses itself in all our relationships with each other. We are an expression of meekness, our confidence in Jesus. I am a Jesus pusher!!!

Jesus PUSHER | 2

I am a Jesus pusher!!!

"Blessed are the meek," (Matthew 5:5). We must always remember the sequence of the Beatitudes. When we accept poverty in our spirits, mourning happens. Mourning is the response of my heart to Jesus as my Source in my state of helplessness. As Jesus comes in His fullness, I come to a realization. All His dealings are trustworthy and true. The circumstances of my life are beyond my control. I cannot govern what people may or may not do to me. I am helpless. I cannot eliminate sickness, events of nature, and reversals of life. He knows my frailties. None of these are greater than He is. He has a plan. Meekness is **"And we know that all things work together for good to those who love God, to those who are the called according to His purpose,"** (Romans 8:28).

This attitude is closely linked with "humility." This attitude eliminates fighting against God. Struggling and contending with Him over the circumstances of my life are quieted by the quality of "meekness." I rest in His loving arms. Self-sourcing is filled with agitation and anxiety. I am quickly exhausted by my exhausting efforts. Little or no progress quickly depresses me. Hopelessness invades the depths of my soul. The awareness of being overwhelmed by the pressures of my life brings me to despair. In my helplessness I must mourn and find meekness in Him. The flow of meekness immediately affects my relationship with others. Self-sourcing expresses agitation and anxiety towards everyone. This complicates my circumstances. I must rest in Jesus in meekness. This brings strength and peace to those around me. Jesus is my only answer. I am a Jesus pusher!!!

Jesus PUSHER | 3

I am a Jesus pusher!!!

"Blessed are the meek," (Matthew 5:5). One of the great misunderstandings of the English term "meek" is its attachment to weakness. Many view meekness as a lack of courage or timidity. The weakling bows in meekness before the bully because he has no choice. But this is not the condition of the Beatitude. If the first Beatitude which declares my helplessness is my dwelling place, this might be true. But I embrace my weakness with mourning as in the second Beatitude. Mourning is my response to Jesus who is sourcing me. All the resource of Jesus is now present in my being. There is no lack of power. This Greek word "prautes," translated **meek**, was used by the Greeks to describe a horse that had been broken. It refers to power under control.

Jesus is the pure demonstration of the Spirit-sourced man. He declared Himself as *"I am gentle* (meek) *and lowly in heart"* (Matthew 11:29). His life was a demonstration of power and might. Demons tremble in His presence; death is revoked by His word. He lives in the sequence of the first three Beatitudes. His meekness is an expression of the Spirit who sourced Him. In His helplessness, Jesus mourned. His mourning is the uniting of His helplessness to the Spirit of His Father. This brings about great power, which can never be used for self-interest or self-assertion. He fulfills the plan of God. This is the picture of your life in Christ. I am a Jesus pusher!!!

Jesus PUSHER | 4

I am a Jesus Pusher!!! Meekness is a focus on God, not described by a God's actions but by His inner Spirit. When man recognizes his helplessness he responds with mourning. The mourning is a response to the presence of the Spirit of Jesus filling the person. Meekness is the atmosphere generated by God as He sources the helpless man, which affects all other relationships, producing peace in the relationships. This peace in the inner soul is so great that this God sourced person is not moved by insults. If we live in a state of unrest over insults, we are at the mercy of those who choose to disturb us, and we are constantly ruffled and upset, always distracted from that which God plans to accomplish through us.

You can tell how close someone is to Jesus if you look at when the person gets angry and what that anger is about. The person who is **meek** is not someone who never gets angry. We see this in Jesus as He cleanses the temple (Matthew 21:12). Do not think that a person who never gets angry is Spirit-sourced. Meekness means we get angry at the right time, at the right things, and never at the wrong time about the wrong things. The self-sourced person finds this impossible. Jesus is our only chance! I am a Jesus pusher!

Jesus PUSHER | 5

I am a Jesus pusher!!! Jesus said, *"Blessed are the meek, for they shall inherit the earth."* This is not a new theme because it is interwoven throughout the Gospel presentation. The spiritual status and physical effects of salvation are coupled together. We can see the Kingdom of God, a spiritual change, in those who are filled with Jesus and enabled by God to embrace their physical world. Think of the truth! The meek, a spiritual attitude of a person who embraces Jesus, possess the physical world.

Moses gave insight into the methodical plan God used in creation. Man was the crowning act and the manifold purpose of God's plan. *Then God blessed them, and God said to them, "Be fruitful and multiply; fill the earth and subdue it; have dominion over the fish of the sea, over the birds of the air, and over every living thing that moves on the earth"* (Genesis 1:28). God purposed that man's existence was connected to the Earth, and He designed the Earth to thrive under the direction and leadership of man. In fact, *the Lord God formed man of the dust of the ground* (Genesis 2:7). God made man from dust. We cannot ignore the interaction of the spiritual and physical life. We manifest our inner spiritual state in our physical responses on a daily basis. Our physical life shapes and molds our spiritual state. Jesus wants to be at the core of this interaction. It is in Jesus that we find spiritual and physical wholeness. I am a Jesus pusher!!!

Jesus PUSHER | 6

I am a Jesus pusher!!! Jesus promised that the meek would inherit the Earth (Matthew 5:5). He declared a link between the physical and the spiritual. Man's sin affects the Earth, which shows the connection between man and the Earth. Listen to what God said, *"Cursed is the ground for your sake; in toil you shall eat of it all the days of your life. Both thorns and thistles it shall bring forth for you, and you shall eat the herb of the field"* (Genesis 3:17-18). Paul recognized that the sin of man infected the offspring of all mankind as well as the earth and all creation. In other words, man is so linked to all creation that his sin ushers everyone and everything under its curse. Paul said, *"For we know that the whole creation groans and labors with birth pangs together until now. Not only that, but we also who have the firstfruits of the Spirit, even we ourselves groan within ourselves, eagerly waiting for the adoption, the redemption of our body"* (Romans 8:22-23).

As the story of redemption unfolds through the patriarchal stories, the writers highlight the "land." God began with Abram, giving him a command with a promise. *"Get out of your country, from your family and from your father's house, to a land that I will show you"* (Genesis 12:1). Israel believed that God had promised and ordained their possession of Canaan. God was also focused on "land" when he said to Jacob, *"Return to the land of your fathers and to your family, and I will be with you"* (Genesis 31:3). Our physical lives are to be blessed by God's spiritual presence in us! Jesus is the answer to our spiritual and physical life! I am a Jesus pusher!!!

Jesus PUSHER | 7

I am a Jesus Pusher!!!

The story of Moses is focused on "the land." God revealed His motivation for delivering Israel from Egyptian land when He said, *"I have surely seen the oppression of My people who are in Egypt, and have heard their cry because of their taskmasters, for I know their sorrows. So I have come down to deliver them out of the hand of the Egyptians, and to bring them up from that land to a good and large land, to a land flowing with milk and honey"* (Exodus 3:7-8). God's chosen role for Moses was that he leads the Israelites to this land. At the end of Moses' life, God allowed him to see "the land" with his own eyes. *"This is the land of which I swore to give Abraham, Isaac, and Jacob, saying, 'I will give it to your descendants'"* (Deuteronomy 34:4).

From the Book of Exodus to the Book of Numbers the thought that God gives Israel the land is common. In the Book of Deuteronomy, Moses' last address to the people prior to their entry into the Promised Land is presented. Possession is possible only because God gave the land to the Israelites and drove out the Canaanites. In the Book of Judah, Joshua received the divine command and repeated it (Joshua 1:2, 10-11). Joshua takes "the land" and divides it by lot to Israel as an inheritance (Joshua 13:1 and 7). Jesus' promised to those who are filled with His spirit will have this physical aspect of "inheriting the land." I am a Jesus Pusher!!!

Jesus PUSHER | 8

I am a Jesus pusher!!! In the full view of the Old and New Testaments, the concept of **inherit** becomes very important. There are three Greek words coming from this word group. "Kleronomeo" is the Greek word for our Beatitude. It is the verb meaning, "to receive an inheritance." "Kleronomia" is a noun referring to the actual inheritance of possession. "Kleronomos" is a noun referring to the heir who receives the inheritance.

Paul is the New Testament writer who most effectively deals with this subject. In reality the Jewish Christians wanted Gentiles to become Jews, meaning only Jews could be Christians. Consider his words carefully as he describes "inheritance." ***Now to Abraham and his Seed were the promises made. He does not say, "And to seeds," as of many, but as of one, "And to your Seed," who is Christ*** (Galatians 3:16).

Paul understood the promise of "the land" being given to ***Abraham and his Seed.*** This was singular and clearly stated by Paul in reference to Christ. Therefore, all Old Testament references that spoke of "the land" as an inheritance belonged to Jesus. "The land" given to Jesus by the Father is the Kingdom of God. This Kingdom is the union of man with the Spirit of God. This union brings wholeness to both the spiritual and physical. This was the reason for Jesus "congratulating" ***the poor in spirit***, ***the Kingdom of Heaven.*** Thank you, Jesus! I am a Jesus pusher!!!

Jesus PUSHER | 9

I am a Jesus pusher!!! Let us clearly say: ***"Blessed are the meek, for they shall inherit the earth"*** (not CONQUER it). The focus of mankind is to conquer, master, and overpower, giving us a sense of power and the right to ownership. We need to be grateful to no one for we have secured our rights by the might of our own resources. But this is not the way of the Kingdom of Heaven. The first Beatitude says, ***"Blessed are the poor in spirit, for theirs is the kingdom of heaven"*** (Matthew 5:3). In our helplessness, we can only possess the Kingdom if we inherit it.

Paul's difficulty with the Jewish Christians was the Law. When the requirement of "doing" is attached to Christianity, it becomes what I conquer by my self-sourcing. I am no longer ***poor in spirit***, and the Kingdom of Heaven is no longer my state of being. Paul said, ***"For if the inheritance is of the law, it is no longer of promise, but God gave it to Abraham by promise"*** (Galatians 3:18). The inheritance is always a promise or it is not an inheritance. Our doing nullifies our helplessness, which enables Jesus to embrace us. It is in this embrace the Kingdom takes place. What part does the Law have in this? Where is the call to "doing?" It is a call to respond and accept! It is all in Jesus. I am joint-heirs with Jesus (Romans 8:17)! I am a Jesus pusher!!!

Jesus
PUSHER | **10**

I am a Jesus pusher!!! ***"Blessed are the meek, for they shall inherit the earth"*** (Matthew 5:5). Throughout Paul's discourse in Galatians about this inheritance, he consistently refers to "faith." He says, ***"But that no one is justified by the law in the sight of God is evident, for 'the just shall live by faith.' Yet the law is not of faith, but 'the man who does them shall live by them'"*** (Galatians 3:11-12). Faith is "invoking the activity of the second party." Faith is admitting and embracing my helplessness in order that One greater than I might source me. Faith is consistently saying: "I cannot; I am not adequate; I am helpless." It is in this state of being that I embrace Jesus; He establishes the Kingdom in me.

The difficulty of this issue is that we all have lived under the Law (doing). This method of self-sourcing became our pattern. We must not misunderstand the role of this Law. Paul wrote: ***"But before faith came, we were kept under guard by the law, kept for the faith which would afterward be revealed. Therefore the law was our tutor to bring us to Christ, that we might be justified by faith. But after faith has come, we are no longer under a tutor. For you are all sons of God through faith in Christ Jesus"*** (Galatians 3:23-26). We must embrace our helplessness and "invoke the activity of Jesus!" No wonder I am a Jesus pusher!!!

Jesus PUSHER | 11

I am a Jesus pusher!!! Let it be clearly said: *"**Blessed are the meek, for they shall inherit the earth"** (not COLLECT it). You cannot earn **the earth** (the Kingdom of God). The idea of **inherit** bespeaks relationship. The reason you inherit is because you are related. As Paul speaks of "inheritance," he equally speaks of "sons." He writes, *"**And if you are Christ's, then you are Abraham's seed, and heirs according to the promise"** (Galatians 3:29). God (the Trinity) made a promise to Abraham and his Seed. It was not plural (seeds) but singular (Seed). It was not dependent on the accomplishment (doing) of the Law, for the promise was given four hundred and thirty years before the Law (Galatians 3:17). The Law was simply a **tutor** and **kept us under guard** until Jesus came (Galatians 3:23 and 25). Now Jesus has received **the promise**. Since we belong to Him, we are **Abraham's seed**. We are heirs to **the promise**; the inheritance is ours! This is all based on our relationship with Jesus.

Jesus is at the core of everything spiritual and physical in our lives. He cannot be isolated to a single function of life. The secret is not in our "doing" but in our "embracing." Intimacy with Jesus is the single factor for both the physical and spiritual realms of my life. No wonder I am a Jesus pusher!!!

Jesus PUSHER | 12

I am a Jesus pusher!!! ***"Blessed are the meek, for they shall inherit the earth"*** (Matthew 5:5). In the embrace of His Person, we enter into the fullness of the Kingdom. The Kingdom of Heaven is the union of the fullness of God and the fullness of man. The Spirit of God sources man in his helplessness. Man receives and responds to all God is within him. This cannot be earned; it is by inheritance. When an individual inherits, he has not worked for it. It is the product or conquest of someone else. When an individual inherits, he enters into the labor of another. If you earn or conquer, you do it in your own strength. But how can we earn or conquer? We are helpless! If our inheritance is a product of Jesus' labor, we must be in relationship with Him. All that the Father did in and through Jesus produced our inheritance. We have yet to discover the wonder of its fullness!

Inherit fits the total concept of the Beatitudes. A person is ***blessed*** when he embraces his helplessness. In responding to Jesus, he has God indwelling and sourcing him. God is the Creator and Sustainer of the universe, all things. Why should anyone who has the Creator in him actively seek that which already belongs to his Father? The ***blessed*** person is a child of God and an heir to His Kingdom. ***The Spirit Himself bears witness with our spirit that we are children of God, and if children, then heirs — heirs of God and joint heirs with Christ,*** (Romans 8:16-17). We are ***blessed***. I am a Jesus pusher!!!

Jesus PUSHER | 13

I am a Jesus pusher!!! Let it be stated: ***"Blessed are the meek for they shall inherit the earth"*** (not CREATE it). An inheritance is solely created, gathered together, and provided by someone else. It is not our making. But how can it be, we are helpless? In our self-sourcing, we create for ourselves. We have many problems to which we must create solutions. There are an abundance of questions to which we must create answers. If we do not create, supply, and resource, how will we survive? Enemies surround us; we must create defense. The list goes on and on!

The Hebrew writer declared a ***rest***. ***"Therefore, since a promise remains of entering His rest, let us fear lest any of you seem to have come short of it*** (Hebrews 4:1). ***There remains therefore a rest for the people of God"*** (Hebrews 4:9). Exactly how do you describe the ***rest*** available to those who are sons of God? Is life to be without purpose and accomplishment? His definition is concise: ***"For he who has entered His rest has himself also ceased from his works as God did from His"*** (Hebrews 4:10). The works of God described by the writer are those of creation (Hebrews 4:4). God rested from creating. We are now to enter into His rest and cease from creating. It is a sourcing issue! He created me helpless; I must rest in His creation. He created me to respond; I must live in the response of mourning. His nature is meek; I must rest in His meekness. The whole earth is His creation; I must rest in my inheritance. ***"But seek first the kingdom of God and His righteousness, and all these things shall be added to you"*** (Matthew 6:33). I am a Jesus pusher!!!

Jesus PUSHER | 14

I am a Jesus pusher!!! ***"Blessed are those who hunger and thirst for righteousness, for they shall be filled"*** (Matthew 5:6). In the year 1820, a great whale rammed and sank the whaling vessel "Essex" in the South Pacific. As it sank, the captain and crew climbed into the three whaleboats. These were twenty-five foot sea going rowboats that would carry the survivors more than three thousand miles, over a period of 93 days, to the coast of South America. Those who survived the journey described the voyage as three months of constant torture. As the first mate, Owen Chase, recorded in his journal, "The privation of water is justly ranked among the most dreadful of the miseries of our life … The violence of raving thirst has no parallel in the catalogue of human calamities." On the twenty-third day after the sinking of their ship, he wrote, "[Our] thirst had become now incessantly more intolerable than our hunger, and the quantity then allowed [half a pint per day] was barely sufficient to keep the mouth in a state of moisture, for about one third of the time … In vain was every expedient try to relieve the raging fever of the throat … Our suffering during these … days almost exceeded human belief." [*In the Heart of the Sea*, p. 116]

We are faced again with another ludicrous Beatitude. Congratulations to those found on a small boat three thousand miles from shore without drinkable water. The physical condition described above, now transferred to a spiritual condition, and only highlights the deep pain contained in the inner soul of the being. How could such a condition be tolerated in the spiritual area of one's life? It is a thirst for Jesus! I am a Jesus pusher!!!

Jesus PUSHER | 15

I am a Jesus pusher!!! We are continually brought back to the progression found in the Beatitudes. It begins with the absolute helplessness and complete dependency of the inner spirit (Matthew 5:3). We never move beyond this condition. When an all-sufficient God and an all-insufficient man embrace, the Kingdom of Heaven is produced. We do not enter into the Kingdom; we become the Kingdom. "A new creature" is born in this embrace. When such poverty of spirit is embraced, mourning is experienced (Matthew 5:4). Mourning is the atmosphere allowing and causing us to respond to our Comforter.

The quality most evident from this relationship is "meekness" (Matthew 5:5). It is a distinct calmness toward God. It is the quality of the heart accepting God's dealing as good in that it enhances the closeness of relationship with Him. I am content in Him and His plan. This gives me one focus, hunger, and thirst (Matthew 5:6). I must have Him! All other drives of the human body and spirit are overridden with this one passion. I realize my need for Jesus as the singular satisfaction of the soul. All other attempts to find satisfaction (from talent, knowledge, materialism, and self-righteousness) are square pegs in round holes. Only Jesus is adequate to fill the deep cavern of my soul! I hunger and thirst for Him! Nothing and no one else is considered. He is my One focus. I am a Jesus pusher!!!

Jesus PUSHER | 16

I am a Jesus pusher!!! Each of the Beatitude contains severe language. The Greek word "ptochos," translated ***the poor,*** is the worst picture of poverty; it is begging poor (Matthew 5:3). It is the person who crouches in shame, totally destitute, helpless, and dependent on others. The Greek word "penthountes," translated, ***who mourn,*** is used throughout the Old Testament Septuagint for "lamenting at death" (Matthew 5:4), describing grief too deep for concealment. This word is often joined with the Greek word "klaio," translated "wee" or "to weep audibly." We discover the same truth in the "meekness" of the third Beatitude (Matthew 5:5). This was radical for the culture of Jesus' day. In fact, the entire idea of humility or gentleness was unused by the Greek writers before the Christian era.

Now we come to ***hunger*** "peinao" ***and thirst*** "dipsao" ***for righteousness*** (Matthew 5:6). The equivalent English word for the Greek word "peinao," is translated "starved" or "famished." It speaks to the deprivation of the substance needed. These severe terms portray the depth of our need and in the greatness of Jesus' provision. Think of what the ***Kingdom of Heaven*** must be in light of our helplessness. If the "mourning" is grief that cannot be concealed, of what must our comfort consist? Our "inheritance" of exaltation will surely be as high as "meekness" was low! The intensity of our ***hunger and thirst*** will be satisfied with an equal filling. Jesus is all of these things for us! I am a Jesus pusher!!!

Jesus PUSHER | 17

I am a Jesus pusher!!! ***"Blessed are those who hunger and thirst for righteousness, for they shall be filled"*** (Matthew 5:6). There is a ROUTINE to be recognized by all that involuntarily ***hunger and thirst***. These are inborn characteristics of our physical existence. **Hunger and thirst** are sourced by the essence of our physical structure. We do not set an alarm to tell us when to be hungry. We do not plan periods of time when we will be thirsty. Both hungering and thirsting are repeated occurrences woven into being alive. The only person who does not get hungry or thirsty is the individual who is either sick or dead.

This parallels our condition of ***poor in spirit***. We are not helpless, hungry, or thirsty due to sin. We are created by God to live in such a state. He created within the very fibers of our existence a craving for His person. We were built for Him! Sin definitely affects this hunger and thirst. The sickness of demonic control attempts to satisfy our soul with substitutes. But the prevenient grace of God will not let us go. When a person is alive in Jesus, he recognizes his hunger and thirst for Jesus. He does not have to try to become hungry or thirsty for Jesus; his nature produces it. His ***hunger and thirst*** are not by effort; ***hunger and thirst*** are from the state of his being in Christ. We are hungry for Jesus. I am a Jesus pusher!!!

Jesus PUSHER | 18

I am a Jesus pusher!!! ***"Blessed are those who hunger and thirst for righteousness, for they shall be filled"*** (Matthew 5:6). What is the RESPONSE of the individual who hungers and thirsts? We do not turn to the resources within to satisfy the hungering or thirsting. Food or water must come from outside the physical being to quench the thirst or satisfy the hunger. Try such an experiment for yourself. Allow your physical structure to satisfy your hunger or thirst for a day. In fact, let nothing external enter your physical body for two days. Extend this experiment to an entire week. You and I do not have the ability within us to either find food or to produce it. We must respond to the raw materials that present themselves to us.

All that feeds, satisfies, and grows our inner spiritual being is found outside of ourselves. Jesus is the supply! Understand our language. Jesus wants to indwell us. He instructed us, ***"He who eats My flesh and drinks My blood abides in Me, and I in him"*** (John 6:56). While He may be within me, supplying every need of my life, He is not "me." I am not discovering the answer to hunger within the existence of myself. He has come! I am helpless; He is my strength! I am mourning; He is my Comforter! I am proud and self-sufficient; He is my meekness! I am hungry and thirsty; He is my sustenance! He is my all in all! I am a Jesus pusher!!!

Jesus PUSHER | 19

I am a Jesus pusher!!! ***"Blessed are those who hunger and thirst for righteousness, for they shall be filled"*** (Matthew 5:6). Contained within the imagery of "hungering and thirsting" is the awareness of continuation, REPEATING. While we may overeat and say, "I will never eat again," it is simply not true. We have satisfaction and sufficiency, but only for a brief time. In the Greek text, "peinao," translated ***hunger,*** and "dipsao," translated ***thirst,*** are participles in the nominative case (verbs acting as adjectives of the subject). The subject becomes "the hungering and thirsting ones." Both of these participles are in the present tense. Some scholars call it the "present durative tense." The present tense indicates durative or continuing action. This indicates that "the hunger and thirst after righteousness" is continuous.

Jesus expressed this truth to the "woman at the well." He asked her to secure Him a drink from the well. He quickly moved the conversation to the reality of what He desired to give her, living water! She did not understand how this could be. Jesus answered and said to her, ***"Whoever drinks of this water will thirst again, but whoever drinks of the water that I shall give him will never thirst"*** (John 4:13-14a). It appears that this contradicts the continual satisfaction of thirst. But notice carefully the rest of His statement: ***"But the water that I shall give him will become in him a fountain of water springing up into everlasting life"*** (John 4:14b). The idea of never thirsting again is in the context of the thirst being continually satisfied by a fountain of water within the individual. It bespeaks man's continual thirsting and Jesus' presence being the satisfaction in our lives. I am a Jesus pusher!!!

I am a Jesus pusher!!! ***"Blessed are those who hunger and thirst for righteousness, for they shall be filled"*** (Matthew 5:6). To the degree you have been hungry or thirsty you understand this fourth Beatitude. Most of us have never experienced the state of thirst in the most severe condition. The saliva becomes thick and foul tasting; the tongue clings to the teeth and the roof of the mouth. The face feels full due to the shrinking of the skin. Many begin to hallucinate. Although none of us may have experienced this extreme, have not we all experienced this in the spiritual realm? Do we have a need for Jesus as strong as our need for water?

Jesus expresses this in the fourth Beatitude. After recognizing my complete helplessness and embracing it to the point of "mourning," I find the nature of God forming the Kingdom of Heaven in me. His nature, as described in "meekness," comforts and supplies every need, even in the physical realm. It is astounding. You would think this would satisfy the individual and bring him into a state of comfort, relaxation, and arrival. However, it appears **hunger and thirst** continues with greater intensity. Obviously, in the sequence of the Beatitudes, it is increased by the presence of Jesus. It is not a destructive thirst, but a vital state of the soul keeping me focused on Him. It is the comforting desire a lover has for his beloved. His love creates such a thirst for her that all other women are forgotten. Jesus created this thirst in us by and for His presence. Once experienced, how can we settle for less? I am a Jesus pusher!!!

Jesus PUSHER | 21

I am a Jesus pusher!!! ***"Blessed are those who hunger and thirst for righteousness, for they shall be filled"*** (Matthew 5:6). This Beatitude pinpoints the intensity of our hunger and thirst for ***righteousness***. The Greek word "dikaiosyne" used here by Matthew is a noun. Its ending "syne" is used for Greek words that develop with an abstract thought. It is in the feminine gender also indicating this abstraction. Ten concrete rules will not bring us to a state of righteousness. Since ***righteousness*** is abstract, we must be careful in our consideration. In the practical aspects of daily life abstractions tend to lead us into areas of no consequence. This is not true for ***righteousness***.

Let au begin with THE DESCRIPTION of ***righteousness***. In both the Old and New Testaments, it is a state commanded by God. It is exclusively determined by God and tested by His judgment. This means ***righteousness*** exists when we conform to all that God commands or appoints. In other words, ***righteousness*** is the standard to which God calls us. Since in both the Old and New Testaments the required standard is God, He becomes the standard of the Christian. In the Old Testament God said to Israel, ***"For I am the Lord your God. You shall therefore consecrate yourselves, and you shall be holy; for I am holy"*** (Leviticus 11:44). He continued, ***"For I am the Lord who brings you up out of the land of Egypt, to be your God. You shall therefore be holy, for I am holy"*** (Leviticus 11:45). Peter echoed this same quote in the New Testament context (1 Peter 1:16). Jesus is the visible expression of this holiness. He is the standard; I must be intimate with Him! I am a Jesus pusher!!!

I am a Jesus pusher!!! ***"Blessed are those who hunger and thirst for righteousness, for they shall be filled"*** (Matthew 5:6). While the definition of **righteousness** does not change from the Old Covenant to the New Covenant, certainly the contextual experience does. If God is **righteousness**, any experienced **righteousness** must require Him. For instance, sin (opposite of **righteousness**) exists in every attempt I make to be like God apart from Him. This was the experience of the Old Testament. God called us to be holy. The Law was an explanation of what this would consist. If a righteous God became a man, the Law demonstrated the actions of His nature. The Law stated how God would live if He were a human being. Man, without the nature of God, desperately attempted to meet that standard. No wonder Paul shouted, ***"Therefore the law is holy, and the commandment holy and just and good. Has then what is good become death to me? Certainly not! But sin, that it might appear sin, was producing death in me through what is good, so that sin through the commandment might become exceedingly sinful"*** (Romans 7:12-13). It was not the Law that was sinful; sin was the attempt to live the law apart from the nature of God. This was the experience of the Old Testament.

Self-sourcing not only produces activities of sin, but is sinful by its existence. The self-sourced individual is sinful in his nature; he is without God who is **righteousness**. The self-sourced individual is sinful in every activity; he cannot conform to the desire of God. ***"But we are all like an unclean thing, and all our righteousnesses are like filthy rags;"*** (Isaiah 64:6). This is not only true in worldly, ungodly living, but it is also true in religious, ceremonial living. Religion in its best performance is still sin when it is self-sourced! The Spirit of Jesus must possess and source us. I am a Jesus pusher!!!

I am a Jesus pusher!!! ***"Blessed are those who hunger and thirst for righteousness, for they shall be filled"*** (Matthew 5:6). In the New Covenant, Jesus gives new contextual experience to **righteousness**. Matthew uses the Greek word "dikaiosyne," translated **righteousness,** six times. Four uses are found in the Sermon on the Mount (Matthew 5:6, 10, 20; 6:33); two uses are found in connection with the ministry of John the Baptist (Matthew 3:15; 21:32). As we mourn over our state of helplessness, we experience the infusion of the nature of God (meekness). The presence of His nature creates the hungering and thirsting to be in a right state before God.

Jesus clearly contrasts **righteousness** in the New Covenant with that of the Old Covenant. ***"For I say to you, that unless your righteousness exceeds the righteousness of the scribes and Pharisees, you will by no means enter the kingdom of heaven"*** (Matthew 5:20). No one can comprehend how any state of **righteousness** could exist beyond him or her. Obviously, if the possibility of entering the Kingdom of Heaven requires **righteousness** beyond the scribes and Pharisees, they are not in the Kingdom. In intimacy with Jesus, the holiness of the Kingdom relationship is found. Righteousness is Jesus! I am a Jesus pusher!!!

Jesus PUSHER | 24

I am a Jesus pusher!!! Jesus clearly contrasts *righteousness* in the New Covenant with that of the Old Covenant. ***"For I say to you, that unless your righteousness exceeds the righteousness of the scribes and Pharisees, you will by no means enter the kingdom of heaven"*** (Matthew 5:20). It is also a bit disturbing to notice the word "***exceeds***" as used by Jesus. The Greek word (perisseuo) translated ***exceeds*** comes from the root Greek word "perissos." It means "abundant." Jesus said that our ***righteousness*** in the New Covenant will "super abound" the ***righteousness*** of the Old Covenant. Immediately you ask, "How can this be possible?" How can anyone do more than the Pharisees did? How can we tithe more carefully than they did? How can we super abundantly keep the ceremonies of the temple more than they? It sounds like a ridiculous statement.

Jesus does not refer to the quantity of righteous deeds; He refers to the quality of ***righteousness***! The quality of ***righteousness*** in the New Covenant is "super abundant" above anything the Pharisees and scribes could imagine. The reason is because of the *source* of the ***righteousness***. The scribes and Pharisees attempted to align their lives with the claim God has upon man through the Law. This attempt was definitely self-sourced. It had to do with outward expression and adherence rather than inward relationship and attitude. Pride was at the core of each activity. The Spirit of Jesus sourcing the believer produces a quality of the life of Christ in all the outward expressions. I am a Jesus pusher!!

I am a Jesus pusher!!! ***"Blessed are those who hunger and thirst for righteousness, for they shall be filled,"*** (Matthew 5:6). A Kingdom person hungers for the food of ***"righteousness."*** But it is not righteousness self-sourced as found in the scribes and Pharisees (Matthew 5:20). Kingdom righteousness as a different quality!

How can the quality of ***righteousness*** actually change? It will require a nature change! The self-sourcing nature of man must be replaced with the sourcing of the nature of Jesus. This is radical! Upon this change, man is called "***a new creation***" (2 Corinthians 5:17). Flowing forth from this ***new creation*** will be the ***righteousness*** of Christ! It will exceed all the forced, disciplined performances of the Old Covenant; this ***righteousness*** leaps forth from the very nature of God. We will have the mind of Christ, operate within the attitude of Jesus, and see with the eyes of God. He will be our "source!" It is "super abounding" ***righteousness***.

Self-sourced righteousness is strained and forced. It must be constantly monitored and measured. It is found only in those who are disciplined and someone prideful. Jesus sourced righteousness is natural and spontaneous. It erupts throughout the life. It appears without thought or effort. It is the expression of the very nature of intimacy with Jesus. No wonder I am a Jesus pusher!!!

I am a Jesus pusher!!! ***"Blessed are those who hunger and thirst for righteousness,"*** (Matthew 5:6). Let's examine a more comprehensive DELINEATION of this ***righteousness***. In our passage (Matthew 5:6), ***hunger and thirst*** is linked with ***righteousness***. The grammar structure of this linkage delineates, portrays, or pinpoints the exact location of this ***righteousness***. The ***righteousness*** of the Old Covenant is not something for which one hungers or thirsts. Jesus calls to those who are trapped in its bondage to ***"Come to Me,"*** (Matthew 11:28). He refers to those individuals as ***"you who labor and are heavy laden."*** He promises ***"rest."*** The New Covenant ***righteousness*** is depicted as ***"Take My yoke upon you and learn from Me, for I am gentle and lowly in heart, and you will find rest for your souls. For My yoke is easy and My burden is light"*** (Matthew 11:29-30).

In the last proclamation of Jesus, He stated seven woes to the scribes and Pharisees. He did not picture their righteousness as something for which they hungered or even desired. He said, ***"Therefore whatever they tell you to observe, that observe and do, but do not do according to their works; for they say, and do not do. For they bind heavy burdens, hard to bear, and lay them on men's shoulders; but they themselves will not move them with one of their fingers"*** (Matthew 23:3-4). Their ***righteousness*** was not sought with passion, but with pride and arrogance. It resulted in compromise and hypocrisy. Outside obligations soon become a burden. Jesus proposes a ***righteousness*** flowing from the hunger of the soul embracing the Spirit of Jesus. I am a Jesus pusher!!!

I am a Jesus pusher!!! ***"Blessed are those who hunger and thirst for righteousness, for they shall be filled,"*** (Matthew 5:6). ***"Righteousness"***, in our passage, is the object of the ***"hunger and thirst."*** One would normally think of this as that which can be satisfied. In other words, you are hungry; you eat at a table with an abundance of food and are satisfied. While it is true, you will be hungry at a later time; it is certainly not a consistent hunger. Depending on the amount of food consumed, you may even feel "over satisfied," thinking that you may not ever need to eat again. In our passage, ***hunger and thirst*** are verbs in the present tense. In the Greek language this expresses present and continual action. Jesus indicates a continual ***hunger and thirst*** in our lives. Doesn't this contradict the final statement of the Beatitude, ***for they shall be filled***? Would not the "***filled***" eliminate the ***hunger and thirst***?

Normally in the Greek language ***hunger and thirst*** would be followed by a genitive. If ***"righteousness"*** were in the genitive it would be a "partitive" genitive. This indicates that only a part of the whole is desired. For instance, when I say, "I am hungry for pie," it means I am hungry for only a piece of pie. However, this is not the case! ***Righteousness*** is in the "accusative" case. This is equal to the "direct object" in the English language. Our hunger ***and thirst*** is focused on the complete ***righteousness*** of Jesus. I hunger and thirst for all that He is in His nature! I am a Jesus pusher!!!

Jesus PUSHER | 28

I am a Jesus pusher!!! ***"Blessed are those who hunger and thirst for righteousness, for they shall be filled,"*** (Matthew 5:6). The verbs ***"hunger and thirst"*** are focused on ***"righteousness."*** We desire the complete ***"righteousness"*** of Jesus! We cannot grasp or explain this actual statement. There is no way to measure or properly describe its content either in quality or quantity. Picture a table spread with meat, vegetables, salads, cakes, pies, fruit, etc. Imagine the table being as wide and as long as you can see. This is all placed into the relationship of embracing the heart of Jesus. The finite has fallen in love with the infinite. We hunger for His being, to know Him in His depth, and to embrace the fullness of His mind. While our capacity is constantly being enlarged, it never seems to be adequate. Thus, we are always in a state of ***"hunger and thirst!"*** This constantly drives us to embrace Him. We are not dissatisfied, yet we are never completely satisfied. Oh, the wonder of the relationship with Jesus, how startling it is.

This will be proven true in eternity. The "forever" state of heaven will be one of discovering the nature of Jesus. At every point within that eternity, we will be "hungering and thirsting" for Him. This bespeaks the depth of who He is. We are continually filled and yet continually hungry. What a Jesus! I am a Jesus pusher!!!

Jesus PUSHER | 29

I am a Jesus pusher!!! ***"Blessed are those who hunger and thirst for righteousness, for they shall be filled,"*** (Matthew 5:6). The DETERMINATION of the state of ***hunger and thirst*** identifies us as healthy. This is the normal Christian's condition. Why would Jesus "congratulate" a person who is not healthy? He paints the picture of a proper relationship with Himself. No wonder this "knocked them out of their senses" (explesso) as expressed at the end of the Sermon on the Mount (Matthew 7:28).

We are prone to the opposite of everything Jesus said. We picture the state of blessedness as one who is overweight and obviously well fed. He sits on a throne of power and strength that cannot be challenged. His conditions are so pleasant he has nothing over which to mourn. There is no indication of helplessness. This is a picture of complete self-sourcing and self-sufficiency. Most of us have lived long enough to know by experience that no matter how picture perfect the life of the self-sourced may appear, it is never reality. A friend of mine was lamenting over a situation he encountered with one of his friends. This individual was the picture of the above condition. He had a beautiful wife and lovely children. His job brought prosperity, providing a beautiful home and all the amenities to make anyone happy. Yet, he left it all for another woman.

Congratulations go to those who embrace their helplessness. Flowing from their inner spirit is the acknowledgment of their total inability. They mourn with a spirit of receptivity to Jesus who infuses them with His nature. They ***"hunger and thirst"*** for all that is contained in Him. Jesus enlarges their capacity to embrace Him even more. He has become their one desire. I am a Jesus pusher!!!

Jesus PUSHER | 30

I am a Jesus pusher!!! ***"Blessed are those who hunger and thirst for righteousness, for they shall be filled,"*** (Matthew 5:6). The Beatitudes have an unmistakable interaction. While each is distinct in meaning and presentation, each is dependent and further explains the others. We noted the sequence in which Jesus stated them. It is as if they are in a pyramid beginning with the foundation. In our fourth Beatitude (Matthew 5:6), congratulations goes to those who ***"hunger and thirst for righteousness." "Hunger and thirst"*** are verbs in the participle form. They act as adjectives and modify the subject of the sentence. In our verse, the subject is the Greek word "ho" often translated "the." Therefore, the subject of the sentence is "the hungering and thirsting ones."

The Greek word (peinao) translated ***hunger*** evolves from the Greek word "peno." It refers to individuals who must toil daily for their food. If they do not work today they will not eat tomorrow. Sometimes it is translated "poor." The Greek word (peinao) in our text means "to be famished, starve, or hungry." In this connection, it is safe to say that the "state of poverty" in the first Beatitude (Matthew 5:3) is linked with the starvation in this fourth Beatitude. The ones who are helpless and destitute experience the ***"hunger and thirst."*** I am helpless in my self-sourcing. I am embraced by my helpless as grief embraces one experiencing the death of a loved one. I must have Jesus! I am a Jesus pusher!!!

Jesus PUSHER | 31

I am a Jesus pusher!!! ***"Blessed are those who hunger and thirst for righteousness, for they shall be filled,"*** (Matthew 5:6). We must continually note the "severity" of Jesus' words. None of them are token statements, but seem to highlight the radical nature of the case. Jesus chooses Greek words like ***"poor"*** (ptochos), which is the most severe word for poverty in that language. This is also seen in the comparison between the reasons they are being congratulated. The ***"poor in spirit"*** are in the state of the **kingdom of heaven**. They are not traveling or even on their way, but are presently experiencing this state. The "mourning one" is ***"comforted"*** by the action of the Comforter who comes to them in the ***"kingdom of heaven."*** The physical world is at the disposal of the ***"meek."*** Those who are starving are ***"filled."***

We encounter difficulties when interpreting a physical illustration of a spiritual truth. Our temptation is to read into the illustration more then what the speaker intended. When we study the parables of Jesus, we must consistently guard against this. In a sense, many of the Beatitudes are parables. This is especially true of the illustration of ***"hunger and thirst."*** In interpreting a physical illustration of a spiritual truth, we must continually focus on the central truth. Whether true or false, there are many side issues, which are not the intent of the speaker. The focus of this beatitude is the "passion" of the inner heart for Jesus. It is an absolute focus of the individual on one subject, Jesus! He is worthy of this focus. I am a Jesus pusher!!!

Jesus PUSHER | 32

I am a Jesus pusher!!! ***"Blessed are those who hunger and thirst for righteousness, for they shall be filled,"*** (Matthew 5:6). The central truth of this physical illustration is the emphasis on the passion of the individual. How does one illustrate the burning desire within the soul for Jesus? Jesus uses severe terms relating to "starvation" and "thirst." We must keep our focus on the passion of these terms; this is the central focus. The passion is ***"for righteousness"***, which is the wonder of Jesus! The craving of the inner soul is for Jesus. The inner drive that controls all of life is Jesus. Our entire system and every area of our being must know Him!

We must beware of the thinking that Jesus is a means to an end. We hunger for food, and the purpose is to satisfy the needs of the physical body, allowing us to experience health, long life, and enjoyment. Food becomes a means to an end. It is the old question of whether we eat to live or live to eat. Jesus is not a means to an end. This is not a process of logic or the end result of reasoning. If I want to have a good life and have it forever, Jesus is the means to achieve this. What I really ***"hunger and thirst"*** for is a good life. Jesus is only an instrument for achieving that for which I ***"hunger and thirst."*** In our passage, I do not ***"hunger and thirst for righteousness"*** as for something apart from Jesus. He is ***"righteousness."*** My passion is for Him alone. I am a Jesus pusher!!!

Jesus PUSHER | 33

I am a Jesus pusher!!! ***"Blessed are those who hunger and thirst for righteousness, for they shall be filled,"*** (Matthew 5:6). Biblically we are portrayed as the bride of Christ. We are preparing for the great wedding. The passion of the bride is for the bridegroom. She cannot stop speaking about him. She is so in love; her passion is for him. If her passion is focused on how much money he has, this indicates a problem. Woe to us if streets of gold or mansions become our passion. How misguided we are when solutions to our problems or health and wealth become our focus. Jesus must captivate us.

Biblically we are portrayed as sons of God. It is tragic when a son only cares about his future inheritance. When his passion is to use his father for the fulfillment of his own personal dream, something has gone wrong. The son loves the father. His father is of greater value than the inheritance. The passion of the son is his father. This is the passion being expressed in this Beatitude. Our ***"hunger and thirst"*** is for the person of Jesus. Everything else shrinks in light of Him. All other issues are minor in light of His embrace. We hunger and thirst exclusively for His embrace. Paul cried, ***"But what things were gain to me, these I have counted loss for Christ. Yet indeed I also count all things loss for the excellence of the knowledge of Christ Jesus my Lord, for whom I have suffered the loss of all things, and count them as rubbish, that I may gain Christ"*** (Philippians 3:7-8). Is this my single focus! He is my righteousness! I am a Jesus pusher!!

Jesus PUSHER | 34

I am a Jesus pusher!!! ***"Blessed are those who hunger and thirst for righteousness, for they shall be filled,"*** (Matthew 5:6). The Greek word (hoti) translated ***"for"*** is used in various ways. It is demonstrative. This means it introduces the object, contents, or argument to which the preceding words refer. It is casual. This means it is particularly equivalent to the phrase "for this reason." Jesus congratulates the hungering and thirsting ones. It is because of the filling. While the verbs ***"hunger*** and **thirst"** are in the active voice, the verb ***"shall be filled"*** is passive. We have nothing to do with "the filling." We are acted upon and supplied with the filling. "Filling" is in His hands exclusively. Our focus must be on directing the ***"hunger and thirst."***

I have discovered that I can direct and control my physical hungers. Those things I used to crave to eat and drink are now distasteful to me. Could Jesus direct me in the focus of my ***"hunger and thirst?"*** I do not have to develop a taste for Him; it is not acquired. He is the fundamental, ever present, and has always been there from the beginning, *'hunger and thirst"* of my life. Will I respond to Him? The "filling" need not concern me! In all of my other **hunger and thirst** my great concern was being filled. How long will it last? When will I need to eat again? "The filling" in every area of my life is His concern. I do not need to select the right foods, drinks, or drugs to bring satisfaction for particular areas of life. Having my needs satisfied is of no concern to me. He knows me; He knows my future; He made me. He supplies; it is all Him. There is no further concern. I am a Jesus pusher!!!

Jesus PUSHER | 35

I am a Jesus pusher!!! ***"Blessed are those who hunger and thirst for righteousness, for they shall be filled,"*** (Matthew 5:6). The Greek word (chortazo) translated ***they shall be filled*** means to feed or to fatten cattle. It comes from the Greek word (chortos) for fodder or grass. In the Pentecost event (Acts 2:1-4) two distinct Greek words were used by Luke to describe the "filling" of the Holy Spirit. The outside God came to be inside man. What a dramatic change this made! The first Greek word (pleroo) translated ***"filled"*** pictures content being placed into a container until it is completely filled (Acts 2:2). The second Greek word (pletho) translated ***"filled"*** pictures a sponge being saturated with a substance (Acts 2:4). Jesus says something different in this Beatitude. In the imagery of starvation and deprivation of water, Jesus depicts the idea of satisfaction. Does anyone question Jesus' embrace? Jesus totally satisfies every need of our lives! The Old and New Testaments present this constant theme. David proclaims, ***"The Lord is my shepherd; I shall not want,"*** (Psalms 23:1). He continued in this favorite Psalm to express the satisfaction of the believer. ***"You prepare a table before me in the presence of my enemies; You anoint my head with oil; My cup runs over"*** (Psalms 23:5). David exclaims, ***"The young lions lack and suffer hunger; but those who seek the Lord shall not lack any good thing,"*** (Psalms 34:10). He boldly proclaims, ***"For He satisfies the longing soul, and fills the hungry soul with goodness,"*** (Psalms 107:9). Jesus fills me! I am a Jesus pusher!!!

I am a Jesus pusher!!! *"Blessed are those who hunger and thirst for righteousness, for they shall be filled,"* (Matthew 5:6). Jeremiah prophesied to Israel concerning the future Kingdom, *"I will satiate the soul of the priests with abundance, and My people shall be satisfied with My goodness, says the Lord."* (Jeremiah 31:14). The revelation of Jesus to the woman at the well in Sychar was astounding. Contrasting the reoccurring thirst from the well water, Jesus said, *"Whoever drinks of this water will thirst again, but whoever drinks of the water that I shall give him will never thirst. But the water that I shall give him will become in him a fountain of water springing up into everlasting life"* (John 4:14). After the miracle of feeding five thousand men plus women and children, Jesus proposed, *"I am the bread of life. He who comes to Me shall never hunger, and he who believes in Me shall never thirst,"* (John 6:35). This same factor was witnessed by John and reported by him in the Book of Revelation. He said, *"They shall neither hunger anymore nor thirst anymore; the sun shall not strike them, nor any heat; for the Lamb who is in the midst of the throne will shepherd them and lead them to living fountains of waters"* (Revelation 7:16-17).

We are able to proclaim with boldness a complete satisfaction in all realms of life in Jesus' embrace. Surely this is the intent of Jesus in this Beatitude. The helpless will know the all-surpassing strength of Jesus' embrace and become the Kingdom. In the infusion of His person, I become the new creation of the Kingdom of God; it is a place of satisfaction. I *"hunger and thirst"* for Him and I am *"filled."* I am a Jesus pusher!!!

Jesus PUSHER | 37

I am a Jesus pusher!!! ***"Blessed are those who hunger and thirst for righteousness, for they shall be filled,"*** (Matthew 5:6). There is a paradox presented to us in the ***"hunger and thirst"*** as seen in light of ***"they shall be filled." "Hunger and thirst"*** are symptoms of being deprived of proper food and water. Once proper food and water are received, ***"hunger and thirst"*** is satisfied and ceases to exist. However, the passage suggests (by the verb tense) that ***"hunger and thirst"*** are continuous, which should negate the satisfaction of being ***"filled."*** This would mean we are never satisfied. We understand this in the physical realm. ***Hunger and thirst*** is satisfied with the proper amount of food and water, but will return again. The satisfaction is only temporary. In fact, we are greatly concerned when we never get hungry or thirsty. It is an unhealthy state!

In the spiritual state, we always seek Jesus and His righteousness. We always want more and never get enough. Yet in this state we experience a satisfaction. It is this satisfaction that seems to make us want more. When we genuinely hunger and thirst for Jesus we find it so satisfying that we desire more and more. We live dissatisfied in a state of satisfaction. Jesus is all we could possibly need in the midst of a growing awareness of our need. I am a Jesus pusher!!!

Jesus PUSHER | 38

I am a Jesus pusher!!! ***"Blessed are those who hunger and thirst for righteousness, for they shall be filled,"*** (Matthew 5:6). Jesus relates this same truth to the woman at the well. In regard to physical water, He clarifies the fact that ***"Whoever drinks of this water will thirst again,"*** (John 4:13). However, in the spiritual realm, we are promised, ***"whoever drinks of the water that I shall give him will never thirst"*** (John 4:14). Immediately we begin to question this reality. How can it be? This is true for the woman at the well. She responded with an immediate desire for this water only because of her regard for physical thirst. Jesus pointed her back to the spiritual need in her life. ***Jesus said to her, "Go, call your husband, and come here"*** (John 4:16). She admitted she had no husband. Jesus told her of her five husbands. The deep need of her inner spiritual life was thirsting and she could never be satisfied by her relationships with men.

Jesus clarifies how this satisfaction can be so perpetual. He tells her and us, ***"Whoever drinks of this water will thirst again, but whoever drinks of the water that I shall give him will never thirst. But the water that I shall give him will become in him a fountain of water springing up into everlasting life"*** (John 4:14). This is the picture of a constant thirst continually being satisfied with the flow of the water for which one thirsts. The embrace of Jesus is a picture of a gushing, flowing, never ceasing fountain, constantly quenching the thirst that is always present and ever growing. We live in a dissatisfied satisfaction! Jesus is capable of being this in our lives for eternity. I am a Jesus pusher!!!

I am a Jesus pusher!!! ***"Blessed are the merciful, for they shall obtain mercy,"*** (Matthew 5:7). The bullies in my grade school would corner me, twist my arm behind my back, and exert pressure. They wanted me to beg for mercy. "Mercy" was identified with weakness. The powerful, those in charge, do not need mercy. When they extend mercy, it is from a sense of pride and arrogance. "Mercy" is strangely a Christian virtue. All the other qualities contained in the Beatitudes are linked to it. "Mercy" is as naturally a part of the Kingdom of God as breathing is to living.

The Roman culture spoke of four cardinal virtues: wisdom, justice, temperance, and courage. "Mercy" is not in the list. "Mercy" begins with Jesus. Even the Old Testament with the laws and punishments was interpreted through the eyes of a merciless world. The traditional Pharisaic theology did not willingly embrace mercy. The Jewish culture of Jesus' day was steeped in "Blessed is the righteous, for God will be merciful to them." The unspoken thought was "for they deserve it." They earned, merited, and owned it. "Mercy" was the result of a self-sourced earning. This enabled them to withhold "mercy" from everyone else who did not obtain their level. But this is not the Kingdom. My helplessness is filled with His great presence; it is mercy in abundance. Who could merit such a relationship? I am a Jesus pusher!!!

I am a Jesus pusher!!! Jesus said, ***"Blessed are the merciful, for they shall obtain mercy"*** (Matthew 5:7). The grammar in this Beatitude follows the common form of the preceding four. Each starts with ***blessed***, which is a translation of the Greek word "makarios." It conveys congratulations, an expression of how fortunate you are. This "congratulations" is followed by the main subject, but has no main verb. It is always the Greek article "ho," which can be translated "the, this, one, that, etc." This subject is followed by an adjective or a participle (a verb acting as an adjective). The Greek adjective in our verse "eleemon" is translated ***merciful***. It is frequently used in the Old Testament (Septuagint).

"Eleemon" is used only twice in this adjective form in the New Testament. Once it is used to describe Jesus. ***Therefore, in all things He had to be made like His brethren, that He might be a merciful and faithful High Priest in things pertaining to God, to make propitiation for the sins of the people*** (Hebrews 2:17). The second time "eleemon" is used is in our passage describes a person filled with Jesus (Matthew 5:7). The Bible insists pure mercy is only comes in relationship with Jesus. Selfish motives extend a counterfeit mercy, always with hidden agendas. Counterfeit mercy is never in Jesus or one filled with Him. No wonder, I am a Jesus pusher!!!

I am a Jesus pusher!!! ***"Blessed are the merciful, for they shall obtain mercy"*** (Matthew 5:7). To understand the fifth Beatitude, we must understand the term ***merciful*** (eleemon), where the FOCUS of mercy is essential to the definition. In the context of our passage, mercy is focused on others. The ability to be ***merciful*** to others results from receiving mercy. Receiving mercy is possible only because it comes from someone else, and the adjective "***merciful***" applies to the giver and not the recipient. "Mercy" flows from one person to another. When we are merciful toward ourselves, we justify, rationalize, and excuse. Therefore, the adjective "***merciful***" can modify only a person who extends mercy toward someone else.

The first four Beatitudes focus on our intimate relationship with Jesus, and this fifth Beatitude is the first that relates to our relationship with others. In the intimate embrace of His person we become the ***kingdom of heaven*** (Matthew 5:3). In response to His presence, we are ***comforted*** (Matthew 5:4). In yielding to Jesus' nature we can conquer our physical world (Matthew 5:5). In seeking His person, we are ***filled*** (Matthew 5:6), and what we experience in relationship to Jesus we focus on others. My attitude and interaction with others must always be the expression of Jesus' presence through me. Oh, how I need Him! I am a Jesus pusher!!!

Jesus PUSHER | 42

I am a Jesus pusher!!! Jesus said, *"Blessed are the merciful, for they shall obtain mercy"* (Matthew 5:7). FEELING is another aspect of *merciful*. Mercy is not an obligation, duty, or law. Law or duty reshapes mercy into pride and arrogance. Mercy motivated by superiority demonstrates self-centeredness. Therefore, mercy is never an act or a performance; it is always an embrace or feeling. One is *merciful* because an emotion is aroused by someone else's affliction.

If being *merciful* is a simple deed, it is a feat we can achieve. Because it is an emotion, no amount of discipline can produce mercy. Genuine mercy flows from a *merciful* individual who has this characteristic because of his internal state of being. Jesus embraces the *poor in spirit* and that individual becomes the **kingdom of heaven** in that relationship. The Comforter comes to abide in the person who mourns. Meekness, the nature of Jesus, brings a new attachment to everything physical. *Hunger and thirst* highlights an expansion and continuation of the believer's filling with Jesus. Who is surprised when mercy flows from the heart of the believer? How can it not? It is an expression of the mind of Christ! The believer is *merciful*; he cannot be other than he is! It is because of Jesus. I am a Jesus pusher!!!

I am a Jesus pusher!!! ***"Blessed are the merciful, for they shall obtain mercy"*** (Matthew 5:7). The FOUNDATION for defining this mercy is in the Septuagint (the Greek translation of the Hebrew Old Testament). The Hebrew word for mercy is "chesedh," and is untranslatable. There is an aspect of the word that means to sympathize with a person in the popular sense of the term. Another aspect is to feel sorry for someone in trouble. But the heart of the word "chesedh" points to the ability to get inside the other person's skin, able to see things with their eyes, think things with their mind, and feel things with their feelings.

"Chesedh" parallels the concept of sympathy. Sympathy does not come from outside a person, but is motivated from within. For instance, **and if children, then heirs — heirs of God and joint heirs with Christ, if indeed we suffer with Him** (sympathy), **that we may also be glorified together** (Romans 8:17). "Sumpascho" (***suffer with Him***) is two Greek words combined. "Sum" means "together with," and "pascho" means "to experience or to suffer." Paul is speaking of the actual suffering in the believer's life and not an emotional concern over Christ's suffering. Is it not obvious that a ***merciful*** person experiences more than an emotional wave of pity for another person. Something happens within the person not given or acquired from outside, because it comes from his nature, his oneness with Jesus. There is identification with the person who is suffering. A ***merciful*** person sees things as the suffering person sees, feeling as they feel. Sympathy means, "experiencing things together with the other person, going through what they go through. Jesus is doing this with me and wants to do it through me for others. I am a Jesus pusher!!!

Jesus PUSHER | 44

I am a Jesus pusher!!! There seems to be a natural division between the first four Beatitudes (Matthew 5:3-6) and the last four Beatitudes (Matthew 5:7-12). The first four Beatitudes focus on our condition; when we embrace this condition and respond to Jesus we experience all He wants us to be. In the last four Beatitudes the focus is on what we become in Him and the unfolding ramifications of such.

Let me illustrate. I am *poor in spirit*, but in this helplessness Jesus embraces me. In that embrace, we (Jesus and me) become the Kingdom of Heaven. I am "mourning," a response to my helpless condition, which allows me to be open to Him. The "mourning" opens the door for the Comforter to come and indwell me. I am *meek*, a state where Jesus comes in power and embraces every circumstance in my life with hope. Praise and adoration fill my heart because the circumstances of the physical realm display the accomplishment of His will. I *hunger and thirst* for Him. Never completely satisfied, I am always satisfied, because His fountain fills me.

Listen closely to the message. Congratulations to the *merciful* ones. They are not *poor in spirit* and being embraced. They are being embraced and are now *merciful*. They are not "mourning" and being indwelt by the Comforter; they have the Comforter and are *merciful*. They are not meek and experiencing His power. They are experiencing His power and are *merciful*. They are not "hungering and thirsting" and are *filled*; they are filled and are *merciful*. This condition of "mercy" is a direct result of what Jesus does in my life through the first four Beatitudes. Thank you Jesus; I am a Jesus pusher!!!

I am a Jesus pusher!!! The condition of a *merciful* one is a state of being (Matthew 5:7), not an achievement and not a discipline, but who we are in Christ. One is not *merciful* because he does deeds of mercy; he does deeds of mercy because he is *merciful*. Jesus sources me because I am "helpless." I continually respond to Him in mourning. I am overwhelmed with the wonder of His person until I am consistently *hungry and thirsty* for Him. The natural state of such an existence is "mercy." How can my heart not respond in "mercy" to the helplessness of my fellowman?

There is a lack of emphasis in the New Testament on "motivating people." The early church had a nature burning in their bones. Evangelism was a natural result of the "mercy" state in which they dwelt. They simply could not help themselves. In the Book of Acts we read of these believers extending "mercy" in every situation. Luke describes the early church as providers to anyone who had need (Acts 2:45), often selling their possessions to participate in this act of mercy. As Peter and John go to the temple for the hour of prayer, the lame beggar cries to them. They can no longer ignore him. "Mercy" will not allow it (Acts 3:1-11). Even the separation of the Jews and Gentiles was eliminated as men came from Cornelius with an invitation (Acts 10). The same spirit that filled the Jews also filled the Gentiles. "Mercy" demanded it! I am a Jesus pusher!!!

Jesus PUSHER | 46

I am a Jesus pusher!!! "Mercy" always has a focus (Matthew 5:7). I extend mercy to someone other than myself. In the culture of Jesus' day, the concept of "mercy" was isolated to two areas. One was the pardon for injuries or wrongs, the content of the word "forgiveness." The second was almsgiving. I am convinced Jesus takes us to a higher level as He addresses this issue in the fifth Beatitude. Since He used severe language in the previous Beatitudes, we can assume this is true concerning "mercy."

Our English word "mercy" comes from the Latin word "misericordia," which is comprised of two words. "Miserans" expresses the idea of pity, the expression of care and concern. "Cor" references the heart. Therefore, "miseria cordis" means "pain of the heart." Of necessity, there are two issues involved in "mercy." There must be an object in distress, suffering, pain or dismay. The inner heart of this person is deeply affected by their condition. Mercy is "a lively emotion of the heart," a response to the discovery of another's misery. This results in physical actions suited to the ability and nature of the individual. A merciful man enters into the pain of the one to whom he extends mercy. He feels and mourns with him. This is a perfect description of Jesus and His involvement in your life. I am a Jesus pusher!!!

Jesus PUSHER | 47

I am a Jesus pusher!!! The sequence of the Beatitudes is important, because they build one on top of the other in Divine formation. The helpless are congratulated because they already dwell in the **kingdom of heaven**. The Comforter embraces those who **mourn** in their helplessness. The nature of the Divine is released through the helpless that respond in mourning. It is demonstrated in "meekness." What the *"blessed"* experience in Jesus is an unfolding greatness, driving them to hunger and thirst for more. While their capacity is always expanding, Jesus is continually filling them. This is not something He gives to us, but it is Jesus within us, a state of dwelling in Him and Him dwelling in us. In this embrace, we experience the Kingdom and exist within it. We find comfort in God's embrace, and as we experience His nature the meekness flows. The physical world is in subjection under the Jesus-filled person. Fullness of satisfaction is known as we know Him. Congratulations are given to the **merciful** ones. This is not a surprise. Is not mercy the heart of Jesus who embraces us? How can those who live in Him not express who He is?

This Beatitude (Matthew 5:7) expresses the nature of a restricted group. You must not take this Beatitude out of its sequence and apply it as the worldview might desire. This is not a call for a judge to have mercy on violators of the law, and this mercy does not apply to a bill collector's attitude toward those who are in debt. This is not a Beatitude for those who gather in an ungodly environment, planning ungodly activities. It is restricted to those who are filled with Jesus. This is why I am a Jesus pusher!!!

I am a Jesus pusher!!! In the fifth Beatitude, (Matthew 5:7) Jesus' focus is on a restricted group highlighted by the definite article "ho," translated ***those***. "Ho" precedes the participle "eleemon", a verb acting as an adjective, and is reinforced with the demonstrative pronoun "autoi," translated ***they***. The pronoun does not need to be stated in the Greek, and is presented to us by the distinctive ending of the verb. In our text, ***"they shall obtain mercy,"*** the pronoun ***they*** is not needed. The Greek verb "eleethesantai" is completely adequate. The pronoun ***they*** indicates the ending of the verb. However, in our text the pronoun is in the ending of the verb and also in the clause stated by the Greek demonstrative pronoun "autoi." It is there twice! Jesus distinguishes a limited group who qualify.

There are many people humanly merciful with a multitude of motives that cause their mercy. When someone extends mercy to another, their action gives a sense of power and superiority, a feeling of satisfaction connected with giving mercy. But mercy sourced from the human spirit is given only for personal benefit. Although one may humanly forgive others, he does not do it in all circumstances, all the time. These acts do not qualify a person to be in the group to whom Jesus refers, a restricted group of people being congratulated. This restricted group is divinely empowered; they become instruments of the Divine mercy from the Divine nature of God. Their helplessness is embraced by the unlimited resource of Jesus. They are instruments for the flow of His nature: mercy! I am a Jesus pusher!!!

I am a Jesus pusher!!! In these studies, we must always return to the concept of being. Jesus does not call us to an action we must accomplish, but to a reality in which He places us. We are not on the way to this destination; this state of existence is our present experience. After the statement of congratulations, Jesus begins with the Greek word "hoti," translated *for* (Matthew 5:7). It is causative in nature and can be translated "for this reason." The next Greek word in the statement is "autoi," which in the Greek language it is not necessary. It is a demonstrative pronoun that will be indicated in the ending of the verb to follow. It is translated *they*. The ones who are *merciful* are those who dwell in the first four Beatitudes. They dwell in Jesus who sources the mercy in their lives. Self-sourced mercy may or may not be present due to selfish motivation; but Divine mercy flows from the nature of God. This is the group receiving congratulations, and mercy belongs to them.

The third and last word in the phrase is "eleethesantai." This verb is in the indicative mood, a simple statement of fact; there is no argument. It is in the future tense as are six of the Beatitudes. The two Beatitudes relating to the *kingdom of heaven* are in the present tense, the first and last Beatitudes. The *kingdom of heaven* is a present state of continual action. Those who are in the embrace of the king and form the *kingdom of heaven* shall experience these six Beatitudes. It is because of Jesus; I am a Jesus pusher!!!

Jesus PUSHER | 50

I am a Jesus pusher!!! The Greek verb "eleethesantai," translated **shall obtain mercy** (Matthew 5:7), is in the passive voice, indicating that because they are **merciful** to others, they will now receive mercy for themselves. But is this correct? The passive voice states that they are not responsible for the mercy they experience. The actual English translation for the Greek verb is "they shall have mercy." Those possessed by the "mercy nature" of Jesus flow mercy to others. Those who are in the flow of mercy will have mercy! There are physical acts of mercy expressed; however, they are an expression of the state of mercy in which we dwell. We are an extension of His mercy, which allows us to experience the state of mercy, His indwelling. Jesus is not saying, "If you do deeds of mercy, you will receive deeds of mercy in return." Neither is he saying, "If you do deeds of mercy, God will have mercy on you." The state of mercy is not the result of doing mercy; it is the cause. The **merciful** ones are those who dwell in mercy.

Jesus speaks with the same emphasis in the remaining Beatitudes. He says, **"Blessed are the pure in heart, for they shall see God"** (Matthew 5:8). Those who see God dwell in a state of purity. He says, **"Blessed are the peacemakers, for they shall be called sons of God"** (Matthew 5:9). Peacemakers are not congratulated because they shall obtain peace. They are peacemakers because they are sons of God. It is a state in which they dwell. Likewise, the **merciful** ones are congratulated because they dwell in a state of mercy. It is found in intimacy with Jesus; I am a Jesus pusher!!!

Jesus PUSHER | 51

I am a Jesus pusher!!! ***"Blessed are the merciful, for they shall obtain mercy"*** (Matthew 5:7). Jesus powerfully illustrates this truth in His life. Peter asked, ***"Lord, how often shall my brother sin against me, and I forgive him?"*** (Matthew 18:21). Jesus' answer was "always forgive!" We are to live in a state of forgiveness or mercy

Then Jesus tells the Parable of the Unforgiving Servant (Matthew 18:23-35). A servant embezzled ten thousand talents (approximately $2,370,000) from his master. The king was moved with compassion, released him, and forgave the entire amount, making the servant debt free. The servant went forth rejoicing in the mercy he had been given. However, upon leaving the presence of the king, he met up with a fellow servant who owed him ***one hundred denarii*** (approximately $16.69). The forgiven servant refused to grant forgiveness and had his debtor thrown into prison, demanding full payment. Hearing this, the master was angry and revoked the mercy. He delivered him to the torturers until he should pay all that was due. The servant was living in a state of mercy. He decided not to continue to live in this state; he would not forgive. This violated mercy; it nullified all the mercy he embraced from the master. The message is clear. Congratulations! We are ***merciful*** ones because we live in a state of mercy. Jesus is this state. We have a passion for Him and find that Jesus Himself fills us. We receive Him in His mercy and extend mercy to our world. Thus, we are Jesus pushers!!!

Jesus PUSHER | 52

I am a Jesus pusher!!! The guarantee of the product is important to me. How secure is forgiveness and mercy? Can I be sure forgiveness will not be revoked? How can I know mercy covers my debt? The strength of the guarantee is found in Jesus' person. He is the guarantee. If He is fickle, then mercy can change to punishment. If He changes His mind, then mercy can be limited. Everything depends on His stability. Listen to the writer of Hebrews. *"Jesus Christ is the same yesterday, today, and forever"* (Hebrews 13:8). *"But He, because He continues forever, has an unchangeable priesthood. Therefore He is also able to save to the uttermost those who come to God through Him, since He always lives to make intercession for them"* (Hebrews 7:24-25). *"Thus God, determining to show more abundantly to the heirs of promise the immutability of His counsel, confirmed it by an oath, that by two immutable things, in which it is impossible for God to lie, we might have strong consolation, who have fled for refuge to lay hold of the hope set before us. This hope we have as an anchor of the soul, both sure and steadfast, and which enters the Presence behind the veil, where the forerunner has entered for us, even Jesus, having become High Priest forever according to the order of Melchizedek"* (Hebrews 6:17-20).

Jesus is my state of mercy. His embrace guarantees my mercy. I must not abandon my state of mercy. The church is not my guarantee. My own goodness is not my guarantee. Only in Him do I find security. I will not stray from Him. I am a Jesus pusher!!!

Jesus PUSHER | 53

I am a Jesus pusher!!! There is a contrast between the focus of purity and the focus on honor and justice. Honor is supreme in the minds of the world. If a daughter of the world is molested, it is not a matter of immorality or sin but the violation of honor. This dishonor can only be rectified by revenge, such as murder, but that is a violation of moral purity. Justice and honor are the high priority in our world, not purity. The Roman culture spoke of four cardinal virtues: wisdom, justice, temperance, and courage. Purity of heart was not found in their most valued assets.

In the Old Covenant, Judaism has an abundance of external laws to govern their moral purity. Jesus did not disagree with the laws given by God demonstrating purity. His cry was for "purity" to go to the depth of man's being. Pharisees from Jerusalem approached Jesus concerning His disciples; *"For they do not wash their hands when they eat bread"* (Matthew 15:2). Jesus answer was, *"Not what goes into the mouth defiles a man; but what comes out of the mouth, this defiles a man"* (Matthew 15:11). In one bold statement, Jesus clearly defined purity as coming from the inner being of man. Purity is never from the external to the internal; it is always from the internal to the external. Purity is never to be claimed because of our outward activities. We can only embrace purity with our hearts. We must experience Jesus; I am a Jesus pusher!!!

Jesus PUSHER | 54

I am a Jesus pusher!!! No one can refute that Jesus links purity with the heart. ***"Blessed are the pure in heart"*** (Matthew 5:8). The actual Greek text reads as follows: "Blessed (makarioi) the (hoi) pure (katharoi) the (te) heart (kardia)." ***Blessed*** (makarioi) is an adjective in the nominative case. ***Pure*** (katharoi) is also an adjective in the nominative case. This means that they both modify and give content to the subject of the sentence. The actual subject is ***the*** (hoi), which can be translated "this one, that one." When the adjectives are placed with the subject, it becomes ***"the blessed*** (congratulated) ***pure ones." "The heart"*** is in the dative, which serves as a direct object. ***The heart*** is receiving the state of the purity. This identifies the location of the purity as being in the heart.

This reference continues in the Sermon on the Mount. In the fulfilled law, Jesus refers to moral purity. He equated it with the heart. ***"But I say to you that whoever looks at a woman to lust for her has already committed adultery with her in his heart"*** (Matthew 5:28). The focus of one's life is very important to Jesus. The ***treasures on earth*** and the ***treasures in heaven*** symbolize this. The conclusion is: ***"For where your treasure is, there your heart will be also"*** (Matthew 6:21). Jesus abundantly placed purity in the heart. He must indwell my heart; I am a Jesus pusher!!!

I am a Jesus pusher!!! ***"Blessed are the pure in heart"*** (Matthew 5:8). The Greek lexicon defines "the heart" (kardia) as the seat of the desires, feelings, affections, passions, and impulses. The Old Testament states the Hebrew concept of the heart. ***"For the life of the flesh is in the blood, and I have given it to you upon the altar to make atonement for your souls; for it is the blood that makes atonement for the soul"*** (Leviticus 17:11). This was the basic concept of the lamb sacrifices offered to God and the Lamb who was to come. Logically, the blood comes from the heart and flows back to the heart. Therefore, the source, seat of the life (blood) of an individual is the heart.

In our language, the heart is what "makes us tick!" It is used to express the human personality, who we are. Therefore, God looks at our hearts rather than at our actions to see our intent toward Him. We are told to seek God with our hearts (our whole person). ***"But from there you will seek the Lord your God, and you will find Him if you seek Him with all your heart and with all your soul"*** (Deuteronomy 4:29). It is the heart God views to determine if we are His people. ***But the Lord said to Samuel, "Do not look at his appearance or at his physical stature, because I have refused him. For the Lord does not see as man sees; for man looks at the outward appearance, but the Lord looks at the heart"*** (1 Samuel 16:7). Purity is a state of existence in my heart; Jesus must dwell there. I am a Jesus pusher!!!

Jesus PUSHER | 56

I am a Jesus pusher!!! ***And they prayed and said, "You, O Lord, who know the hearts of all, show which of these two You have chosen"*** (Acts 1:24). The Greek word "kardiognostes," translated ***"who knows the hearts,"*** is "heart (kardio)" "knower (gnostes). The human personality is made up of a variety of different functions of our being. It includes how we think, remember, feel, desire and will. The heart is used as an image of all of these. We are created in the image of God (Genesis 11:26-27). God, as revealed in the Scriptures, is a person who thinks, feels, desires, and chooses. The Book of Hosea is a story of God displaying through a prophet what He experiences, feels, and desires personally. God promised not to destroy Israel for their rebellion. This decision was not easy; it was a result of God's inner struggle. He cries out from deep within, ***"My heart churns within Me; My sympathy is stirred. I will not execute the fierceness of My anger; I will not again destroy Ephraim. For I am God, and not man, The Holy One in your midst; And I will not come with terror"*** (Hosea 11:8-9). God justified changing His mind on the basis of His divinity. Mankind naturally destroys when angered, but God is Divine and pure in His heart! No wonder Jesus said, ***"Blessed are the pure in heart"*** (Matthew 5:8).

Paul shared great insight with Titus. He wrote, ***"To the pure all things are pure, but to those who are defiled and unbelieving nothing is pure; but even their mind and conscience are defiled"*** (Titus 1:15). This is based on the premise that purity is in the heart. Nothing can be pure when sourced by an impure heart. An impure heart influences every action of the being. The heart is the center of man. I want Jesus in my heart! I am a Jesus pusher!!!

Jesus PUSHER | 57

I am a Jesus pusher!!! ***"Blessed are the pure in heart"*** (Matthew 5:8). The heart of man in the New Testament is more than an organ of the body. It contains within its imagery all an Israelite would consider as the Holy of Holies. As the high priest entered the heart of the temple he approached the sanctuary, the area most sacred containing the Holy Place and the Holy of Holies. The high priest in the Holy Place made sacrifices behind the enormous veil separating the Holy of Holies. This was the dwelling place of God. In the imagery of the New Covenant, you and I are the temple of the Spirit of God. *"**Do you not know that you are the temple of God and that the Spirit of God dwells in you**"* (1 Corinthians 3:16)? The heart is the Holy of Holies in which the encounter with God is realized in either the positive or negative sense. This is the foundation, the firm ground, of religious life. All the ethical conduct of a person is determined from this location. *"**And because you are sons, God has sent forth the Spirit of His Son into your hearts, crying out, 'Abba, Father!'"**"* (Galatians 4:6). The confirmation of being sons of God is placed in our hearts. Paul's prayer for us was *"**that Christ may dwell in your hearts through faith**"* (Ephesians 3:17). I want Jesus in my heart! I am a Jesus pusher!!!

I am a Jesus pusher!!! ***"Blessed are the pure in heart"*** (Matthew 5:8). While purity may be in the heart, the opposite is true as well. ***"Beware, brethren, lest there be in any of you an evil heart of unbelief in departing from the living God"*** (Hebrews 3:12). Unbelief takes place in the heart of man. Thus the stage of the battle for the soul of men is in his heart. The heart can be overrun with lusts. ***"Therefore God also gave them up to uncleanness, in the lusts of their hearts, to dishonor their bodies among themselves"*** (Romans 1:24). This took place ***"because, although they knew God, they did not glorify Him as God, nor were thankful, but became futile in their thoughts, and their foolish hearts were darkened"*** (Romans 1:21).

Jesus does not meet us on a superficial, external level of living. He is not interested in being an additional aspect of my physical life such as another hand. He is not going to be a garment I wear or an exterior protection for some difficulty of life. He meets me in the location of my heart. Here in the center of my being, the seat of my affections, the source of all activities, and the determiner of my attitude is where He comes. This places Him at the core of my being, my very existence. To refuse or accept Him on this level is my choice. He is not my business partner, my counselor giving advice, or my instructor on proper activities; He is a lover of my heart! I am a Jesus pusher!!!

I am a Jesus pusher!!! ***"Blessed are the pure in heart"*** (Matthew 5:8). Jesus' presence in my heart is the determining factor of salvation! This is the core of the message. I must embrace Jesus in my heart. Jesus solved the debate concerning the greatest of the commandments; He said, ***"You shall love the Lord your God with all your heart, with all your soul, and with all your mind"*** (Matthew 22:37). This is a quotation from the Old Testament (Deuteronomy 6:5), and congregation started the religious service by quoting this. Was it so familiar they had forgotten it?

I ask you to consider your "heart condition." Consider this statement; "The heart is every man's best part, the shrine of his affections, the ocean of his thoughts, the store-house of the energies of his will; insomuch that there is not one of the multifarious responsibilities of life which he can worthily bear, nor one of its great duties that he can effectively discharge, until he has learned to put his heart into it. Least of all is it possible for religion to be of value unless it be suffused with the tenderness, glowing with the ardour, and resolute with the purpose of the heart. As we ourselves know that we have never won a man until we have gained his affection, so He who created and redeemed us insists that we have given nothing to Him until we yield our love. Consent of the intellect alone is nothing. Conviction of the judgment alone is nothing. Service of the hands alone is nothing. His grave, sweet voice still calls to, us out of heaven, 'My son, give Me thy heart;' and only when this is done can we be counted among His disciples. The seat of His religion is the heart; its effect is to produce purity of heart; its reward is to open the eyes of the heart." ("The Heirs of the Kingdom," by Rev. W. J. Woods, in *The Christian World Pulpit*, Dec. 31, 1890.). I am a Jesus pusher!!!

I am a Jesus pusher!!! ***"Blessed are the pure in heart"*** (Matthew 5:8). The subject of purity has several fundamental issues. These are not just ideas or suggestions, but they are the hardcore realities of God's heart. They are the essential building blocks for our outlook on life. What you decide about these issues will determine your practical manner of living. All your relationships will be colored by your view, and the relationships you allow in your life come under the control of these issues. We will be discussing these issues as we progress in our saturation in the Scriptures.

Picture yourself standing at the crossroads of your life. What you decide about purity at this intersection will determine whether you turn left or right. It is not about choosing a high road or a low road when both going in the same direction. The decision involves roads going in opposite directions. The decision you make will not dictate whether your life has ups and downs or a level path. Your life's road will sometimes have curves and other times are straight. The right decision about of purity will not eliminate suffering or obstacles in the road. You are not deciding about ease of travel or number of rest stops. The issue under discussion is the direction in which you are headed. Jesus is purity! There is no purity in the heart outside of intimacy with Him. I am a Jesus pusher!!!

Jesus PUSHER | 61

I am a Jesus pusher!!! ***"Blessed are the pure in heart"*** (Matthew 5:8). As we progress through these Beatitudes, we discover the first four are focused on who we are in relationship with Jesus. Immediately we are congratulated as if we are especially fortunate. There is an emphasis of congratulations in all eight Beatitudes. Jesus does not begin congratulating us for purity but for being ***poor in spirit***. However, could this helpless state be the core of purity? It is the mourning that embraces the Comforter. Could the response of mourning be the fiber interwoven through purity? It is the meek who experience the nature of God in His fullness in their physical world as intended. Could this be the source of all purity? Hungering and thirsting allows fullness, which increases hungering and thirsting that brings fullness. Could this be the activity of purity? These individuals are enabled to extend mercy because they live in the state of His mercy. Is this mind-boggling awareness of His mercy the attitude of purity? Perhaps in all the Beatitudes Jesus promotes the standard of purity.

If the entire prior Beatitudes were an explanation of purity, we would assume the condition of purity is the standard of all previous Beatitudes. If you and I were congratulated for the condition of purity, we would assume it is our state and present location. We would also assume it is a standard in which we can and do dwell. It is obviously not a hope for the future or an idealistic impossibility. Jesus intends this for our lives now. Congratulations! Purity is in Him! I am a Jesus pusher!!!

I am a Jesus pusher!!! ***"Blessed are the pure in heart"*** (Matthew 5:8). Throughout the law structure of the Old Covenant a basic premise is proposed. The presupposition is that impurity and Jehovah are irreconcilable opposites. Purity is the norm qualifying one to take part in worship; impurity separates one from worship and from God's people. The Old Testament Scriptures declaring our premise are too many to list. God called out to His people through the prophet Isaiah saying, ***"Behold, the Lord's hand is not shortened, that it cannot save; nor His ear heavy, that it cannot hear. But your iniquities have separated you from your God; and your sins have hidden His face from you"*** (Isaiah 59:1-2). The Hebrew word "awon," translated ***iniquities,*** is one of four main words indicating sin in the Old Testament. It conveys the idea of twisting or perverting deliberately. In the noun form, it carries along with it the idea of guilt from conscious wrongdoing. "Iniquities" is sin involving an impure heart.

The blockage of God's power in the desperate situation of Israel was not because God lacked power. His hand or arm was not too short to reach them. He was not hard of hearing, therefore unable to answer their need. It was their personal impurity that separated them from Him. Regardless of how much He loved them, their impure hearts would not allow God to intervene. Impurity and God are irreconcilable opposites. No wonder I am a Jesus pusher!! He is the only possibility we have of a pure heart allowing intimacy with God.

Jesus PUSHER | 63

I am a Jesus pusher!!! ***"Blessed are the pure in heart"*** (Matthew 5:8). The law structure of the Old Covenant constantly proposed a basic premise. The purity of Jehovah's heart could not tolerate the impurity of sin. This is demonstrated forcibly to Israel during the leadership of Joshua. He led the Israelites into the promise land. They advanced through Canaan, step by step conquering the cities. The walls of Jericho have fallen. Ai is the next city in their quest. Joshua sends spies into the city; they report it to be an easy victory for Israel. A reduced army attacks the city only to be completely slaughtered. Joshua is grief stricken and falls on his knees in prayer. God reveals sin in the camp of Israel, which hinders His involvement. After searching through the camp, they find Achan disobeyed the desires of God by hording the spoils of previous victories. Victory again becomes theirs when they correct this sin (Joshua 7). Impurity stayed the hand of God in the battle. All of Israel suffered because of one man's sin. This highlights the severity of the proposition of the Old Covenant. Impurity and God are irreconcilable opposites.

Your life might be in total despair; what chance do you have to live above sin in purity? Purity is the message of Jesus! He not only provides forgiveness for my sin, but victory over my sin. In His cleansing of sin, He sources me with His pure nature. Jesus becomes the source of my living. The Gospel means "good news." It is the good news of Jesus who brings victory over impurity. You and I can be the people God calls us to be through Jesus. No wonder I am a Jesus pusher!!!

Jesus PUSHER | 64

I am a Jesus pusher!!! ***"Blessed are the pure in heart"*** (Matthew 5:8). The laws of God for the people of Israel consistently highlight purity. There are clean (pure) and unclean (impure) animals. Touching certain things would bring them into impurity and defilement. While the high priest must adhere to certain ceremonies, dress, and mannerisms before going into the Holy of Holies, the intent of the numerous requirements is purity. Even the fire on the sacrifice altar must be pure fire, ever burning and maintained. If "strange" or "unholy" fire is brought to the altar, it is not acceptable to God (Leviticus 6:8-13).

If this standard was proposed and upheld in the Old Covenant, the New Covenant will support an even higher requirement. The Hebrew author wrote, ***"For if the blood of bulls and goats and the ashes of a heifer, sprinkling the unclean, sanctifies for the purifying of the flesh, how much more shall the blood of Christ, who through the eternal Spirit offered Himself without spot to God, cleanse your conscience from dead works to serve the living God?"*** (Hebrews 9:13-14). The intent of this statement by the Hebrew author was not to condemn or impose guilt. He was revealing the tremendous, increased, and extravagant possibility found in Jesus! The blood of Jesus, meaning His life, extends to us a state of purity. We are cleansed and living in the presence of Jesus! I am a Jesus pusher!!!

Jesus PUSHER | 65

I am a Jesus pusher!!! ***"Blessed are the pure in heart"*** (Matthew 5:8). The conflict between Jesus and the Pharisees focused on the issue of purity. Jesus elevated purity to a higher level. In the Sermon on the Mount He cried, ***"For I say to you, that unless your righteousness exceeds the righteousness of the scribes and Pharisees, you will by no means enter the kingdom of heaven"*** (Matthew 5:20). How could anyone be more righteous than the legalistic Pharisee? It could only take place in "purity of the heart." Jesus proceeds by listing external activities of the law; He calls for the attitude of the heart to match each external deed. Refraining from murder must be replaced by the purity of love (not hating). Not participating in immoral activities must be superseded by purity of thought. The acts of separation must be overcome with purity of forgiveness. Swearing or oaths must be replaced inwardly with pure honesty. Controlled revenge must give way to pure love for your enemies.

The conflict between Jesus and the Pharisees raged over the defilement laws and activities. Jesus always returned to the high standard of a pure heart. He said, ***"Do you not yet understand that whatever enters the mouth goes into the stomach and is eliminated? But those things which proceed out of the mouth come from the heart, and they defile a man"*** (Matthew 15:17-18). He painted a vivid picture of the Pharisees when he said, ***"Woe to you, scribes and Pharisees, hypocrites! For you are like whitewashed tombs which indeed appear beautiful outwardly, but inside are full of dead men's bones and all uncleanness"*** (Matthew 23:27). He was calling them to the standard of a pure heart. This can only happen in Jesus. I am a Jesus pusher!!!

I am a Jesus pusher!!! ***"Blessed are the pure in heart"*** (Matthew 5:8). Obviously the Old Covenant's focus on pure actions changed to inward purity in the New Covenant. What is the content of this purity? The Greek word "katharos," translated ***pure,*** does not play a dominate role in New Testament language. However, "katharos" is linked in usage with "holy," "obedience," "sanctification," and "love." These words must be viewed against the opposite state of "sin."

The message of the angel to Joseph before Jesus was born is startling. Joseph needed instruction because he concluded not to ***make her a public example***. He decided to ***put her away secretly*** (Matthew 1:19). During the revelation the angel spoke, ***"And she will bring forth a Son, and you shall call His name Jesus, for He will save His people from their sins"*** (Matthew 1:21). The mission of Jesus was to rescue us from sin. The Book of Matthew unfolds in revealing that the opposite of sin is purity of heart. The deed or external action is not the determining factor, but the motive and intent of the heart. Therefore the substance of purity is found in the attitude of the heart. This truth complicates the issue of purity. I cannot conquer my outward actives and force them into purity; I must conquer my inner motive and it will change my actives. I cannot do this! I need Jesus! He is my only answer for heart purity! I am a Jesus pusher!!!

Jesus PUSHER | 67

I am a Jesus pusher!!! ***"Blessed are the pure in heart"*** (Matthew 5:8). John Wesley proposed the idea of "Christian Perfection." Then and now people respond in a negative way regarding the wordage. Yet, in the Sermon on the Mount, Jesus calls us to this substance of heart. ***"Therefore you shall be perfect, just as your Father in heaven is perfect"*** (Matthew 5:48). Neither Wesley nor Jesus referred to perfect outward actions, perfect judgments, or perfect service. They both spoke of the substance found in a pure heart. Jesus gave this statement at the end of the Sermon on the Mount, speaking of loving your enemies. It is easy to love those who love you. Even the tax collector has this level of love. Therefore, how can one boast of love if he does not love more than those who cheat for their own self-centered betterment? We are to love like our heavenly Father who ***makes His sun rise on the evil and on the good, and sends rain on the just and on the unjust*** (Matthew 5:45). The perfection to which we are called is a perfection of heart purity, perfect love.

The legalistic Pharisees asked, ***"Teacher, which is the great commandment in the law?"*** (Matthew 22:36). The answer was a Scripture they quoted at the start of every worship service. ***"You shall love the Lord your God with all your heart, with all your soul, and with all your mind." This is the first and great commandment. And the second is like it: "You shall love your neighbor as yourself.' On these two commandments hang all the Law and the Prophets"*** (Matthew 22:37-40). All the words describing the inner aspects of who we are (***heart, soul*** and ***mind***) are to be focused in love with ***the Lord your God***. This same motive spills forth in how you treat and view your neighbor. Is this not heart purity? Only Jesus can accomplish this in my heart! I am a Jesus pusher!!!

Jesus PUSHER | 68

I am a Jesus pusher!!! ***"Blessed are the pure in heart"*** (Matthew 5:8). We have often discussed the difference between what God has and who God is. The Trinity has *omnipresence*. God's ability to be in every place at the same time is incomprehensible to those of us limited to one spot. Think of the effort, expense, time, and thought we put into going from one place to another. Each member of the Trinity has *omniscience*. The ability of knowing everything, past and future cannot be fathomed by one limited in his thinking. The *omnipotence* of the three persons of the Trinity is a frightening thought to one full of weakness. What chance do we have against such a powerful, all knowing, and ever present God? If He is fickle, irritable, mean, selfish, and a tyrant, we are in desperate trouble. No one can dispute the fact that what God has in power is under the control of who He is! Since this is true, we are safe!!! ***God is love*** (1 John 4:8, 16).

This cannot be questioned; Jesus is the visible image of the invisible God (Colossians 1:15). ***No one has seen God at any time. The only begotten Son, who is in the bosom of the Father, He has declared Him*** (John 1:18). Jesus is the second member of the Trinity. He set aside everything He had as God in order to completely demonstrate everything He is as God. What we see in Jesus is the pure heart of God. The reason the Trinity provided Jesus as a means of our forgiveness is because ***"God is love!"*** The only explanation for the Trinity not eliminating us is ***"God is love!"*** He brought all those things He has under the control of who He is. We are safe; He is love! I am a Jesus pusher!!!

Jesus PUSHER | 69

I am a Jesus pusher!!! ***"Blessed are the pure in heart"*** (Matthew 5:8). There is a radical difference between having and being! God never gave up who He is (love) but emptied Himself of all He had, omnipresence, omniscience, and omnipotence were all surrendered. This is Jesus! It is amazing news. However, brace yourself for an additional startling reality. God invites you into His heart. He is not inviting you to possess what He has; He wants you to be a part of who He is. He wants to share His heart with you. It is a pure heart. We have many attributes as a natural part of our humanity, stupidity, human limitations, weakness, insufficiencies, and many others. There are many things we have as a result of the Fall, damaged emotions, sickness, misunderstandings, and many more shortcomings. We have these things: but what if who we are could be filled with Him? Could His heart dominate us? Is it possible for my helplessness to join His unlimited loving heart? All that I have can come under the control of all that I am in Him. My human limitations, weaknesses, damaged emotions, misunderstandings, and many more will be controlled by the single motive of His love.

Congratulations! You have a pure heart. Jesus marvelously pulls you into Himself until you are one with His heart. You are the demonstration of how He feels. You are driven with one motive and desire. You have perfect love. Congratulations! No wonder I am a Jesus pusher!!!

I am a Jesus pusher!!! ***"Blessed are the pure in heart, for they shall see God"*** (Matthew 5:8). The Jews listening to Jesus' message were a product of the four hundred years between the Old and New Testaments. They knew their difficulties were due to their disobedience of God's law and vowed never to let this to happen again. Groups of leaders, such as the Pharisees, arose to lead them in this commitment. They were totally focused on pleasing God through obedience of the law. However, they became aware that total observance of all the religious requirements was impossible. This was difficult for conscientious and honest Jews. Feelings of guilt, frustration, and anxiety plagued them. The life of the Jew revolved around his religion. His education, political and social life, and employment came under the control of his religion. Yet, they could not fulfill everything their religion demanded. The laws were too many; the ceremonies were complex with attention given to detail.

How does an honest believer cope with failure in keeping their religious beliefs? It seems some of the religious leaders fostered an alternate idea. If a person could perfectly keep just a few of the laws, God would understand. This in itself was a compromise. How is the selection going to be made? Which laws are the most important? This proved to be impossible. Therefore, some narrowed the requirement to one law perfectly kept. ***"Blessed are the pure in heart, for they shall see God"*** (Matthew 5:8). This Beatitude contains Jesus' marvelous summation both in statement and in experience. I must have Him! I am a Jesus pusher!!!

I am a Jesus pusher!!! ***"Blessed are the pure in heart, for they shall see God"*** (Matthew 5:8). The Jewish religion of Jesus' day drew to a startling conclusion. If the laws of God in their multiplicity actually served their purpose, they would drive every person to desire a pure heart. The fact they concluded one law might be kept perfectly brought them to the awareness they needed a focus. They must focus on only one thing if they were to accomplish it. This presented a problem. What is the one thing (law) above all others? What is the most important law, which should command their entire attention and effort? This created such a controversy that the Pharisees used it to test Jesus (Matthew 22:35). They selected a ***lawyer*** skilled in debate and argument. His question was, ***"Teacher, which is the great commandment in the law?"*** (Matthew 22:36). In other words, if all of the laws and religious requirements were to be integrated into a single goal, what would be the focus? This was evidently a raging controversy in the religion of that day.

Another lawyer in another situation asked a similar question to test Jesus. ***"Teacher, what shall I do to inherit eternal life?"*** (Luke 10:25). His life had been focused on meeting the requirements of his religion. His studies and career were contained in the boundaries of Judaism. This is why he was a "law expert." He joined with his fellow scholars in believing that laws and religious requirements were integrated into one focus. Jesus presents the one focus as ***"pure in heart."*** If you are not pure in your heart you are not pure regardless of actions! Jesus must be this in us! I fully embrace Him today! I am a Jesus pusher!!!

Jesus PUSHER | 72

I am a Jesus pusher!!! ***"Blessed are the pure in heart"*** (Matthew 5:8). Nicodemus was a ruler of the Jews. He came to Jesus in the night hour. He had a question, but began with a testimony. ***"Rabbi, we know that You are a teacher come from God; for no one can do these signs that You do unless God is with him"*** (John 3:2). This testimony combined with Jesus' immediate answer conveyed the question Nicodemus wanted to ask. He wanted to know how to be righteous. In the midst of all the pressure of the Jewish requirements, how can an individual know God? Every Jewish law integrated into this single focus.

A rich young ruler at the prime of his successful career came "running" to Jesus. The urgency is found in his question. ***"Teacher, what good thing shall I do that I may have eternal life?"*** (Matthew 19:16). Jesus quoted a list of the commandments; this young man claimed to have kept them all. However, he sensed a lack in himself. All his religious observances had not given any satisfaction to the integrated goal of ***eternal life***. He focused his religious experience on this single desire.

Do you see the common element in every one of these illustrations? All the laws and religious activities are integrated into one driving passion of the soul. This is the end we all come to! We want to see God! I want such intimacy with Him that I see Him. If you say, "I want love," ***God is love*** (1 John 4:8, 16). If you say, "I want holiness." ***"He who called you is holy,"*** (1 Peter 1:15). Is not our cry singular? Is it not Him that we want? Jesus is our only chance! I am a Jesus pusher!!!

I am a Jesus pusher!!! ***"Blessed are the pure in heart"*** (Matthew 5:8). It is the statement of all the Beatitudes. Jesus highlights one idea, one focus. The absolute helpless are embraced by the unlimited resource of His person; thus, in His embrace the Kingdom of Heaven is formed. What is the focus of need for the helpless? It is Jesus! The Comforter comforts those who mourn in their helplessness. It is in Him we find comfort. What is the focus of need for the comfortless? It is Jesus! The meek experience their physical world on a new level. His nature of meekness brings us to this experience. We need Him. Hunger and thirst for righteousness can only be filled in Him. He is the fullness of life. We experience mercy because of His presence; therefore we live and extend mercy. It is because of Jesus that I want to have a pure heart; my desire is for Him. In Him I find purity. Everything I need or desire for my life is integrated in Jesus.

In the Book of Ephesians, Paul highlighted the phrase ***"in Him"*** repeatedly in the first chapter. Everything God wants you to have is in Jesus. All spiritual blessings provided by God we find in Jesus. We have spent enough energy and valuable time looking elsewhere. Now is the time to come back to Jesus alone! We are not coming to Jesus along with other religious issues. We are coming only to Jesus, the Person. No wonder I am a Jesus pusher!!!

Jesus PUSHER | 74

I am a Jesus pusher!!! ***"Blessed are the pure in heart, for they shall see God"*** (Matthew 5:8). All laws, ceremonies, and requirements of religion are integrated in one focus. This focus is to ***see God***. If this is true, can a state of being ***pure in heart*** be isolated from the ability to ***see God***? Is one more important than the other? Does purity of heart cause me to ***see God***? Perhaps it is the opposite. If I ever ***see God***, I will be ***pure in heart***. Any attempt to isolate one from the other will end up in the destruction of both.

This reality is found in the nature of God Himself! If you give attention to the attribute of God (what He has), you will be impressed with God's ability. In comparison to your ability, you will shrink in fright. But as it is with all beings, "what He has" is brought under the control of "who He is." His omnipotence is always under the control of His nature. If His nature is safe, then we view His heart. What He does or has done is only viewed for the sake of seeing His heart. Once we see His heart, how do we describe it? He is ***pure in heart***.

But ***pure in heart*** is the description of those who are receiving congratulations! Could it be that His heart and my heart have become one? In fact, what He is inside is what I am inside, because He has come inside of me. This is the message of the Beatitudes. No wonder I am a Jesus pusher!!!

I am a Jesus pusher!!! ***"Blessed are the pure in heart, for they shall see God"*** (Matthew 5:8). This is the conclusion of all the preceding Beatitudes. The helpless are invaded by the unlimited resource of the Divine. In this invasion, they become the Kingdom of Heaven. Those who mourn are responding to the Comforter who embraces them. The assurance and security of His being invades the heart of one who responds in mourning. The meek are only congratulated because His nature of meekness invades the core of their being. This indwelling Meek One affects your physical life. To be in a state of mercy is to be merciful. Congratulation is ours because we are merciful. We are only merciful because we receive Him who is mercy. The purity found in our hearts is because we see Jesus. We see Jesus because we are pure in our hearts,

The Hebrew author wrote: ***"Pursue peace with all people, and holiness, without which no one will see the Lord"*** (Hebrews 12:14). The main verb of the statement is ***"pursue."*** It is an imperative, a command. This is a translation of the Greek word "dioko," the same Greek word translated ***persecuted*** in the last Beatitude (Matthew 5:10). This Greek word can be positive or negative. "Force, zeal, and earnestness" is the undercurrent of the word. ***Peace*** and ***holiness*** are in the dative (direct object). They receive the action of this passion. The Greek word "choris," translated ***without,*** means "separately, by itself, or apart." In other words, no one will ***see the Lord*** apart from ***holiness*** and ***peace***. The next Beatitude (Matthew 5:9) highlights ***peacemakers***. To ***see God*** and not be ***pure in heart*** is impossible; to be pure in heart and not ***see God*** is impossible. I must embrace Jesus for the reality of purity and seeing God. I am a Jesus pusher!!!

I am a Jesus pusher!!! ***"Blessed are the pure in heart, for they shall see God"*** (Matthew 5:8). ***"See God"*** is a Hebraism; it signifies possessing God. The Greek word "optanomai," translated ***see,*** has the idea of gazing with wide-open eyes at something remarkable. It should be noted there are five other Greek words that can be translated ***see.*** Therefore Jesus had several choices of Greek words to express what occurs in the life of one who is ***pure in heart.*** An individual being in possession of God is a radical concept. It is more understandable and acceptable to say that God possesses us. But the New Covenant brings about such a new linkage between God and man that it refers to it as "having God." The early church Fathers referred to Christianity as "having religion." In the Scriptures it is not indicated that people possess demons; however, demons possess people. In order for one to possess the other, there must be surrender, yielding oneself. God yields Himself to us who are ***pure in heart.***

Jesus placed this verb "optanomai" in the middle voice. We are not being acted upon as we ***see God.*** This would be the passive voice. The pure in heart are not causing their ability to ***see God.*** This would be the active voice of the verb. The middle voice of a verb means "personal preference." This becomes the heart's cry of the individual who is ***pure in heart.*** Once the nature of God is experienced, the heart cries for the revelation of all that is God. Seeing and possessing Jesus is the driving passion of those who are pure. You can gauge your heart's purity by how passionate you are to possess Jesus. Congratulations, those of you who have purity of heart. You possess Jesus and are a Jesus pusher!!!

Jesus PUSHER | 77

I am a Jesus pusher!!! ***"Blessed are the peacemakers"*** (Matthew 5:9). The Greek word "eirene," translated peace in the New Testament, is a familiar word. It is used ninety-two times and appears in every book of the New Testament except 1 John. Before the birth of Jesus, Zacharias prophesied concerning his son, John the Baptist. In his preparatory ministry, John would ***"guide our feet into the way of peace"*** (Luke 1:79). At the birth of Jesus, there was a multitude of heavenly host praising God and saying, ***"Glory to God in the highest, and on earth peace"*** (Luke 2:14).

The Bible contains four hundred direct references to peace and many more indirect references. The Bible opens with man living in peace in the Garden of Eden and closes with the eternal peace of heaven. The call of the Gospel message is one of "peace." Jesus linked peace with the fullness of the New Covenant contained in the Holy Spirit. He said to His disciples, ***"Peace I leave with you, My peace I give to you; not as the world gives do I give to you"*** (John 14:27). While the Bible is filled with announcements and promises of peace, where is it? Someone said, "Peace is that glorious moment in history when everyone stops to reload." Peace in Jesus is much more than a lull in the battle. It is a removal of the inner battle. The Hebrew author called it ***"rest"*** (Hebrews 41-11). Security in Jesus brings inner peace. I am a Jesus pusher!!!

Jesus PUSHER | 78

I am a Jesus pusher!!! ***"Blessed are the peacemakers"***
(Matthew 5:8). In 1968 a major newspaper reported that there
had been to that date 14,553 known wars since thirty-six years
before Jesus. Since 1945 there have been over seventy wars and
nearly two hundred internationally significant outbreaks of
violence. While peace is promoted as desirable, the heroes of
our world are warriors. Men of peace are considered weak and
compromising. Our favorite sports are those of violence, and the
video games supplanting the time of our youth are filled with the
opposite of peace. "Peace" is heard in the background of battle
noise, strife, and quarreling. Television does not promote peace.

Where is the source of this constant clamor of strife and
battle? Is it not the root or being of sin? It is self-centered
carnality. I am determined to have my own way. I am willing
to compromise only when it benefits my greater self-centered
desires. When conflict is found, selfishness is present. The
prominent, dominating philosophy of our world is to put self
first. It is blaringly promoted in television advertisements and
strongly recommended by many psychologists and counselors.
When self is first, peace is last. Self-centered carnality is the fuel
for strife, division, hatred, resentment, and war. It is the core of
all sin; it is the opposite of a pure heart from which peace comes.
Our only chance for a pure heart is Jesus. When "self" is lord of
my life, there is conflict; when Jesus is Lord of my life, there is
peace. I am a Jesus pusher!!!

I am a Jesus pusher!!! ***"Blessed are the peacemakers"*** (Matthew 5:8). The Beatitude of peace does not just happen to be the seventh Beatitude. The opening Beatitude is about the Kingdom of Heaven. It is not a place or location, but a relationship. In my complete helplessness, I respond to the unlimited strength and resource of Jesus. I recognize that I am created helpless in order that I might merge with Him. In the embrace of His person, we become the Kingdom. This is maintained in my life through mourning. Mourning is the constant recognition of my helplessness, which produces a constant dependency on Jesus. This releases His nature to flow through me. I live in meekness, which is "a distinct calmness toward God." I will submit every aspect of my life under His supervision and be energized by Him alone. The more I see Him the more I hunger for Him. Jesus always fills this hunger, which only creates more hunger.

As His nature flows through me, I am merciful. I live in constant mercy, so I always express mercy. As His nature flows through me, I am pure in heart. I live in purity, so I always possess God. I am also a peacemaker. This is a direct result of Him. He is the source of all peace. I am not merciful because of my superior discipline. I am certainly not pure in my heart because I have reformed my life. In both cases it is His presence. He is the source of mercy and purity. With no less fervor I can say He is my peace. I am only a peacemaker because of Him. I am a Jesus pusher!!!

I am a Jesus pusher!!! ***"Blessed are the peacemakers"*** (Matthew 5:8). In both the Old and New Testaments, God is the source of peace. The only possibility of peace is to receive it as a gift from God. Our God is a Trinity. He is three persons in One. Each member of the Trinity contributes to the sourcing of peace. In the Old Testament, Jehovah is seen as the supply of peace. ***The Lord*** (Jehovah) ***will give strength to His people; the Lord*** (Jehovah) ***will bless His people with peace*** (Psalms 29:11). ***"But upon David and his descendants, upon his house and his throne, there shall be peace forever from the Lord*** (Jehovah)" (1 Kings 2:33).

How will this peace come to us? ***"But now in Christ Jesus you who once were far off have been brought near by the blood of Christ. For He Himself is our peace"*** (Ephesians 2:13-14). In this same passage, Paul uses the word ***reconcile***. It is translated from the Greek word "apokatallosso." It was never used prior to the New Testament and only found in Colossians and Ephesians. It describes the act of establishing a relationship of peace not before present. Paul said, ***"God was in Christ reconciling the world to Himself, not imputing their trespasses to them, and has committed to us the word of reconciliation"*** (2 Corinthians 5:19). Through Jesus peace has come between you and God. Rest in His love! I am a Jesus pusher!!!

I am a Jesus pusher!!! ***"Blessed are the peacemakers"*** (Matthew 5:8). Don Richardson wrote a book entitled *Peace Child*, (Glendale, California: Regal, 1979). The basis of the book is the description of the long struggle to bring the gospel to the cannibalistic, headhunting Sawi tribe of Irian Jave, Indonesia. The central focus of this ministry was to communicate the heart of the Gospel message. They had great difficulty in getting this tribe to understand the Gospel message, especially the significance of Christ's atoning death on the cross.

The Sawi tribe highly honored treachery, revenge, and murder; there seemed to be no hope for peace. Each village made war against their neighboring village. They were constantly fighting among themselves. However, the tribe had a legendary custom. If one village gave a baby boy to another village, peace prevailed between the two villages as long as the child lived. This baby was called a "peace child."

This custom created an open door for the message of the Gospel. The missionary used it as an analogy of the reconciling work of Jesus. Jesus is God's Divine Peace Child. He gave Jesus to us! Hear the prophet of old: ***"For unto us a Child is born, unto us a Son is given; and the government will be upon His shoulder. And His name will be called Wonderful, Counselor, Mighty God, Everlasting Father, Prince of Peace. Of the increase of His government and peace there will be no end"*** (Isaiah 9:6-7). Jesus lives eternally; therefore His peace will never end. This analogy was the key that unlocked the Gospel for the Sawi Tribe. God, the Father, is the source of all peace; Jesus, the Son, is the manifestation of that peace. Jesus is given to you! I am a Jesus pusher!!!

I am a Jesus pusher!!! ***"Blessed are the peacemakers"*** (Matthew 5:8). Again we say that the Beatitude of peace does not just happen to be the seventh Beatitude. It does not accidently follow the Beatitude of purity. It is as if they are the same! Listen to the declaration of the Psalmist, ***"Mercy and truth have met together; righteousness and peace have kissed"*** (Psalms 85:10). We find the importance of this in the heart of Jesus' definition of peace. Peace is not the absence of war, strife, or argument. It is not only the negative but also the positive. It is the presence of purity, which is holiness. In other words, it is the absence of sin and the presence of Jesus! Individuals can stop fighting without purity, but they cannot live in peace without purity. Purity not only brings an end to harm, but it flows with the healing of love. In fact, the Scriptures shout, ***"God is holy!"*** (1 Peter 1:16). The same Scriptures proclaim, ***"God is love"*** (1 John 4:8, 16). God is both, for they are the same. "Holiness" is "perfect love." Purity is the attitude of perfect love's motive. Therefore, peace does not exist without purity flowing forth with love.

Peace is the creative, aggressive presence of Jesus for goodness. In the Hebrew language of the Old Testament the Jewish greeting was "Shalom." It is an expression of "peace" and a desire that the one who is greeted will have all the purity and goodness God can give. The deepest meaning of the expression is "God's highest good to you." The actual Hebrew word "shalom" has the meaning of "wholeness." Since the state of peace is one of "wholeness," the relationship is complete. Paul cried, ***"You are complete in Him"*** (Colossians 2:9). I am a Jesus pusher!!!

I am a Jesus pusher!!! *"Blessed are the peacemakers"* (Matthew 5:8). To the woman who washed Jesus' feet with her tears and wiped them with her hair, He said, *"Your faith has saved you. Go in peace"* (Luke 7:50). In the Old Testament the "peace offering" is called the "salvation offering." The author of Hebrews encourages us with these words. *"Pursue peace with all people, and holiness, without which no one will see the Lord"* (Hebrews 12:14).

In light of this, many of us struggle with this statement of Jesus to His disciples, *"Do not think that I came to bring peace on earth. I did not come to bring peace but a sword"* (Matthew 10:34). Jesus' statement must be seen in the context of "ministry." The imagery of this ministry is *"Behold, I send you out as sheep in the midst of wolves"* (Matthew 10:16). This does not sound peaceful. Jesus climaxes the Beatitudes with a blessing on those who are being persecuted for purity's sake (Matthew 5:10). This does not sound peaceful. Jesus clearly says that His proposal is not peace at any cost. When perfect love comes to a world of perfect hate, one can expect conflict. When purity is present in a wicked situation, one can expect conflict. War will be declared; but our state must be one of peace in the midst of war. Let us cling to Jesus as conflict rages until His peace dominates our world. I am a Jesus pusher!!!

I am a Jesus pusher!!! ***"Blessed are the peacemakers"*** (Matthew 5:8). The Greek word "eirenopoieo," is translated **peacemakers**. It is a combination of two Geek words. "Eirene" is peace, and "poieo" is to make or do. We have examined "eirene," the first aspect of our word. Let's discuss "poieo." "Poieo" is contrasted with the Greek word "prasso." Both words can be properly translated "to do, or make." However, we often discuss the difference in the motive of these words. "Prasso" highlights routine, duty, or obligation. It is rote action, mechanical or habitual repetition of something to be learned. "Poieo" is the Greek word used to express trees "bearing" fruit. It is a result of something from within the nature of the tree springing forth to accomplish fruit. Jesus "did" or "made" miracles. He is always "poieo." His miracles were a result of the inner movement of the Spirit of God, which could not be contained. Ministry springs forth from the indwelling of the Spirit of God.

You cannot learn peace. This Beatitude does not propose a seminar on "conflict management." This is not a study of personality types and how to appeal to their differences. Jesus proposes we embrace God's Spirit, making us the Kingdom of Heaven. Our helplessness embraces His unlimited resource and we become the Kingdom. This is a Kingdom of peace; we cannot help ourselves. It flows from our inner most being. It is because of the presence of Jesus! I am a Jesus pusher!!!

I am a Jesus pusher!!! ***"Blessed are the peacemakers, for they shall be called sons of God"*** (Matthew 5:9). When someone called me names to hurt me, my mother would always say, "Consider the source." There is some name-calling in this Beatitude. Ultimately it is God who is the source. From what we know about Him, it must be good. Congratulations, God is speaking about you. He has nothing but good to say about you.

There is a parallel passage written by Paul. He opens his letter to the Ephesians with these words: ***"Blessed be the God and Father of our Lord Jesus Christ, who has blessed us with every spiritual blessing in the heavenly places in Christ"*** (Ephesians 1:3). The Greek word "eulogetos, "is translated ***blessed***. It is a synonym of "makarios," translated ***blessed*** in the Beatitudes. It means, "to speak good things." It is the root of our English word "eulogy." Paul uses the word "eulogetos" three times in this one verse. It is used as an adjective, verb, and noun. In the context of this passage, Paul reveals all the good that God speaks about us. What is awesome about this is that they have all come into existence in Jesus. In fact, Jesus is the reality of their existence. Everything good that God desires for your life is in Jesus. There is no need in your life outside of intimacy with Jesus. He is all we need. I am a Jesus pusher!!!

I am a Jesus pusher!!! ***"Blessed are the peacemakers, for they shall be called sons of God"*** (Matthew 5:9). When God speaks, He creates. God spoke the worlds into existence as recorded in the Book of Genesis. Jesus is the Word of God; therefore, all creation came through Him. Congratulations, God is speaking about you. He calls you a "son of God." The evidence of the creative power of this speaking is found in the congratulations. He will not refer to you as fortunate if it is not true. But once again, God speaks through Jesus. Jesus is the creative Word of God. We are sons of God because of Him. Everything He wants us to be He placed in Jesus. Jesus does not extend it to us; we have it because of Him.

Let us never misunderstand the reality of this truth. Jesus is our prototype. Everything He is, we are to be. If it is not in Jesus, we do not want or need it. We are totally focused on Him. ***"The Spirit Himself bears witness with our spirit that we are children of God, and if children, then heirs — heirs of God and joint heirs with Christ"*** (Romans 8:16-17). We are His brothers (Hebrews 2:11). What Jesus receives from the Father, we receive; what Jesus is, we are to be! We are called ***sons of God***. The life of God that sourced the life of Jesus is now sourcing us. We come from the same life source. Therefore we are brothers with Him. This is another description of the merger we experience with God. Our helplessness merged with His nature produces a "son of God." It is all because of Jesus. I am a Jesus pusher!!!

I am a Jesus pusher!!! ***"Blessed are the peacemakers, for they shall be called sons of God"*** (Matthew 5:9). Congratulations! We are in a state of helplessness, ***"poor in spirit."*** We are destitute of every resource needed. How did we get in such a position? God created us this way. It was His intent from the beginning. We were created to be dependent not independent. His unlimited resource comes to embrace us. In the unity of our helplessness and His Person, we become the Kingdom of God. This is the new creature of the New Covenant. We mourn in our state of helplessness. We never step outside the boundary of our helplessness. It enables us to respond to His comfort. The Comforter comes to embrace us. As His nature fills us meekness fills our lives. We relate to our physical existence in a healthy manner. Our hunger and thirst for Him is filled, only to experience expanded hungering and thirsting to be filled again and again. No wonder we are being congratulated.

The state of mercy in which we dwell produces mercy extended to all our relationships. In the embrace of His person we experience His heart. It is a heart of purity. Within us and from us peace reigns. How would you characterize such a relationship? What would be an adequate title for this intimacy? Is there a descriptive term to capture how He has reached us? It is **sons of God**. What a position of honor we now have! It describes the depth of His involvement in sourcing our lives as well as the depth of intimacy He has with us. We are one with Him. I am a Jesus pusher!!!

Jesus PUSHER | 88

I am a Jesus pusher!!! ***"Blessed are the peacemakers, for they shall be called sons of God"*** (Matthew 5:9). The Greek word "huios," translated **sons,** and the Greek word "teknon," translated **children,** are used in the New Testament to speak of our relationship to God. It appears they are used interchangeably. However, there is a legitimate distinction between the two uses. It is important to notice that "child" (teknon) is never used to describe Jesus' relationship to His Father. He is the "son" (huios) of God. "Children" (teknon) is a term of tender affection and endearment as well as of relationship (John 1:12; Ephesians 5:8; 1 Peter 1:14). "Sons" (huios) expresses the dignity and honor of the relationship of a child to his parent.

In this Beatitude, **sons**, the Greek word "huios," is used instead of "teknon." The distinguishing factor is that "teknon" expresses the origin and "huios" expresses the fellowship of life. John wrote, ***"But as many as received Him, to them He gave the right to become children of God, to those who believe in His name"*** (John 1:12). This stresses the initial establishment of a relationship of God as a Father. However, the peacemaker is seen in light of the other six Beatitudes. In relationship to God, the tender affection of being a "child" (teknon) is not missing; but the highest degree of fellowship is experienced as a "son" (huios). As we embrace the nature of God we experience partnership with Him. We are ***"sons of God."*** I am a Jesus pusher!!!

I am a Jesus pusher!!! ***"Blessed are the peacemakers, for they shall be called sons of God"*** (Matthew 5:9). We are ***"sons*** (huios) ***of God."*** We experience the fellowship of His life. This spiritual truth is emphasized by the absence of the definite article before the Greek word "huios," translated ***sons***. When the definite article is used, the emphasis is placed on the origin and the belonging. Without the definite article the emphasis is placed on the fellowship of life. In other words, the reason we are peacemakers is because we are in the fellowship of life with Him. We are ***sons of God*** and actually share His life or nature; therefore, we are ***peacemakers***. This does not merit you the right to be called a "son of God." However, you are a "son of God." Therefore, you live in the fellowship of His life and are a peacemaker. Peacemaking is a result of fellowship and the full realization of our relationship with our Father. What a privilege.

This is understood clearly from the premise of the Sermon on the Mount. We are absolutely helpless, ***"poor in spirit."*** Therefore, any thought of earning or meriting is absurd. We could never accomplish the fellowship of life found in being a son of God. He shares His life with us in our helplessness. We are new creatures; we are called ***"sons of God."*** The moment I move from my helplessness to earn or merit, I destroy the relationship. Therefore, I constantly embrace my helplessness that I might experience Him. Jesus is my source. I am a Jesus pusher!!!

I am a Jesus pusher!!! ***"Blessed are the peacemakers, for they shall be called sons of God"*** (Matthew 5:9). The word order in the Greek text of this beatitude is different than all the others. The Greek text begins with "hoti," translated ***for***. It is causative and gives the reason for the congratulations. ***"They"*** is the second word translated from the Greek word "autos." It is in the nominative case meaning it is the subject of the statement. It is an intensive pronoun giving stress and emphasis to the ***peacemakers***, the antecedent of ***they***.

The third Greek word is "huios" and is translated ***sons***. It is also in the nominative case meaning it is the subject of the statement. This may mean sons is the antecedent of the pronoun, ***they***. There is a double emphasis on ***sons***. **God** (theos) is the next word. It is in the genitive, which establishes relationship with ***sons***. The verb is ***shall be called*** translated from "kaleo." It is indicative meaning a simple statement of fact with no argument. At the end of this verb the pronoun ***they*** is indicated. This means the subject is suggested and stated three times. This statement might be translated: "Congratulations, peacemakers, for you yourselves are sons of God and shall be called this by God." God places us as peacemakers in this honored position. We not only share in the fellowship of His life, but also are honored by the position He gives us. The ***peacemakers*** not only share in His life, which is the accomplished work of Jesus, but also they share in the process and method by which that accomplishment is achieved. I am a Jesus pusher!!!

I am a Jesus pusher!!! ***"Blessed are the peacemakers, for they shall be called sons of God"*** (Matthew 5:9). The verb of the statement is ***"shall be called."*** It is in the indicative mood, which means it is a simple statement of fact without argument. It has a passive voice, which means ***sons*** or ***they*** (the subject) are not responsible for the action of the calling. This presupposes that God is the actor of the calling. The source of being a son is not "peacemaking." The source of being a son comes from God. This removes it from all earnings, performance, or self-promotion. *Today's English Version* translates this statement, ***"God will call them his children!"*** (Matthew 5:9).

The Greek word "kaleo," translated ***shall be called,*** is used in a variety of ways. However, in this context, it is used in the sense of "to call to any station, appoint, or choose." Paul used this in reference to his position as an apostle to the Gentiles (Galatians 1:15). The Hebrews writer said, ***"And no man takes this honor to himself, but he who is called by God, just as Aaron was"*** (Hebrews 5:4). The idea of ***"shall be called"*** means "to become." This is verified by many Old Testament examples. In the prophecy of Isaiah, God said, ***"For My house shall be called a house of prayer for all nations"*** (Isaiah 56:7). God told Abraham, ***"For in Isaac your seed shall be called"*** (Genesis 21:12). We are ***"sons of God"*** not because we are peacemakers. We are ***"sons of God"*** because of the intense desire coming from the heart of God as He calls us. I am a Jesus pusher!!!

I am a Jesus pusher!!! ***"Blessed are the peacemakers, for they shall be called sons of Go"*** (Matthew 5:9). In the Greek text, there is no definite article before the word **God** in the statement **sons of God**. In comparing this with the preceding Beatitude congratulating the **pure in heart**, Jesus says in the Greek text, "For they shall see **the** God" (Matthew 5:8). Why does He not use the same wordage here? The scholars tell us that when the definite article is omitted in such cases, it refers to God in His totality, in His general make-up and infinity. This causes us to conclude that the pronouncement of "being a son" comes from the entire Trinity, not just one member. All three personalities of the Godhead declare our position. Jesus, the visible manifestation of God, makes this statement. But the statement does not just belong to Him but to the entire Godhead, to God in His unity, in His eternity, and in His infinity.

What an unbelievable statement this is! In our absolute helplessness we become invaded by the unlimited resource of the complete Trinity. All three persons of the Triune God take part in bringing the work of their nature to our world through us. Is this what Paul meant when he said, ***"For in Him dwells all the fullness of the Godhead bodily; and you are complete in Him"*** (Colossians 2:9-10)? God, the Trinity, has made us His own! We are sons of the Triune God! It is all through Jesus! I am a Jesus pusher!!!

I am a Jesus pusher!!! ***"Blessed are the peacemakers, for they shall be called sons of God"*** (Matthew 5:9). The manifestation of peace is contained in the Kingdom of God. In our helplessness, we are embraced by the unlimited resource of His nature. In this unity the Kingdom of God is formed. The Kingdom is not a place, a location. It is the manifestation of the new creature formed by God and man. This manifestation is one of peace. We receive this peace as we are diffused with His presence. The peace-receivers become transformed into peace-diffusers. The nature of God is reflected in them. The family likeness becomes manifested; we are the ***sons of God***.

This is not a strain or a discipline. We are not trained or taught. This does not come from education or talent. It is a declaration of His nature. It does not take energy; it is not exhausting. It is not a burden, duty, or obligation. It is spontaneous and expressed without awareness. It is not found in striving, trying, or controlling. It is in the category of *not* being able to help ourselves. It is His nature of peace. We are ***sons of God***.

Think of the honor and the dignity of such a designation! We share in the activity of the Divine Persons. We are co-workers in the embrace of His unlimited resources, the Kingdom of God. Fenelon, the great saint, was reported to have such communion with God his very face shone. Lord Peterborough, a skeptic, through circumstances had to spend the night with him at an inn. In the morning he rushed away saying, "If I stay another night with that man I shall be a Christian in spite of myself." This is the presence of Jesus in us! I am a Jesus pusher!!!

Jesus PUSHER | 94

I am a Jesus pusher!!! ***"Blessed are those who are persecuted for righteousness' sake"*** (Matthew 5:10). My childhood heroes were the New Testament's men of faith. I discovered a book containing an artist's perception of each of the twelve disciples. His drawings were inspired by descriptions from history. In my admiration for these twelve men, I carefully removed the pictures from the book and framed them. Many of these disciples died a martyr's death. John, the beloved, was exiled to the Isle of Patmos. One of my favorite chapters is the roll call of the heroes of faith (Hebrews 11). The list of sufferings includes ***mockings and scourgings, yes, and of chains and imprisonment. They were stoned, they were sawn in two, were tempted, were slain with the sword. They wandered about in sheepskins and goatskins, being destitute, afflicted, tormented — of whom the world was not worthy. They wandered in deserts and mountains, in dens and caves of the earth*** (Hebrews 11:36-38).

Fox's Book of Martyrs is a classic. I was raised on its information. These individuals were so captured by Jesus that nothing could deter them. They lived with the long-range view of eternal values. What could not be seen in the immediate was crystal clear through the eyes of faith. With great admiration we honor them; but we do not want to join them. We desire relief, reduced pressure, and life without problems. We do not begin our day with internal cravings for suffering through persecution. Perhaps we have missed the mind of Christ! How does He think? Is it found in this climatic Beatitude? I am a Jesus pusher!!!

I am a Jesus pusher!!! ***"Blessed are those who are persecuted for righteousness' sake"*** (Matthew 5:10). It may be we have developed into a self-absorbed evangelical church. Our focus in programming is determined by the apparent meeting of the immediate needs. No church seems to extend the invitation to "Come and die!" "Join our church; suffer with the afflictions of Christ!" This challenge does not resonate with today's church.

Yet, there are those of us who desperately want the "mind of Christ." How does He think? He must be from another world; everything He says in the Beatitudes is exactly opposite to the flow of my world. Congratulating the ***poor in spirit*** does not produce confidence in His viewpoint. "Mourning" is not attractive; meekness is not a longing of our hearts. ***Righteousness*** is questionable in every situation; ***mercy*** is only spoken of among the weak. ***Pure in heart*** is only a dream among the religious idealists. My heroes are warriors not ***peacemakers***. But the most ludicrous of all is the preposterous idea of being congratulated for being persecuted. Perhaps the idea could be suggested at the beginning of the discussion of the Kingdom of God; but why would Jesus climax the presentation of the Beatitudes with ***persecution***? Is this the inevitable experience of those who are one with Him? Would the helpless man who finds the resource of His presence even care? Does the greatness of Jesus overshadow all circumstances and discomforts? I am a Jesus pusher!!!

Jesus PUSHER | 96

I am a Jesus pusher!!! The helpless state of being ***poor in spirit*** is a condition sourced by God. We are not this way because we have sinned through disobedience; we are this way because He created us to be so. The reason is that the unlimited resource of His person might unite with our helplessness; the Kingdom of Heaven is formed in this embrace. "Mourning" ushers forth from that embrace. It is the constant response of the heart being wooed by Jesus. It allows the embrace to be closer and closer. It allows the Comforter to extend His presence in and through us. The very nature of God permeates our lives; meekness is experienced. This enables us to experience the physical world on a new level. His presence creates a hunger and thirst that He alone can fill. As He fills us our hunger is expanded; this enables Him to fill us more. We dwell in a state of mercy; as we experience His mercy we are able to extend mercy. Because we are one with Him we have a pure heart; our pure heart allows us to be one with Him. In it is unity and our position as sons is secured. Peace flows within and from us into our world (Matthew 5:3-9).

Jesus' presentation of the state of the Kingdom is focused on one source. He is the source. None of these Beatitudes would be true in our lives except for His embrace. Regarding this final Beatitude of persecution, one could make the argument that if it were not for His embrace, persecution would not take place. As described in the further explanation of the Beatitude, it is for ***"My sake"*** (Matthew 5:11). This same emphasis is highlighted in the Beatitude. ***"Blessed are those who are persecuted for righteousness' sake"*** (Matthew 5:10). Therefore, indirectly Jesus is the source of the persecution. Is He more valuable to me than my own comfort and safety? I am a Jesus pusher!!!

I am a Jesus pusher!!! The Beatitude on persecution is uniquely different from all the rest. This is not an intervention of Jesus producing something wonderful in our lives; persecution is sourced from the evil of another kingdom. The Greek word "dioko," translated *"who are persecuted"* is in the passive voice. This means they are not the source of the persecution; they do not do the action of persecution. They receive the action from another. It is in this Beatitude that Jesus sets the stage for the rest of His discourse. We are going to be **salt** in the midst of a flavorless world (Matthew 5:13). Our lives will shine like **light** in a dark world (Matthew 5:14). All the law of the Old Covenant, which was sourced by self-doing, is fulfilled in this New Covenant relationship. Self will not easily relinquish its hold (Matthew 5:17). Throughout the Sermon on the Mount Jesus continues to contrast the state of dwelling in Him, and He in you, with the world that wants to live out of itself. There are two kingdoms opposed to each other. Persecution is sourced from an evil kingdom.

Do not become so enamored with the wonder of the **kingdom of heaven** that you are surprised at opposition. The two kingdoms are certainly not equal in power. We are not fighting a losing battle. All Jesus describes in the wonder of His presence is far more than adequate for complete victory. Just be aware of the enemy. But focus on Jesus! I am a Jesus pusher!!!

I am a Jesus pusher!!! The Greek word "dioko" is translated "persecuted ones" (Matthew 5:10). This is a participle; it is a verb acting as an adjective. It gives content to the subject. It is in the perfect tense. There are two other Beatitudes using this participle form to describe a subject. They are the Beatitudes on "mourning" and "hungering and thirsting." In each case, they are in the present tense. Jesus changes this in the last Beatitude. In fact, this is the only Beatitude in which the perfect passive participle is used. The perfect tense is used to give a consistency to the action. It speaks of an action occurring in the past, which has continual effects into the present. This means the translation of this verse should read, "who have been persecuted" instead of *"who are persecuted."*

In other words, persecution is not just attached to being **peacemakers**. It begins the moment you and I respond to Jesus and begin the journey in His presence. When we are first embraced by His presence in our helplessness and become the Kingdom of God, we are going to be persecuted. Our response to Him through "mourning" is going to foster persecution. "Meekness" does not excite or thrill our self-seeking world. They cannot understand anyone who hungers and thirsts for something other than themselves. Who would want to be **merciful**? Purity in heart is not the craving of a self-focused individual. One who is bent on their way does not care for *"peacemaking."* Therefore, persecution is present from the beginning. Jesus is not saying, "Blessed are those who shall be persecuted or are being persecuted." He boldly says, "Blessed are those who have been persecuted from the outset of this relationship." They are now full-fledged "persecuted ones!" Focus on Jesus! I am a Jesus pusher!!!

Jesus PUSHER | 99

I am a Jesus pusher!!! Jesus highlights the absolute certainty of persecution (Matthew 5:10-11). Paul writes to the Thessalonians concerning his love for them. His desire was *that no one should be shaken by these afflictions; for you yourselves know that we are appointed to this. For, in fact, we told you before when we were with you that we would suffer tribulation, just as it happened, and you know* (1 Thessalonians 3:3-4). Paul seemed to think that persecution is inevitable. He predicted it; it came to pass.

Some years ago a popular national magazine took a survey to determine the things that make people happy. The responses revealed several things: happy people enjoy other people but are not self-sacrificing; they refuse to participate in any negative feelings or emotions; and they have a sense of accomplishment based on their own self-sufficiency. Consider the opposite approach of Jesus as He calls us *"Blessed."* We are helpless in our spirit, so there is no self-sufficiency. We consistently acknowledge this fact through mourning. We are meek, never seeking our own way. We are hungering and thirsting for Him instead of self. We live in a state of mercy and give mercy; we have a pure heart and make peace. The state of happiness *from* the world and the state of happiness *in* Jesus are extremely opposite. Each time the state of the Christian intersects the state of the world there will be conflict. It is called "persecution." I am a Jesus pusher!!!

I am a Jesus pusher!!! Paul used the term ***tribulation*** to describe persecution (1 Thessalonians 3:3-4). Persecution is one form of ***tribulation*** that God permits and for which Jesus calls us ***"Blessed"*** (Matthew 5:10). This word comes from the Latin word "tribulum." It describes a threshing sledge or flail. This is a threshing instrument consisting of a staff with a short heavy stick dangling on the end. The farmer would use the flail to beat and bruise the sheaves. This enabled him to separate the golden grain from the chaff and straw. Persecution is a picture of God's threshing instrument in our lives. His purpose is not to destroy us, but to separate what is good, heavenly, and spiritual within us from what is wrong, earthly, and fleshly. It will take the blows of adversity and persecution to accomplish this. This is the final desire of the relationship. He embraces us in our helplessness and the Kingdom of Heaven is established. We respond by mourning and experience the Comforter in the embrace. His nature of meekness gives us a new relationship to our physical world. We are filled only to hunger and thirst for more. We live in a state of mercy, purity of heart, and peace as we rest in His embrace. The purpose for all of this is to reveal His person through us. He allows persecution for the final refining of His image in our lives. Jesus is allowed to see Himself in us and others see His reflection through our lives. I am a Jesus pusher!!!

Jesus PUSHER | 101

I am a Jesus pusher!!! The prophets of old wrote, *"He will sit as a refiner and a purifier of silver; He will purify the sons of Levi, and purge them as gold and silver, that they may offer to the Lord an offering in righteousness"* (Malachi 3:3). A Bible study group, wondering about the deeper meaning of this verse, made an appointment with a silversmith. As the silversmith revealed to them the process of refining, he was asked, "Do you sit while the refining is going on?" To that he replied, "Oh, yes, indeed. I must sit with my eyes steadily fixed on the surface. If the time necessary for refining is exceeded to the slightest degree, the silver is sure to be injured." Then the silversmith gave the most revealing statement of all. He said, "I only know when the process is complete by seeing my own image reflected on the silver." Is this why Jesus calls us *"blessed"* when we are persecuted (Matthew 5:10)?

Jesus presented the imagery for ministry as *"sheep in the midst of wolves"* (Matthew 10). This virtually reeks of persecution. However, He urged His disciples not to focus on the persecution. How easy it is to major on being hurt, the pain, or how unfair it is. We are to focus on being like Him. Jesus said, *"It is enough for a disciple that he be like his teacher, and a servant like his master"* (Matthew 10:25). This is the supreme cry of the heart of one who embraces Him. *"It is enough,"* means the fulfillment of the passionate priority of my life. This is the supreme desire of my being. I am a Jesus pusher!!!

I am a Jesus pusher!!! Persecution is something that each of us at some time or another has certainly thought was being bestowed on us. In school I wrote what I thought was an excellent paper only to have my teacher persecute me with a poor grade. In my insecurity I was sure a group of my peers were standing in the hall talking about me. That was persecution. My parents unfairly persecuted me every time they did not permit me to participate in certain activities. When I failed to get the desired job promotion I just knew the foreman was persecuting me. Over the years I have sensed persecution in the church. People simply do not recognize my true value and worth. In my opinion, my life is consistently plagued with persecution.

Then we come to our present study in Matthew (5:10-12). I am now having difficulty placing the things I have spoken of into Jesus' description of persecution. In fact, I feel a little embarrassed. My many inconveniences do not seem to merit the title of persecution. Jesus said, "I am to be **persecuted for righteousness' sake**." This disqualifies every suffering spawned by stubbornness and selfishness. I wonder if I have ever experienced real persecution. I shrink into insignificance in comparison to the Apostle Paul who said, **"From now on let no one trouble me, for I bear in my body the marks of the Lord Jesus"** (Galatians 6:17). I absolutely have no right to complain about my meager sufferings. I have no marks! Jesus, forgive me! I am a Jesus pusher!!!

Jesus PUSHER | 103

I am a Jesus pusher!!! There is one fact of which I am deeply aware. The call of Christianity is a call to suffer. This is the "shouting" message of the Beatitudes (Matthew 5:3-12). We are not off on our own. We do not experience persecution in isolation. We are embraced by and filled with the essence of His being. Any persecution we experience only takes place by participating with Jesus in His movement in our lives and our world. Why would we hesitate to be a part of it? If Jesus' death were the result of **lawless hands** (Acts 2:23), would I not experience the same persecution in His death? Peter used this phrase to describe the Jewish religious leaders. Persecution comes from the self-sourcing in our world as well as within the religious organization. It comes from self-sourcing because this is the core of all sin.

We are in the middle of the essence of Cross Style. It is fundamental to the Christian experience; we have summarized it into a phrase. We cannot embrace Jesus without embracing His style. His style is the cross. The cross was not just one event in the life of Jesus. It was not something He had to go through and then it was over. The cross is the core of His thought process, His nature. He leaped off His throne as God and became man; it is the cross style. He was born in a stable; it is cross style. He did miracles and wanted nothing in return; it is cross style. As Master, He washed the disciples' feet; it is cross style. He never ever thought about Himself, but poured out His life for others; it is cross style. Was He persecuted? Indeed, yes! It is cross style. Is not persecution a natural result of cross style in a self-sourced world? I am a Jesus pusher!!!

I am a Jesus pusher!!! Jesus viewed the fulfillment of the Beatitudes in the experience of persecution (Matthew 5:10-12). The virtues of the Beatitudes are seen clearly and expressed most forcibly in the crucifixion. The cross style is only experienced in relationship with Jesus. Cross style is impossible to accomplish outside of intimacy with Him. In its essence it is not something we do; it is the way we think, exist, and function. If we develop a list of activities to achieve the status of cross style, we automatically violate the nature of the cross. If the master washing the disciples' feet is viewed as a cross style activity, there are a variety of subjects to be addressed. How many feet are required to meet the condition? How thoroughly must the feet be washed? How often should I wash feet? Asking these questions violates the heart of "cross style."

Paul speaks of the ***fellowship of His sufferings***. He explains that this ***fellowship of sufferings*** brings me into ***being conformed to His death*** (Philippians 3:10). The Greek word "koinonia," translated ***fellowship,*** portrays the idea of partnership. It originally portrayed the picture of a government official giving business advice. We become "business partners." Paul proclaimed this in the mystery of his statement, ***"I now rejoice in my sufferings for you, and fill up in my flesh what is lacking in the afflictions of Christ, for the sake of His body, which is the church"*** (Colossians 1:24). How can my sufferings mingle with His to redeem the world? It is a mystery, but He has included me. I am a Jesus pusher!!!

I am a Jesus pusher!!! Throughout the ministry of Jesus, He always placed His call to the style of the cross in the context of relationship. A major shift takes place in chapter sixteen of Matthew. The Galilean ministry has drawn to an end. Jesus withdraws from the crowd. He focuses on training His disciples. The heart of this training is to prepare them for the cross. He desperately wants them to join Him in this journey to redeem the world. He begins by quizzing His disciples about Himself. Peter's great confession is a startling confirmation: ***"You are the Christ, the Son of the living God"*** (Matthew 16:16).

While Jesus is greatly pleased with this confession, He has a concern. Do they understand the content of "being the ***Christ?***" Jesus shares with them His first prediction of His death, the cross (Matthew 16:21), creating a major uproar within the group. In the discussion, Jesus says, ***"If anyone desires to come after Me, let him deny himself, and take up his cross, and follow Me. For whoever desires to save his life will lose it, but whoever loses his life for My sake will find it"*** (Matthew 16:24-25). At the core of the suffering involving the cross is relationship. Cross style is about denying self and embracing Jesus. No one takes up a cross without following Jesus. If we lose our lives it will be for His sake. This is not about acts of sacrifice; this is about embracing Jesus. No wonder Jesus considers us blessed when we are persecuted (Matthew 5:10-12). I am a Jesus pusher!!!

Jesus PUSHER | 106

I am a Jesus pusher!!! Persecution must be seen in the context of **righteousness**. There is a strong focus in the Beatitude on **righteousness' sake**. It is an amazing statement. In many English translations the word "**for**" is there twice (Matthew 5:10). In the statement, "**for theirs is the kingdom of heaven**" the Greek word translated *for* is "hoti." It introduces the object, content, or argument to which the preceding word refers. In our Beatitudes, "hoti" appears to give the reason or argument for the congratulations. In other words, congratulations go to the persecuted ones because they are the "**kingdom of heaven**." But the statement "**for** righteousness' **sake**" is a different word. Actually "**for sake**" is a translation of the Greek word "heneka." It means "for this cause" or "for this reason." Jesus clearly states why the persecuted one is suffering such treatment. It is because of **righteousness**. The Greek word "dikaiosune," translated **righteousness** is used both in the Old and New Testaments as the stated commanded by God and standing the test of His judgment.

In light of this cause, let us examine the "completeness of the cause." If the underlying cause of persecution is **righteousness** and if it is described as "a state commanded by God which stands the test of His judgment," then the cause is far beyond any activity. You cannot simply eliminate a deed connected to Christian ceremonies that might offend a non-believer. **Righteousness** is actually all of the Beatitudes brought together. All of the Beatitudes describe the state of righteousness in which the believer dwells. He is the helpless one who merges with Jesus. This merger causes persecution. But it is a state of blessedness because of Jesus. I am a Jesus pusher!!!

I am a Jesus pusher!!! The believer is an individual who is absolutely helpless. He consistently responds to Jesus and experiences God's nature of meekness. He hungers and thirsts and is constantly being filled with mercy, purity, and peace. What do we call such a person? He is the **kingdom of heaven**, **comforted**, **inherit**or of **the land**, **filled**, one who experiences **mercy**, one who has a vision of God, a son of God, and again he is the **kingdom of heaven**.

If the cause of persecution is a state of **righteousness** then there is a "cause within the cause." The ones who persecute are those who are not righteous. Obviously the righteous ones are not doing whatever is contained within persecution. As we walk through the Beatitudes, we see the evidence of this. The absolute destitute embrace the unlimited resource of Jesus and can do nothing but love. Those who are filled with the Comforter can do nothing but extend comfort. The meek ones extend concern and care. Those filled proclaim the location of fullness. Those dwelling in a state of mercy and purity share mercy and righteousness. The spirit of persecution is not the spirit of the **kingdom of heaven**! Therefore if you are a persecutor, you are not in the Kingdom. How could you embrace Jesus and persecute others? Jesus compels us in the Spirit of the Beatitudes, meekness, mercy, purity, and peace. We live in Him. I am a Jesus pusher!!!

Jesus PUSHER | 108

I am a Jesus pusher!!! Jesus concludes the presentation of the Beatitudes with that of persecution. ***"Blessed are those who are persecuted for righteousness' sake, for theirs is the kingdom of heaven"*** (Matthew 5:10). This is the only beatitude to which He gives additional explanation and encouragement. Such a statement raises some real questions. Why am I being persecuted? Do you find the "conflict of the cause" perplexing? Why does someone who lives out the essence of these Beatitudes irritate others? If you are someone who loves and cares, why are you hated? Why is it that people do not like righteousness? Solomon wrote, ***"And he who is upright in the way is an abomination to the wicked"*** (Proverbs 29:27).

We must understand what is already stated in the previous studies. It is the "consistency of the cause." The Greek word (dioko) translated ***"who are persecuted"*** is in the perfect tense. This tense reflects something happening in the past but reoccurs in the present. In other words, the focus of the statement is not just on a single event of persecution, but also on the continuous element of it. This places persecution in the first Beatitude and carries it through to the last. Persecution is present from start to finish. If one is to endure the consistent conflict of persecution, they must know the One who is greater than the persecution. It is Jesus! Only those who in their helplessness have merged with His greatness will consider persecution a mere irritation in comparison. Jesus is greater than my persecution. I am a Jesus pusher!!!

I am a Jesus pusher!!! There are some common truths spoken by all of the Beatitudes (Matthew 5:3-12). Jesus advocates from the first Beatitude an intimate relationship with Him. One by one the Beatitudes highlight an aspect of this relationship. My helplessness is matched with the unlimited resource of His person; together we become the Kingdom of Heaven. Mourning is my constant response to the embrace of the Comforter. In this intimacy His nature of meekness is known. The more I hunger and thirst for His mind and heart, the more He reveals Himself to me. I dwell in His mercy, purity, and peace. These are all characteristics of who He is. All of these Beatitudes are mere descriptions of an intimate relationship with Him.

Jesus also advocates a second truth from the first Beatitude. Through this relationship everything He is will be manifested in us. His mind will become our mind; His heart will become our heart. We will become the visible image of His person in our world. We are people of mercy because we dwell in the embrace of His mercy. We have pure hearts because He who is pure dwells in us. We are peacemakers because we dwell in His peace. As this takes place, the way the world treated Him is the way the world will treat us. It is inevitable; we will be persecuted. But the delight of knowing Him overshadows the persecution. It is a joy to join Him in His suffering. I am a Jesus pusher!!!

I am a Jesus pusher!!! We must consider "severe persecution." This is the only Beatitude that has more than one verse (Matthew 5:10-12). Jesus expands this Beatitude with two additional verses to address persecution. He begins with **"Blessed are those who are persecuted"** (Matthew 5:10). Remember that the verb is in the perfect tense that translates **"have been persecuted."** He emphasizes this again in the next verse by saying, **"Blessed are you when they revile and persecute you"** (Matthew 5:11). This is further stressed in the following verse, **"So they persecuted the prophets who were before you"** (Matthew 5:12). The restatement of the word three times presents to us the severity of His message.

In all three of these statements, the Greek word "dioko" is translated **persecute**. This word has the basic meaning of chasing, driving away, or pursuing. It is presents the picture of physical affliction or infliction of physical pain. This should not be a surprise to us since the third Beatitude speaks directly to our connection to the physical world. Our relationship with Jesus does not simply dwell in some mystical, unseen world. Because of His nature we embrace our physical existence in a new way. There are definite physical ramifications to being Kingdom people. But the joy of embracing Him overshadows persecution. He is our focus! I am a Jesus pusher!!!

I am a Jesus pusher!!! Jesus compels us to consider "slanderous persecution." He says, *"Blessed are you when they revile and persecute you, and say all kinds of evil against you falsely for My sake"* (Matthew 5:11). The Greek word "oneidizo," translated *revile* suggests the idea of reviling, upbraiding, or seriously insulting. It means to cast in one's teeth. Jesus definitely describes this condition with the additional statement of *"and say all kinds of evil against you falsely for My sake."* The crucifixion event gives a vivid example of such activity. The crowds who were passing by wagged their heads; they made fun of His teachings. The leaders of Israel mocked Jesus with words promoting disgust. They struck blows of criticism against the most precious and sacred possession of Jesus, His relationship with His Father. But over and above all of this, *even the robbers who were crucified with Him reviled* (oneidizo) *Him with the same thing* (Matthew 27:44). This covered every aspect of society.

Not only was there physical persecution, but there was mental, verbal, and emotional persecution. Persecution is not simply about physical pain; there is an emotional pain as well. This aspect of persecution is often harder to bear than the physical aspect. It reveals a total misunderstanding of what is really happening. For instance, in the case of Jesus, He shared His heart with the individuals who were berating Him. He healed and loved them. They demonstrated no comprehension of anything He shared with them. Even if the physical aspect of the cross were removed, the isolation and rejection would be paramount. As He fills us, will we not experience this in our world? But intimacy with Him overshadows all persecution! I am a Jesus pusher!

I am a Jesus pusher!!! Jesus suggests another kind of persecution. "Sham persecution" is a focus on "**all kinds of evil against you falsely for My sake**" (Matthew 5:11). Insults are abusive words said to your face, but **all kinds of evil** are primarily abusive words said behind your back. This suggests major war taking place about which we do not know. There are multitudes of incidents, plots, and demonic strategies assaulting us. We may never know the full employment of the forces of evil being hurled against us.

But the final word is "It does not matter!" We are to **"rejoice and be exceedingly glad"** (Matthew 5:12). The final word about persecution from Jesus is "focus." Do not focus on the hurt, the pain, or the slander; we must focus on Jesus. Do not focus on the negative, the wrong, or what is unfair; focus on Jesus. Do not focus on what others are doing to you; focus on what Jesus wants to do through you to them. He is always redemptive. The wonder of what we experience in the Beatitudes so overshadows anything negative that we hardly notice it. After all it is all **"for My sake."** Any persecution you experience is linked intimately with Him. What a privilege to suffer for Jesus' sake! If He is not more important to you than your personal comfort, you do not know Him! I am a Jesus pusher!!!

I am a Jesus pusher!!! Matthew is an author who writes with a fundamental goal in view, an evangelist writing with an evangelistic fervor. He wants to win the Israelite nation to Jesus. They must be convinced of who Jesus is. The hopes and dreams of Jewish history are focused on the Messiah. Their Messiah appears, only to be rejected and crucified by His own. It is the greatest of tragedies. Matthew plays the role of a lawyer, piling evidence upon evidence, building a strong case for Jesus. Jesus is the Kingly Messiah.

Obviously this places the Kingdom of Heaven at the heart of his presentation. It was the core of the forerunner's message, John the Baptist. John preached, *"Repent, for the kingdom of heaven is at hand!"* (Matthew 3:2). Jesus followed up with the identical message (Matthew 4:17). The heart of the devil's temptation of Jesus focused on the Kingdom. The last of the recorded forty-day temptations deals directly with the Kingdom. The devil took Jesus to an elevation where He could see all the kingdoms of the earth (Matthew 4:8). They were already established and could be His. Why construct something already in existence?

Now Jesus presents a three-chapter discourse giving the "Manifesto of the Kingdom of Heaven!" Here are the fundamental principles of Kingdom living and the core heartbeat of that Kingdom. It is significant that the first statement of the Sermon on the Mount contains the Kingdom's declaration. In other words, the Beatitudes begin with the reality of the Kingdom's presence. Now as we come to the end of the Beatitudes, the closing is a statement of the Kingdom's reality. The reality of the Beatitudes is the reality of the Kingdom. The Kingdom is the merger between your helplessness and His Person. Jesus in you is the Kingdom. I am a Jesus pusher!!!

I am a Jesus pusher!!! There are eight Beatitudes. The first one ends with the statement, *"For theirs is the kingdom of heaven"* (Matthew 5:3). The eighth or last Beatitude states, *"For theirs is the kingdom of heaven"* (Matthew 5:10). These two statements are exactly alike in words and grammar structure. This is an example of a literary device known as "inclusion." It signals the beginning and the end of a section. It is a presentation of the theme, concept, or proposition of the sermon. It implies that the Kingdom sums up all the other results listed in the second clauses of the Beatitudes.

It is important to note that the six Beatitudes sandwiched between the first and last are all in the future tense. The reality of the present tense Kingdom is presented in the first Beatitude; we are reminded of this present reality in the last Beatitude. In my state of helplessness, I am embraced by the unlimited resource of Jesus. We become the Kingdom in this union. This is present tense! In this present tense reality Jesus begins to manifest in my life all the resources of His person. As I mourn in response to His presence, I experience more of the Comforter. My physical existence takes on the shape of Jesus' presence as I embrace Him. The satisfaction of my hungering and thirsting marvels my mind. I experience mercy in an ever-unfolding reality. His face becomes clearer in my sight. I can hear His voice whispering softly in my ear, "You are my son." These unfolding wonders exist in the *kingdom of heaven*. What a wonder to *be* the Kingdom of Heaven, embraced by Jesus. I am a Jesus pusher!!!

I am a Jesus pusher!!! The values of the Kingdom of Heaven and the kingdoms of the world have a startling contrast. The values of the Kingdom of Heaven are sandwiched between the first and the last Beatitudes. These six Beatitudes between give us the elements from which all things in the Kingdom exist. As stated above they are in the future tense, while the first and last Beatitudes state the Kingdom in the present tense. Any attempt to discover value of the Kingdom not mentioned in these six Beatitudes is futile. These are the core values.

Each one seems to be presented in a contrast. The first of the six between Beatitudes is ***"Blessed are those who mourn."*** "Mourning" is contrasted with "comfort." "Mourning" is distinctly connected to the "helpless state." It is this state that makes us suitable to be embraced by the unlimited resource of His presence. This embrace is the existence of the Kingdom. "Mourning" is the consistent recognition of my state of helplessness; it is the consistency of my helplessness embracing Him. His presence fills my life; He is the Comforter. He comes alongside (inside) to nurture, encourage, empower, and enable all I need. I am living in a state of "comfort."

Consider this kind of "comfort" in contrast to the kingdom of the world. "Comfort" is seen in terms of materialism, power, and prestige. It is a false sense of having no needs, being in charge, or acquiring my own desires. It is the satisfaction of getting what I want. "Living comfortably" is a phrase to describe possessing what I want, all needs being met. Yet, this sense of completeness quickly fades; it is because I do not have what I need. I am a Jesus pusher!!!

I am a Jesus pusher!!! The Beatitudes are a presentation of the core values given by Jesus. He begins the Beatitudes with a declaration of the Kingdom (Matthew 5:3) and ends it with the same (Matthew 5:10). The values of the Kingdom are in extreme contrast to the values of the world! For instance, ***"Blessed are the meek, for they shall inherit the earth"*** (Matthew 5:5). This is such a radical concept. The ***meek***, gentle, and caring individual gives expression to the nature of Christ. The haughty, proud, and domineering give expression to the nature of the kingdom of darkness. Those in the Kingdom of Heaven embrace their physical world in a relational matter. In becoming one with the physical world, all the benefits of this world become theirs. The haughty and proud use the physical for selfish ends. They pollute their physical world with the darkness of their souls. While they value possessing physical things, those physical things never become one with them.

"Blessed are those who hunger and thirst for righteousness" declares another core value (Matthew 5:6). Hungering and thirsting for righteousness brings a filling. But the nature of such fulfilled desires establishes greater expansion. The filling creates a hunger for the potential of completion. It spurs one into the consistent unfolding of His revelation. The hungering and thirsting of the kingdom of darkness never produces filling. The more you eat, the more you lack. Unrighteousness diminishes a person's capacity of the heart. I want the values of Jesus in my life. I am a Jesus pusher!!!

Jesus PUSHER | 117

I am a Jesus pusher!!! The core values of the Kingdom of Heaven are the discussion of the Beatitudes. **Mercy**, *pure in heart*, and **peacemakers** are not valued in the kingdom of darkness (Matthew 5:7-9). Ruthlessness, domination, power, and the ability to master every situation for self-benefit are held supreme. Yet, everyone of this persuasion is soon brought to a position of crying for mercy. They define peace as the removal of conflict because they are superior. They live in the world of "what can I get by with" and "what can I get." The heartbeat of purity brings forth integrity and honesty is polluted with greed and selfishness.

Jesus battled the devil in spiritual warfare for forty days and nights (Matthew 4:1-11). The final temptation climaxed in no tricks or manipulations. Evidently, the devil was willing to bargain with Jesus in order to survive. He took Jesus to an ***exceedingly high mountain, and showed Him all the kingdoms of the world and their glory***. The Greek word "doxa," translated **glory** refers to viewpoint and perspective. Jesus came to earth to establish a Kingdom. If Jesus could take over the kingdoms of the world, would He not rush to the opportunity?

In glee and delight, Satan pointed out all the wonders of his kingdoms. All the filth of sin, all the perversion of sexual desires, all the corruption of dishonesty and greed, all the destruction of addictions, and all the cancer of carnality were revealed. Jesus could have it all. He could be King over this domain. The devil thought this would allure Jesus, when in fact it repulsed Him. The values of the Kingdom of Heaven are completely opposite of the values of the kingdoms of the world. I want the values of Jesus! I am a Jesus pusher!!!

I am a Jesus pusher!!! The values of the Kingdom of Heaven are vastly different from the kingdoms of the world. According to the dictionary, a viewpoint is "a particular attitude or way of considering a matter." We refer to it as posture or position. When an individual is within the relationship that produces the Kingdom of Heaven, he sees from this viewpoint. When one exists in the kingdoms of the world, he sees everything from a different position.

Let's return to the first Beatitude (Matthew 5:3). It is the *poor in spirit* who are experiencing the *kingdom of the heaven*. They are not "in" the *kingdom of heaven* from the sense of location. They have become the Kingdom. In the helplessness of their state, they are filled with His unlimited resource. In this embrace and oneness, the Kingdom of Heaven is formed. God has chosen not to be the Kingdom of Heaven without us; we cannot possibly exist as the Kingdom without Him.

This means that the viewpoint, position, or posture for the "Kingdom person" is Jesus. The "mind of Christ" is now ours. We have His attitude. In each of the "between" Beatitudes, we are congratulated for a virtue. However, each particular virtue is really "Jesus." Those who *mourn* are being congratulated for "being comforted." In previous studies we discovered the Greek word "parakaleo," translated *comforted* is a title for the Holy Spirit, the Spirit of Jesus! The strong arms of Jesus embrace us; He is our comfort. It is from this position we view our world. I am a Jesus pusher!!!

I am a Jesus pusher!!! We are not **meek** due to our own effort (Matthew 5:5). Our lives are filled with meekness because we experience His nature. As we live in Jesus, in the Kingdom's embrace, we experience all He is. This is our posture. We experience our physical world from this position. We know the truth about our own body and its desires. Jesus is our viewpoint. The core of hungering and thirsting is found in the content of desire. For what do we hunger in the deep heart of our being? In experiencing Him, we hunger for Him only! Indeed, He fills us and fulfills us. He is consistently enlarging our capacity for Himself. He is our hunger and our filling.

We find **mercy** in the Kingdom of Heaven. If the Kingdom of Heaven is His embrace, He is this **mercy**. Extending mercy to others is to extend Him. In the state of **pure in heart**, I see God. Could it be that I am in a state of seeing God and have a pure heart? In oneness with Him my heart becomes pure. He is my purity! It is impossible to have peace and to impart it to others without His embrace. The nature of selfishness produces conflict and dissention within and without. Peace can only be defined as the presence of Jesus. The values of the Kingdom of Heaven are not the values of the kingdoms of the world. The values of the Kingdom are found in King of the Kingdom. Therefore, the values of the Kingdom are not many; they are the person of Jesus. In His embrace, I have His mind. In intimacy with Him; I care as He cares. We become the Kingdom of Heaven. I am a Jesus pusher!!!

Jesus PUSHER | 120

I am a Jesus pusher!! The helpless state of being ***poor in spirit*** is a condition sourced by God. We are not this way because we have sinned through disobedience; we are this way because He created us to be so. The reason is that the unlimited resource of His person might unite with our helplessness; the Kingdom of Heaven is formed in this embrace. "Mourning" ushers forth from that embrace. It is the constant response of the heart being wooed by Jesus, allowing greater closeness in the embrace. It allows the Comforter to extend His presence in and through us. The nature of God permeates our lives; we experience meekness. This enables us to experience the physical world on a new level. His presence creates a hunger and thirst that He alone can fill. As He fills us our hunger is expanded; this enables Him to fill us more. We dwell in a state of mercy; as we experience His mercy we are able to extend mercy. Because we are one with Him we have a pure heart; our pure heart allows us to be one with Him. In oneness we have unity and our position as sons is secured. Peace flows within and from us into our world.

Jesus' presentation of the state of the Kingdom is focused on one source. He is the source. None of these Beatitudes would be true in our lives except for His embrace. Regarding this final Beatitude of persecution, one could make the argument that if it were not for His embrace, persecution would not take place. As described in the further explanation of the Beatitude, it is for ***"My sake"*** (Matthew 5:11). This same emphasis is highlighted in the Beatitude. ***"Blessed are those who are persecuted for righteousness' sake"*** (Matthew 5:10). Therefore, indirectly Jesus is the source of the persecution. Any discomfort I might experience is overshadowed by His presence. I am a Jesus pusher!!!

Jesus PUSHER | 121

I am a Jesus pusher!!! ***"Blessed are those who are persecuted for righteousness' sake"*** (Matthew 5:10). This Beatitude is uniquely different from all the rest. This is not an intervention of Jesus producing something wonderful in our lives; persecution is sourced from the evil of another kingdom. The Greek word "dioko," translated ***"who are persecuted,"*** is in the passive voice. This means those persecuted are not the source of the persecution; they do not do the action of persecution. They receive the action from another.

It is in this Beatitude that Jesus sets the stage for the rest of His discourse. We are going to be **salt** in the midst of a flavorless world (Matthew 5:13). Our lives will shine like **light** in a dark world (Matthew 5:14). All the law of the Old Covenant, which was sourced by self-doing, is fulfilled in this New Covenant relationship. Self will not easily relinquish its hold (Matthew 5:17). Throughout the Sermon on the Mount Jesus continues to contrast the state of dwelling in Him, and He in you, with the world that wants to live out of itself. There are two kingdoms opposed to each other. Persecution is sourced from an evil kingdom.

Do not become so enamored with the wonder of the **kingdom of heaven** that opposition surprises you. The two kingdoms are certainly not equal in power. We do not fight a losing battle. All Jesus describes in the wonder of His presence is far more than adequate for complete victory. Just be aware of the enemy. He will provide some obstacles. But continue to be a Jesus pusher!!!

I am a Jesus pusher!!! ***"Blessed are those who are persecuted for righteousness' sake"*** (Matthew 5:10). The Greek word "dioko" is translated "persecuted ones," a participle, a verb acting as an adjective. It gives content to the subject and is in the perfect tense. There are two other Beatitudes using this participle form to describe a subject. They are the Beatitudes on "mourning" and "hungering and thirsting." In each case, they are in the present tense. Jesus changes this in the last Beatitude. In fact, this is the only Beatitude in which the perfect passive participle is used. The perfect tense is used to give a consistency to the action. It speaks of an action occurring in the past, which has continual effects into the present. This means the translation of this verse should read, "who have been persecuted" instead of ***"who are persecuted."***

In other words, persecution is not just attached to being ***peacemakers***. It begins the moment you and I respond to Jesus and begin the journey in His presence. When we are first embraced by His presence in our helplessness and become the Kingdom of God, we are going to be persecuted. Our response to Him through "mourning" is going to foster persecution. "Meekness" does not excite or thrill our self-seeking world. They cannot understand anyone who hungers and thirsts for something other than themselves. Who would want to be ***merciful?*** Purity in heart is not the craving of a self-focused person. One who is bent on their way does not care for ***"peacemaking."*** Therefore, persecution is present from the beginning. Jesus is not saying, "Blessed are those who shall be persecuted or are being persecuted." He boldly says, "Blessed are those who have been persecuted from the outset of this relationship." They are now full-fledged "persecuted ones!"

I am a Jesus pusher!!! ***"Blessed are those who are persecuted for righteousness' sake"*** (Matthew 5:10). Jesus highlights the absolute certainty of persecution. In writing to Timothy, Paul speaks of two men, Jannes and Jambres in the Old Testament who evidently were the magicians or sorcerers of Pharaoh in Egypt. They resisted the truth and stood against Moses, but made no progress. But Timothy did not respond like these magicians of old. He ***carefully followed*** Paul's ***doctrine, manner of life, purpose, faith, longsuffering, love, perseverance, persecutions, afflictions*** (2 Timothy 3:10-11). Timothy saw how Jesus delivered Paul in each case. Then Paul declares to Timothy, ***"Yes, and all who desire to live godly in Christ Jesus will suffer persecution"*** (2 Timothy 3:12).

In Galatians, Paul gives the example of Isaac. He is a "child of promise" and is an example for us. But there is one who was born ***according to the flesh***. Paul concludes, ***"But, as he who was born according to the flesh then persecuted him who was born according to the Spirit, even so it is now"*** (Galatians 4:29). Paul traces this back to the days of Abraham and his two sons. His son who was born of Hagar is born of the flesh. His son who was born of Sarah is born of the Spirit. They war against each other; they are not the same. Persecution is inevitable. Is Jesus worth it? All suffering is overshadowed by His indwelling presence. I am a Jesus pusher!!!

I am a Jesus pusher!!! ***"Blessed are those who are persecuted for righteousness' sake"*** (Matthew 5:10). Paul writes to the Thessalonians concerning his love for them. His desire was ***that no one should be shaken by these afflictions; for you yourselves know that we are appointed to this. For, in fact, we told you before when we were with you that we would suffer tribulation, just as it happened, and you know*** (1 Thessalonians 3:3-4). Paul seemed to think that persecution is inevitable. He predicted it; it came to pass.

Some years ago a popular national magazine took a survey to determine the things that make people happy. The responses revealed several things: happy people enjoy other people but are not self-sacrificing; they refuse to participate in any negative feelings or emotions; and they have a sense of accomplishment based on their own self-sufficiency. Consider the absolute opposite approach of Jesus as He calls us ***"Blessed."*** We are helpless in our spirit, so there is no self-sufficiency. In fact, we consistently acknowledge this fact through mourning. We are meek, never seeking our own way. We are hungering and thirsting for Him instead of self. We live in a state of mercy and give mercy; we have a pure heart and make peace. The state of happiness *from* the world and the state of happiness *in* Jesus are extremely opposite. Each time the state of the Christian intersects the state of the world there will be conflict. It is called "persecution." It is inevitable! Yet, contained within the persecution is the element of redemption. Are we willing to be redemptive? I am a Jesus pusher regardless of the consequence!!!

I am a Jesus pusher!!! ***"Blessed are those who are persecuted for righteousness' sake"*** (Matthew 5:10). Paul used the term **tribulation** to describe persecution as quoted above (1 Thessalonians 3:3-4). Persecution is one form of **tribulation** that God permits and for which He calls us ***"Blessed."*** This word comes from the Latin word "tribulum." It describes a threshing sledge or flail. This is a threshing instrument consisting of a staff with a short heavy stick dangling on the end. The farmer would use the flail to beat and bruise the sheaves. This enabled him to separate the golden grain from the chaff and straw. Persecution is a picture of God's threshing instrument in our lives. His purpose is not to destroy us, but to separate what is good, heavenly, and spiritual within us from what is wrong, earthly, and fleshly. It will take the blows of adversity and persecution to accomplish this.

The prophets of old wrote, ***"He will sit as a refiner and a purifier of silver; He will purify the sons of Levi, and purge them as gold and silver, that they may offer to the Lord an offering in righteousness"*** (Malachi 3:3). A Bible study group, wondering about the deeper meaning of this verse, made an appointment with a silversmith. As the silversmith revealed to them the process of refining, he was asked, "Do you sit while the refining is going on?" To that he replied, "Oh, yes, indeed. I must sit with my eyes steadily fixed on the surface. If the time necessary for refining is exceeded to the slightest degree, the silver is sure to be injured." Then the silversmith gave the most revealing statement of all. He said, "I only know when the process is complete by seeing my own image reflected on the silver." Will I allow Jesus to form His image in me? I am a Jesus pusher!!!

I am a Jesus pusher!!! ***"Blessed are those who are persecuted for righteousness' sake,"*** (Matthew 5:10). Jesus embraces us in our helplessness and the Kingdom of Heaven is established. We respond by mourning and experience the Comforter in the embrace. His nature of meekness gives us a new relationship to our physical world. We are filled only to hunger and thirst for more. We live in a state of mercy, purity of heart, and peace as we rest in His embrace. The purpose for all of this is to reveal His person through us. He allows persecution for the final refining of His image in our lives. Jesus is allowed to see Himself in us and others see His reflection through our lives.

Jesus gathers His disciples together because of the deep burden He has for the needs of others. He takes the power He has and transfers it to them. He qualifies them for ministry. Before He sends them forth, He gives a discourse on ministry (Matthew 10). He presents the imagery for this ministry as ***"sheep in the midst of wolves."*** This virtually reeks of persecution. He continues to describe the persecution forth coming as religious, political, and family. However, He urges His disciples not to focus on the persecution. How easy it is to major on being hurt, the pain, or how unfair it is. We are to focus on being like Him. Jesus said, ***"It is enough for a disciple that he be like his teacher, and a servant like his master"*** (Matthew 10:25). This is the supreme cry of the heart of one who embraces Him. ***"It is enough,"*** means the fulfillment of the passionate priority of my life. This is the supreme desire of my being. I want to look like Him. I want to be so filled, embraced, and permeated by Him that His domination can be seen in me. I am not to focus on the hurts and persecutions. I must focus on Him. He has captured me. I am a Jesus pusher!!!

I am a Jesus pusher!!! ***"Blessed are those who are persecuted for righteousness' sake"*** (Matthew 5:10). Persecution is something that each of us at some time or another has certainly thought was being bestowed on us. In school I wrote what I thought was an excellent paper only to have my teacher persecute me with a poor grade. In my insecurity I was sure a group of my peers were standing in the hall talking about me. That was persecution. My parents unfairly persecuted me every time they did not permit me to participate in certain activities. When I failed to get the desired job promotion I just knew the foreman was persecuting me. Over the years I have sensed persecution in the church. People simply do not recognize my true value and worth. In my opinion, my life is consistently plagued with persecution.

Then we come to our present study in Matthew. I am now having difficulty placing the things I have spoken of into Jesus' description of persecution. In fact, I am feeling a little embarrassed. My many inconveniences do not seem to merit the title of persecution. Jesus said, "I am to be ***persecuted for righteousness' sake.***" This disqualifies every suffering spawned by stubbornness and selfishness. I wonder if I have ever experienced real persecution. I shrink into insignificance in comparison to the Apostle Paul who said, ***"From now on let no one trouble me, for I bear in my body the marks of the Lord Jesus"*** (Galatians 6:17). I absolutely have no right to complain about my meager sufferings. I have no marks! Jesus is worthy! I am a Jesus pusher!!!

I am a Jesus pusher!!! ***"Blessed are those who are persecuted for righteousness' sake,"*** (Matthew 5:10). There is one fact of which I am deeply aware. The call of Christianity is a call to suffer. This is the "shouting" message of the Beatitudes. We are not off on our own. We do not experience persecution in isolation. We are embraced by and filled with the essence of His being. Any persecution we experience only takes place by participating with Jesus in His movement in our lives and our world. Why would we hesitate to be a part of it? If Jesus' death were the result of ***lawless hands*** (Acts 2:23), would I not experience the same persecution in His death? Peter uses this phrase to describe the Jewish religious leaders. Persecution comes from the self-sourcing in our world as well as within the religious organization. It comes from self-sourcing because this is the core of all sin.

We have marched into the middle of the essence of Cross Style. It is fundamental to the Christian experience; we have summarized it into a phrase and painted it on our wall. We have taken it as the slogan and expression of our basic belief. We cannot embrace Jesus without embracing His style. His style is the cross. The cross was not just one event in the life of Jesus. It was not something He had to go through and then it was over. The cross is the core of His thought process, His nature. He leaped off His throne as God and became man; it is the cross style. He was born in a stable; it is cross style. He did miracles and wanted nothing in return; it is cross style. As Master, He washed the disciples' feet; it is cross style. He never ever thought about Himself, but poured out His life for others; it is cross style. Was He persecuted? Indeed, yes! It is cross style. Is not persecution a natural result of cross style in a self-sourced world? I am a Jesus pusher!!!

I am a Jesus pusher!!! ***"Blessed are those who are persecuted for righteousness' sake"*** (Matthew 5:10). The cross style is persecution and only experienced in relationship with Jesus. In its essence it is not something we do; it is the way we think, exist, and function. Throughout the ministry of Jesus, He always placed His call to the style of the cross in the context of relationship. A major shift takes place in chapter sixteen of Matthew. The Galilean ministry has drawn to an end. Jesus withdraws from the crowd. He focuses on training His disciples. The heart of this training is to prepare them for the cross. He begins by quizzing His disciples about Himself. Peter's great confession is a startling confirmation: ***"You are the Christ, the Son of the living God"*** (Matthew 16:16).

While Jesus is greatly pleased with this confession, He has a concern. Do they understand the content of "being the ***Christ*****?" Jesus shares with them His first prediction of His death, the cross (Matthew 16:21), creating a major uproar within the group. In the discussion, Jesus says, ***"If anyone desires to come after Me, let him deny himself, and take up his cross, and follow Me. For whoever desires to save his life will lose it, but whoever loses his life for My sake will find it"*** (Matthew 16:24-25). At the core of the suffering involved in the cross is relationship. Cross style is about denying self and embracing Jesus. No one takes up a cross without following Jesus. If we lose our lives it will be for His sake. This is not about acts of sacrifice; this is about embracing Jesus. I am a Jesus pusher!!!

I am a Jesus pusher!!! ***"Blessed are those who are persecuted for righteousness' sake"*** (Matthew 5:10). The cross style is persecution and is only experienced in relationship with Him! In its essence it is not something we do; it is the way we think, exist, and function. If we develop a list of activities to achieve the status of cross style, we automatically violate the nature of the cross. If the master washing the disciples' feet is viewed as a cross style activity, there are a variety of subjects to be addressed. How many feet are required to meet the condition? How thoroughly must the feet be washed? How often should I wash feet? The asking of these questions violates the heart of "cross style."

Paul speaks of the ***fellowship of His sufferings***. He explains that this ***fellowship of sufferings*** brings me into ***being conformed to His death*** (Philippians 3:10). The Greek word "koinonia," translated ***fellowship,*** portrays the idea of partnership. It originally portrayed the picture of a government official giving business advice. We become "business partners." Paul proclaimed this in the mystery of his statement, ***"I now rejoice in my sufferings for you, and fill up in my flesh what is lacking in the afflictions of Christ, for the sake of His body, which is the church"*** (Colossians 1:24). How can my sufferings mingle with His to redeem the world? It is a mystery, but He has included me. Why would I shrink from persecution or the reproaches resulting from bearing His name? What a privilege to share in His redemptive ministry! I am a Jesus pusher!!!

I am a Jesus pusher!!! ***"Blessed are those who are persecuted for righteousness' sake, for theirs is the kingdom of heaven"*** (Matthew 5:10). Persecution must be seen in the context of ***righteousness***. There is a strong focus in the Beatitude on ***righteousness' sake***. It is an amazing statement. In many English translations the word *"**for**"* is there twice (Matthew 5:10). In the statement, *"**for theirs is the kingdom of heaven"*** the Greek word translated ***for*** is "hoti." It introduces the object, content, or argument to which the preceding word refers. In our Beatitudes, "hoti" appears to give the reason or argument for the "congratulations." In other words, congratulations go to the persecuted ones because they are the "***kingdom of heaven***." But the statement *"**for** righteousness' **sake**"* is a different word. Actually *"**for sake**"* is a translation of the Greek word "heneka" means "for this cause" or "for this reason." Jesus clearly states why the persecuted one is suffering such treatment. It is because of ***righteousness***. The Greek word "dikaiosune," translated ***righteousness,*** is used both in the Old and New Testaments as the state commanded by God and standing the test of His judgment.

Any suffering outside this context is not considered ***"blessed."*** The state of ***"blessed"*** is found in the merger between my helplessness and His resource. In this relationship I experience His redemptive flow intersecting with my world. This brings persecution because I express His righteousness. Any conflict results from my selfish preferences are not in this category. I must be filled with Him! I am a Jesus pusher!!!

I am a Jesus pusher!!! ***"Blessed are those who are persecuted for righteousness' sake"*** (Matthew 5:10). The Greek word "heneka" is translated ***"for sake."*** It means "for this cause" or "for this reason." Jesus clearly states why the persecuted one is suffering such treatment. It is because of ***righteousness***. The Greek word "dikaiosune),"translated ***righteousness,*** is used both in the Old and New Testaments as the state commanded by God and standing the test of His judgment. In light of this cause, let us examine the "completeness of the cause." If the underlying cause of persecution is ***righteousness*** and is described as "a state commanded by God which stands the test of His judgment," then the cause is far beyond any activity. You cannot simply eliminate a deed connected to Christian ceremonies that might offend a non-believer. ***Righteousness*** is all of the Beatitudes brought together describing the state of righteousness in which the believer dwells. The believer is an individual who is absolutely helpless. He consistently responds to Jesus and experiences God's nature of meekness. He hungers and thirsts and is constantly being filled with mercy, purity, and peace. What do we call such a person? He is the ***kingdom of heaven, comforted, inheritor of the earth, filled***, one who experiences ***mercy***, one who has a vision of God, a son of God, and again he is the ***kingdom of heaven***. The cause of persecution is not one thing about the Kingdom person, but the complete and whole person. He is merged with Jesus. It isn't his personality that is not liked it is His connection with Christ. It is not his religious activities that are not appreciated; it is the atmosphere of Jesus, the mind of Christ, or the attitude of God expressed through the believer's life. It is Jesus seen in and through the Kingdom person. He is a Jesus pusher!!!

I am a Jesus pusher!!! *"Blessed are those who are persecuted for righteousness' sake"* (Matthew 5:10). The cause of persecution is *"righteousness."* Consider the "cause within the cause." If the cause of persecution is a state of *righteousness* then the ones who persecute are those who are not righteous. Obviously the righteous ones are not doing whatever is contained within persecution. As we walk through the Beatitudes, we see the evidence of this. The destitute embrace the unlimited resource of Jesus and can do nothing but love. Those who are filled with the Comforter can do nothing but extend comfort. The meek ones extend concern and care. Those filled proclaim the location of fullness. Those dwelling in a state of mercy and purity share mercy and righteousness. The spirit of persecution is not the spirit of the *kingdom of heaven*! Therefore if you are a persecutor, you are not in the Kingdom.

Do you find the "conflict of the cause" perplexing? Why does someone who lives out the essence of these Beatitudes irritate others? If you are someone who loves and cares, why are you hated? Why is it that people do not like righteousness? Solomon wrote, *"And he who is upright in the way is an abomination to the wicked"* (Proverbs 29:27). We must understand what is already stated in the previous studies. It is the "consistency of the cause." The verb is in the perfect tense. This places persecution in the first Beatitude and carries it through to the last. Persecution is present from start to finish. Persecution is inevitable in a merger with Jesus. What a privilege to be a Jesus pusher!!!

I am a Jesus pusher!!! From the first Beatitude Jesus advocates an intimate relationship with Him. One by one the Beatitudes highlight an aspect of this relationship. My helplessness is matched with the unlimited resource of His person; together we become the Kingdom of Heaven. Mourning is my constant response to the embrace of the Comforter. We know meekness in intimacy with His nature. The more I hunger and thirst for His mind and heart, the more He reveals Himself to me. I dwell in His mercy, purity, and peace. All of these Beatitudes are mere descriptions of an intimate relationship with Him. Jesus also advocates a second truth from the first Beatitude. Through this relationship everything He is will be manifested in us. His mind will become our mind; His heart will become our heart. We will become the visible image of His person in our world. We are people of mercy because we dwell in the embrace of His mercy. We have pure hearts because He who is pure dwells in us. We are peacemakers because we dwell in His peace. As this takes place, the way the world treated Him is the way the world will treat us. It is inevitable; we will be persecuted.

Now we must consider "severe persecution." This is the only Beatitude that has more than one verse. Jesus expands this Beatitude with two additional verses to address persecution. He begins with ***"Blessed are those who are persecuted"*** (Matthew 5:10). Remember that the verb is in the perfect tense that translates "***have been persecuted***." He emphasizes this again in the next verse by saying, ***"Blessed are you when they revile and persecute you"*** (Matthew 5:11). This is further stressed in the following verse, ***"So they persecuted the prophets who were before you"*** (Matthew 5:12). This is a severe of message. It is not a trite issue to be a Jesus pusher!!!

I am a Jesus pusher!!! ***Blessed are those who are persecuted"*** (Matthew 5:10). Remember that the verb is in the perfect tense that translates ***"have been persecuted."*** He emphasizes this again in the next verse by saying, ***"Blessed are you when they revile and persecute you"*** (Matthew 5:11). Jesus stresses this further in the following verse, ***"So they persecuted the prophets who were before you"*** (Matthew 5:12). In all three of these statements, the Greek word "dioko" is translated **persecute**. This word has the basic meaning of chasing, driving away, or pursuing. It presents the picture of physical affliction or infliction of physical pain. This should not be a surprise to us since the third Beatitude speaks directly to our connection to the physical world. Our relationship with Jesus does not dwell in some mystical, unseen world. Because of His nature we embrace our physical existence in a new way. There are definite physical ramifications to being Kingdom people.

Our spiritual merger with Jesus will demonstrate itself in our physical world. The materialistic world around us is the platform for the demonstration of the Spirit of Christ within us. One cannot disconnect the physical from the spiritual. In a sinful world, one should expect that intimacy with Jesus in the spiritual would cause discomfort and negative results in the physical world. You must value Jesus in your life of greater worth than all the physical comfort around you! I have found Him worthy! I am a Jesus pusher!!

I am a Jesus pusher!!! Jesus compels us to consider "slanderous persecution." He says, ***"Blessed are you when they revile and persecute you, and say all kinds of evil against you falsely for My sake"*** (Matthew 5:11). The Greek word "oneidizo," translated ***revile,*** suggests the idea of reviling, upbraiding, or seriously insulting. It means to cast in one's teeth. Jesus definitely describes this condition with the additional statement of ***"and say all kinds of evil against you falsely for My sake."***

The crucifixion gives a vivid example of such activity. The crowds who were passing by wagged their heads; they made fun of His teachings. The leaders of Israel mocked Jesus with words promoting disgust. They struck blows of criticism against the most precious and sacred possession of Jesus, His relationship with His Father. But over and above all of this, ***even the robbers who were crucified with Him reviled*** (oneidizo) ***Him with the same thing*** (Matthew 27:44). This covered every aspect of society.

Not only was physical persecution present, but there was mental, verbal, and emotional persecution. This aspect of persecution is often harder to bear than the physical aspect. It reveals a total misunderstanding of what is happening. For instance, in the case of Jesus, He shared His heart with the individuals who were berating Him. He healed and loved them. They demonstrated no comprehension of anything He shared with them. Even if the physical aspect of the cross were removed, the isolation and rejection would be paramount. In this context Jesus said, "Forgive them." I want to be like Him! I am a Jesus pusher!!!

I am a Jesus pusher!!! We must also consider "sham persecution." ***"Blessed are you when they revile and persecute you, and say all kinds of evil against you falsely for my sake"*** (Matthew 5:11). It is a focus on "***all kinds of evil against you falsely for My sake.***" Insults are abusive words said to our face, but ***all kinds of evil*** are primarily abusive words said behind our back. This suggests major war taking place about which we do not know. There are multitudes of incidents, plots, and demonic strategies assaulting us. We may never know the full employment of the forces of evil being hurled against us.

But the final word is "It does not matter!" We are to ***rejoice and be exceedingly glad*** (Matthew 5:12). The wonder of what we experience in the Beatitudes so overshadows anything negative so that we hardly notice. We must not focus on the hurt, pain, or slander; we must focus on Jesus. It is for His sake! This is the picture of a helpless individual (Matthew 5:3) who embraces his helplessness (Matthew 5:4). He is filled with the Comforter (Matthew 5:4). His life becomes the expression of all Jesus' qualities such as meekness, mercy, peace, purity, and even persecution. What a privilege! The privilege of His presence overshadows all discomforts. The story of the early church is a testimony of such experiences. It is what brought about the redemptive expression in their world transforming from evil! Perhaps the love of God can only be truly manifested and understood by evil men against the backdrop of persecution. I am available for this expression! I am a Jesus pusher!!!

I am a Jesus pusher!!! Matthew is an author who writes with a fundamental goal in view. He is an evangelist writing with an evangelistic fervor. He wants to win the Israelite nation to Jesus. They must be convinced of who Jesus is. The hopes and dreams of Jewish history are focused on the Messiah. Their Messiah appears, only to be rejected and crucified by His own. It is the greatest of tragedies. Matthew plays the role of a lawyer. He piles up the evidence, building a strong case for Jesus. Jesus is the Kingly Messiah. Obviously this places the Kingdom of Heaven at the heart of his presentation. It was the core of John the Baptist's message, the forerunner of Christ. John preached, ***"Repent, for the kingdom of heaven is at hand!"*** (Matthew 3:2). Jesus followed up with the identical message (Matthew 4:17). Now He presents a three-chapter discourse giving the "Manifesto of the Kingdom of Heaven!" Here lie the fundamental principles of Kingdom living and the core heartbeat of that Kingdom. It is significant that the first statement of the Sermon on the Mount contains the Kingdom's declaration. In other words, the Beatitudes begin with the reality of the Kingdom's presence. Now as we come to the end of the Beatitudes, the closing is a statement of the Kingdom's reality.

The Kingdom is not a location to which you arrive; it is a relationship of merger with Him. None of the beatitudes are possible, especially the last calling us to rejoice in persecution, without a merger with Jesus. We are helpless in resource to accomplish such standards. The Kingdom is relationship with Jesus in which He and I merge together become the new creature, the Kingdom of God. I am a Jesus pusher!!!

I am a Jesus pusher!! There are eight Beatitudes in all. The first one ends with the statement, ***"For theirs is the kingdom of heaven"*** (Matthew 5:3). The eighth or last Beatitude says, ***"For theirs is the kingdom of heaven"*** (Matthew 5:10). These two statements are the same in words and grammar structure. This is an example of a literary device known as "inclusion." It signals the beginning and the end of a section. This secures the Beatitude as a prologue to the Sermon on the Mount. It is a presentation of the theme, concept, or proposition of the sermon. Jesus will flesh out the structure He has presented in the Beatitudes. It implies that the Kingdom sums up all the other results listed in the second clauses of the Beatitudes.

It is important to note that the six Beatitudes sandwiched between the first and last are all in the future tense. The reality of the present tense Kingdom is presented in the first Beatitude; we are reminded of this present reality in the last Beatitude. In my state of helplessness, I am embraced by the unlimited resource of Jesus. We become the Kingdom in this union. This is present tense! In this present tense reality Jesus begins to manifest in my life all the resources of His person. As I mourn in response to His presence, I experience the Comforter. My physical existence takes on the shape of Jesus' presence as I embrace Him. My mind marvels at the satisfaction of my hungering and thirsting. I experience mercy in an ever-unfolding reality. Jesus' face becomes much clearer in my sight. I can hear His voice whispering softly in my ear, "You are my son." These unfolding wonders exist in the ***kingdom of heaven***. What a wonder to *be* the Kingdom of Heaven, embraced by Jesus. I am a Jesus pusher!!!

I am a Jesus pusher!!! The values of the Kingdom of Heaven and the kingdoms of the world have a startling contrast. The values of the Kingdom of Heaven are sandwiched between the first and last Beatitudes. These six Beatitudes between give us the elements from which all things in the Kingdom exist. They are in the future tense, while the first and last Beatitudes state the Kingdom in the present tense. The emphasis is that we are presently "in" the Kingdom of Heaven and these are the values, the qualities, resulting from this state of existence. Any attempt to discover a quality or value of the Kingdom of Heaven not mentioned in these six Beatitudes is futile. These are the core values.

Jesus presents each one in a contrast. The first of the six between Beatitudes is ***"Blessed are those who mourn."*** "Mourning" is contrasted with "comfort." "Mourning" is distinctly connected to the "helpless state." It is this state that makes us suitable to be embraced by the unlimited resource of His presence. This embrace is the existence of the Kingdom. "Mourning" is the consistent recognition of my state of helplessness; it is the consistency of my helplessness embracing Him. His presence fills my life; He is the Comforter. He comes alongside (inside) to nurture, encourage, empower, and enable all I need. I live in a state of "comfort." Consider this kind of "comfort" in contrast to the kingdom of the world. "Comfort" is seen in terms of materialism, power, and prestige. It is a false sense of having no needs, being in charge, or acquiring my own desires. It is the satisfaction of getting what I want. "Living comfortably" is a phrase that describes having everything I want, all needs being met. Yet, this sense of completeness quickly fades; it is because I do not have what I need. It is Jesus! I need to merge with Him. I am a Jesus pusher!!!

I am a Jesus pusher!!! ***"Blessed are the meek, for they shall inherit the earth"*** (Matthew 5:5). This is such a radical concept. The ***meek***, gentle, and caring individual gives expression to the nature of Christ. This is contrasted with the haughty, proud, and domineering that give expression to the nature of the kingdom of darkness. Those in the Kingdom of Heaven embrace their physical world in a relational manner. In becoming one with the physical world, all the benefits of this world become theirs. The haughty and proud use the physical for selfish ends. They pollute their physical world with the darkness of their souls. While they value possessing physical things, those physical things never become one with them.

Hungering and thirsting for righteousness brings a filling. But the nature of such fulfilled desires establishes greater expansion. The filling creates a hunger for the potential of completion. It spurs one into the consistent unfolding of His revelation. This is contrasted with the hungering and thirsting of the kingdom of darkness that never produces filling. The more you eat, the more you lack. Unrighteousness diminishes a person's heart capacity. What was satisfying yesterday cannot satisfy today. The void at the heart of life continually increases. What am I to do? Embracing our helplessness opens the door for His merger with our lives! We must become Kingdom people, filled with Him. I am a Jesus pusher!!!

I am a Jesus pusher!!! **Mercy**, **pure in heart**, and **peacemakers** (Matthew 5:3-10) are not valued in the kingdom of darkness. Ruthlessness, domination, power, and the ability to master every situation for self-benefit are held supreme. Yet, everyone of this persuasion is soon crying for mercy. They define peace as the removal of conflict because they are superior. They live in the world of "what can I get by with" and "what can I get." The heartbeat of purity that pumps forth integrity and honesty is polluted with greed and selfishness.

Jesus battled the devil in spiritual warfare for forty days and forty nights (Matthew 4:1-11). In an all out effort, Satan launched three last attempts. The final temptation climaxed in no tricks or manipulations. Evidently, the devil was willing to bargain with Jesus to survive. He took Jesus to an **exceedingly high mountain, and showed Him all the kingdoms of the world and their glory**. The Greek word "doxa," translated **glory,** refers to viewpoint and perspective. Satan is sure Jesus will bow to this temptation. It is a deal far too great not to accept. Jesus came to earth to establish a Kingdom; He is the only one in this Kingdom at this point. If Jesus could take over the kingdoms of the world, why would He not rush at the opportunity? In glee and delight, Satan pointed out all the wonders of his kingdoms. All the filth of sin, all the perversion of sexual desires, all the corruption of dishonesty and greed, all the destruction of addictions, and all the cancer of carnality were revealed. Jesus could have it all. He could be King over this domain. The devil thought this would allure Jesus, when in fact it repulsed Him. The values of the Kingdom of Heaven are completely opposite of the values of world's kingdoms. I want the values of Jesus! I am a Jesus pusher!!!

I am a Jesus pusher!! The reason the values of the Kingdom of Heaven are vastly different from the kingdoms of the world is viewpoint. According to the dictionary, a viewpoint is "a particular attitude or way of considering a matter." We refer to it as posture or position. When an individual is within the relationship that produces the Kingdom of Heaven, he sees from this viewpoint. When one exists in the kingdoms of the world, he sees everything from a different position.

Let's return to the first Beatitude (Matthew 5:3). It is the *poor in spirit* who experience the *kingdom of the heaven*. They are not "in" the *kingdom of heaven* from the sense of location. They have become the Kingdom. In the helplessness of their state, they are filled with His unlimited resource. In this embrace and oneness, the Kingdom of Heaven is formed. God has chosen not to be the Kingdom of Heaven without us; we cannot possibly exist as the Kingdom without Him.

This means that the viewpoint, position, or posture for the "Kingdom person" is Jesus. The "mind of Christ" is now ours. We have His attitude. In each of the "between" Beatitudes, we are congratulated for a virtue. However, each particular virtue is really "Jesus." Those who *mourn* are being congratulated for "being comforted." In previous studies we discovered the Greek word "parakaleo," translated *comforted,* is a title for the Holy Spirit, the Spirit of Jesus! The strong arms of Jesus embrace us; He is our comfort. It is from this position we view our world. I am a Jesus pusher!!!

I am a Jesus pusher!!! We are not **meek** due to our own effort (Matthew 5:5). Our lives are filled with meekness because we experience His nature. As we live in Jesus, in the Kingdom's embrace, we experience all He is. This is our posture. We experience our physical world from this position. We know the truth about our body and its desires. Jesus is our viewpoint.

The core of hungering and thirsting is found in the content of desire. For what do we hunger in the deep heart of our being? Our embrace of the Kingdom determines this. In experiencing Him, we hunger for Him only! Indeed, He fills us and fulfills us. In this filling we find new arenas of Him for which to hunger. He is consistently enlarging our capacity for Himself. He is our hunger and our filling. We find **mercy** in the Kingdom of Heaven (Matthew 5:7). If the Kingdom of Heaven is His embrace, He is this **mercy**. Extending mercy to others is to extend Him. In the state of **pure in heart**, I see God (Matthew 5:8). Could it be that I am in a state of seeing God and have a pure heart? It is a Kingdom embrace. In oneness with Him my heart becomes pure. He is my purity! It is impossible to have peace and to impart it to others without His embrace. The nature of selfishness produces conflict and dissension within and without. Peace can only be defined as the presence of Jesus.

The values of the Kingdom of Heaven are not the values of the kingdoms of the world. How can they be? The values of the Kingdom of Heaven are found in who Jesus is. He is the King of the Kingdom. Therefore, the values of the Kingdom of Heaven are not many; they are one. They are the person of Jesus. In His embrace, I have His mind. In intimacy with Him, I care as He cares. In oneness with His Spirit, I contain His values. We become the Kingdom of Heaven. I am a Jesus pusher!!!

Jesus PUSHER | **145**

I am a Jesus pusher!!! ***"Blessed are you when they revile and persecute you, and say all kinds of evil against you falsely for My sake"*** (Matthew 5:11). All that is valuable to me is in Jesus. He is the pearl of great price (Matthew 13:45-46). I would sell all other pearls to have Him. He is the great treasure hidden in a field (Matthew 13:44). I would sell all I have to have this one treasure. His heart and mind are mine in the embrace of the Kingdom. I desire only what He desires. I have His viewpoint. Now He produces the cravings of my life. The framework of victory in my life is Jesus. He is my victory. Any separation from His mind and heart is defeat. All that lessens His embrace in my life is labeled destruction. Persecution is seen from this relationship. It is not defeat; it is victory. I do not hold it in dread and fear; I embrace Him. In persecution, I experience the depth of Jesus' heart, the cross. The throbbing heart of His being is expressed in suffering. The principle capturing His mind, shared with my thinking, plays out in action. I do not run from Jesus; I embrace Him. All experienced persecution having value is for His sake. I want to be an extension of His life but also His redemption. Redemption is only found in suffering. When I embrace persecution as the style of the cross, a redemptive force is released into the life of the persecutor. He cannot be the same. When I resist persecution with complaining and rebellion, I become like the persecutor and do not know Jesus. I belong to Jesus in life, death, and in suffering. I am a Jesus pusher!!!

I am a Jesus pusher!!! ***"Blessed are you when they revile and persecute you, and say all kinds of evil against you falsely for My sake"*** (Matthew 5:11). Jesus also said, ***"For whoever desires to save his life will lose it, but whoever loses his life for My sake will find it"*** (Matthew 16:25). It is in losing that I win; it is in dying that I live; it is in giving that I get; it is being a slave that I become free. How can I dread being like Him? ***"It is enough for a disciple that he be like his teacher, and a servant like his master. If they have called the master of the house Beelzebub, how much more will they call those of his household!"*** (Matthew 10:25). Should not my concern be they do not call me "Beelzebub?" I must never fear being persecuted: I must fear not being persecuted.

A famous classical story is told of John Chrysostom. He was a saint in the fourth-century who preached so strongly against sin that he offended the ungodly Empress Eudoxia. Many of the church officials were also disturbed. John was bound and delivered before the Emporia Arcadius. His preaching was challenged and he was threatened with banishment if he did not cease. His response was, "Sir, you cannot banish me, for the world is my Father's house."

The Emperor cried, "Then I will slay you."

John replied, "Nay, but you cannot, for my life is hid with Christ in God."

"Your treasurers will be confiscated" was the next threat.

John replied, "Sir; that cannot be, either. My treasurers are in heaven, where none can break through and steal."

"Then I will drive you from man, and you will have no friends left!" was the Emperors final, desperate warning.

"That you cannot do, either," answered John, "for I have a Friend in heaven who has said, 'I will never leave you or forsake you.'"

This is victory! I am a Jesus pusher!!!

I am a Jesus pusher!!!

Numerous times we have reminded you of the crowd's reaction to the Sermon on the Mount. ***And so it was, when Jesus had ended these sayings, that the people were astonished at His teaching"*** (Matthew 7:28). The Greek word "explesso," translated ***were astonished*** means, "to be knocked out of your senses." It appears that every statement in this sermon had this same affect. The first Beatitude is not less ludicrous than the last Beatitude. In the progression of going from one to the other, the astonishment accumulates until the last one is too much to embrace. We are being congratulated for being persecuted. How can this be? It becomes obvious He is not discussing the minor irritations of life, but the spiritual warfare between two Kingdoms. The fierceness of this war is as major as the contrast between the Kingdom values stated in the Beatitudes and the values of the world. It obviously becomes physical, extends into the mental, and affects the character. Our reaction to this fierce persecution is to be ***"rejoice and be exceedingly glad."*** Why didn't He use words like "endure patiently," "control your negative responses," or "silently bear your burden?" He indicates we should respond like we have won the ballgame, received a substantial raise at our job, or won the new car! There is, however, one ray of hope in this matter. Jesus gives a focus. He turns our attention completely away from the actual persecution and highlights all that is happening in Him, fostered by the persecution. We are not called to look at the pain and be glad about it. We are to look at Him until He becomes greater than the pain. Jesus establishes a pattern He will follow throughout His teaching ministry. He is our focus! I am a Jesus pusher!!!

Jesus PUSHER | 148

I am a Jesus pusher!!! ***"Blessed are you when they revile and persecute you, and say all kinds of evil against you falsely for My sake"*** (Matthew 5:11). At the high point in Jesus' ministry, He is compelled to duplicate Himself in the lives of the disciples. He challenges them to pray; He allows them to be the answer to their own prayers (Matthew 9:37-38). Jesus shares the Divine power of the Spirit with them, which enables them to duplicate His ministry (Matthew 10:1). This lifts them from "disciples" to "apostles." Before He sends them forth, Jesus gives them a great discourse on ministry (Matthew 10:5-24). In the section of His instruction discussing the core of ministry, He highlights "persecution" (Matthew 10:16-24). He presents it in the imagery of His ministry, ***sheep in the midst of wolves***.

This picture, however, is not allowed to remain as imagery. He vividly describes "religious persecution," "political persecution," and "family persecution." He begins this section with a warning. ***"But beware of men"*** (Matthew 10:17). The Greek word "prosecho," translated ***beware,*** is two words combined, "pros" meaning "toward," which is a directional term, and "echo" meaning "to have." In other words, you are to set your mind in a direction; it is a focus. Twice in the next few verses He speaks of ***"for My sake"*** (Matthew 10:18, 22). We are not to focus on the persecution, but we are to focus on being like Him (Matthew 10:25). Focusing on the hurt and pain of persecution will cause you to become a wolf; you begin to act just like those who are persecuting you. Focus on Jesus! I am a Jesus pusher!!!

I am a Jesus pusher!!! ***"Blessed are you when they revile and persecute you, and say all kinds of evil against you falsely for My sake"*** (Matthew 5:11). The call of the Beatitudes is not to focus on the persecution, but to focus on Jesus. What is being done to you is not fair; do not focus on this. The reviling and false accusations bring pain to your heart; do not focus on that. There is physical pain which creates extreme discomfort; do not focus on that pain. We are to focus on Jesus. How could Paul and Silas fill a jail in Philippi with singing at midnight? Pain and suffering are present from the beatings. This circumstance has hindered the purpose of Paul's journey to this city. The punishment is completely unfair considering the good deed that Paul had done. How could they have such joy? Their focus was on Jesus!

The final Beatitude is in verse ten. Jesus uses the third person to address those who are listening. It is expressed as "***those***" and "***theirs***." Now as He amplifies this Beatitude beyond the basic statement, He addresses the disciples directly. He changes to the second person and says, ***"Blessed are you," "and say all kinds of evil against you," "your reward,"*** and ***"before you."*** This is a personal conversation between you and Jesus. In this personal conversation Jesus gives an imperative. He commands, ***"Rejoice and be exceedingly glad."*** It is hard to distinguish between the Greek word "chairo," translated ***rejoice,*** and the Greek word "agalliao," translated ***be exceedingly glad***. In other words, they are statements made in connection with each other to highlight one concept. Jesus describes a definite response we are to have toward persecution. Jesus does not command this strong reaction to persecution without giving reason for such. He is the reason. I am a Jesus pusher!!!

I am a Jesus pusher!!! ***"Blessed are you when they revile and persecute you, and say all kinds of evil against you falsely for My sake"*** (Matthew 5:11). One is forced to come to the conclusion that Jesus is the cause of the persecution. The persecution He discusses is ***for righteousness' sake.*** I must remind you! Jesus congratulates those who "have been persecuted" (Matthew 5:10). This verb is a perfect, passive, participle. The perfect tense means, "It happens in the past and has continual effects and action into the present." Persecution does not start at the end of the Beatitudes, but at the beginning.

Congratulations to all who are helpless or destitute. The unlimited resource of His Person will embrace you and together you will be the Kingdom of God. The natural result of the righteousness of this relationship will be persecution. Living in His embrace will bring persecution. Do not be shocked! He is the cause. Congratulations go to those who continually respond to Jesus in their helplessness. They will live in the embrace of the Comforter. Don't be fooled! You can experience this comfort in the midst of persecution. This comfort in your life will cause jealously and ridicule from others. Congratulations to you who experience the nature of God permeating your life. You will experience and express meekness. You will embrace your physical world in a new way. Don't be naïve; this expression of Jesus through your life will create persecution; many will take advantage. It is all right for it is for His sake. I am a Jesus pusher!!!

I am a Jesus pusher!!! Hungering and thirsting for righteousness is a natural for persecution. ***"Blessed are those who are persecuted for righteousness' sake"*** (Matthew 5:10). This will constantly expand in and through your life as you are filled only to hunger and thirst for more of Him. Living in a state of mercy naturally extends mercy. This is who Jesus is in your life. Will this be viewed with kindness by a merciless world? Is not the ***pure in heart*** the one who craves for righteousness? It can only be experienced because this one has eyesight clear enough to see Jesus. ***Peacemakers*** are people of peace. Oh, how blessed to dwell in the peace of Jesus and extend that peace to others. But it is not peace at any cost. Persecution is inevitable.

Do not be self-focused. In your self-sourcing, you might take persecution personally. You might then feel guilt; what have I done? Why am I not liked? I have done my best and yet I am still not accepted. If you are self-focused then this Beatitude does not apply to you. This is persecution of which Jesus is the cause. Could I propose this persecution becomes a badge, an announcement, or verification of your intimacy with Jesus? Is there any greater privilege than being like Him? Is there any greater privilege than being an extension of His redemption to the world? Persecution becomes the platform for the expression of the love of Christ. This is the redeeming factor that moves the heart of the world. You and I are called to such an experience. But it is not persecution; it is your attitude! Jesus calls us to ***"rejoice and be exceedingly glad"*** (Matthew 5:12). He is worthy! I am a Jesus pusher!!!

I am a Jesus pusher!!! ***"Blessed are you when they revile and persecute you, and say all kinds of evil against you falsely for My sake"*** (Matthew 5:11). This is a DECLARATION OF HIS PRIORITY in your life. Jesus never presents His relationship with you as an escape. He never baits us with the allurement of comfort, ease, and wealth. Jesus boldly declares that proper relationship with Him will equal persecution. The heart of the Christian faith is a cross not a rocking chair. Let it be known up front, let it be a key factor in your decision, your life will be changed when you have relationship with Jesus, and it will mean persecution. The choice of all who are Christian is choosing Jesus and inevitable persecution over personal safety!

Persecution is not the fine print of the contract. It is not hidden and revealed after a time. There is no honeymoon period and then it will strike your life. The radical nature of choosing Christ is an abandonment of self and all of its concern. We do not sugarcoat or soft peddle this message. But let me boldly declare, intimacy with Jesus is worth more than an escape from persecution. There is no sacrifice too great to know Him; in fact, any sacrifice quickly ceases to be sacrifice. Every suffering of persecution becomes a minor irritation, a small discomfort, and an unnoticed hindrance. Jesus is so great that He overshadows all else. The presence of persecution reveals His priority in my life. He is more important than personal comfort. Jesus is worthy! I am a Jesus pusher!!!

I am a Jesus pusher!!! ***"Blessed are you when they revile and persecute you, and say all kinds of evil against you falsely for My sake"*** (Matthew 5:11). This is a DECLARATION OF YOUR PERSONAL LINKAGE with Him. It is ***for my sake***. Persecution is directly linked to Him. As described in the sequence of the Beatitudes, the Kingdom of Heaven is an intimate embrace with His person. The nature of His person flows through the Kingdom person. The qualities being expressed out of the life of the believer are a direct by-product of His being.

My father was a pastor of a church focused on the social, liberal aspects of Christianity. Intimacy with Jesus was not their primary concern. After a couple of years of preaching and living Jesus among them, they asked us to leave. The district superintendent of the denomination asked the pulpit committee, "What is the problem, the reason, for the request?" One possibility was his preaching; but their answer was that the preaching was the best they had ever heard. Perhaps their reason was his theology; but their answer was that he always preached the Bible. Finally a person on this committee blurted out, "He just can't make chili like our last pastor." Now everyone understood that this was not the reason, but because they could not put their real reason into words, they blamed it on the chili.

May I be so in love with Jesus, it is the only thing about me that irritates people. When true persecution comes, it is a testimony of my personal linkage with Jesus. The Beatitudes are a declaration of His nature filling my life; people can see Him in every area of my living. There are no activities, attitudes, or spoken words emerging from my life that do not highlight Jesus. Persecution is a declaration of my personal linkage with Him. I am a Jesus pusher!!!

Jesus PUSHER | 154

I am a Jesus pusher!!! ***"Blessed are you when they revile and persecute you, and say all kinds of evil against you falsely for My sake"*** (Matthew 5:11). This is a DECLARATION OF YOUR LIFE AS A PLATFORM of labor. I realize a martyr's attitude might develop within us. We are always seeing ourselves as sufferers. This is not healthy. But here is a Biblical fact. ***"And according to the law almost all things are purified with blood, and without shedding of blood there is no remission"*** (Hebrews 9:22). We consider the suffering and persecution of Jesus as the means by which we are saved. ***"In Him we have redemption through His blood, the forgiveness of sins, according to the riches of His grace"*** (Ephesians 1:7). While the suffering of Jesus for us was the Divine plan, we know God used the suffering of persecution as a platform for redemption. Peter preached, ***"Him, being delivered by the determined purpose and foreknowledge of God, you have taken by lawless hands, have crucified, and put to death"*** (Acts 2:23).

Is He not asking us to join Him is this same redemptive flow? ***"And they overcame him by the blood of the Lamb and by the word of their testimony, and they did not love their lives to the death"*** (Revelation 12:11). History reveals the growth of the church is greatest during days of persecution. Can ministry flow through our lives without the cost of persecution? Is this not a great privilege? Would we not be honored to be an extension of His suffering? I am a Jesus pusher!!!

I am a Jesus pusher!!! ***"Rejoice and be exceedingly glad, for great is your reward in heaven, for so they persecuted the prophets who were before you"*** (Matthew 5:12). The final verse in the Beatitude of persecution sets the tone for the Sermon on the Mount. If you can rejoice in the midst of physical pain, slander, and falsehood, you can rejoice in any state. This elevates the relationship Jesus presents in the Kingdom to a level above all hindrances or difficulties. If ***rejoice and be exceedingly glad*** is to be the state in persecution, how much more this will be true in times of blessing. The Kingdom embrace brings enough joy to override all persecution.

Jesus begins with the Greek word "chairo," translated **rejoice**. It is a verb in the present tense. This plants the activity of rejoicing directly in the moment of persecution. To ***rejoice*** before or after the persecution is not an option. Jesus proposes that the state of deep inward joy must resonate in the midst of adverse circumstances. It is also in the imperative mood. This gives force to the command to live in this state. It is in the active voice which compels us to respond to everything we received and experienced in the previous Beatitudes. Nothing, not even persecution, is to interfere with the wonder of the Kingdom we are called to experience. There is a stability and security experienced in merging with Jesus that cannot be shaken by persecution. There is an understanding that comes in merging with the mind of Christ. It encompasses the reality beyond the pain of persecution. We understand the total picture. No wonder we rejoice in Him! I am a Jesus pusher!!!

I am a Jesus pusher!!! *"Rejoice and be exceedingly glad, for great is your reward in heaven, for so they persecuted the prophets who were before you"* (Matthew 5:12). Jesus begins with the Greek word "chairo," translated **rejoice,** a verb in the present tense. This plants the activity of rejoicing directly in the moment of persecution. This is a "word group" coming from the rood word "char." "Chara" is a noun; it is the Greek word for "joy." "Chairo" is the verb for "rejoice." We must also note that "charis" is the Greek word for "grace." From this comes the verb "charizomai" meaning "to bestow favor." "Charisma" also comes from this root word. Therefore, there is a connection between "rejoicing" and "grace."

Jesus congratulates us on being helpless (Matthew 5:3). This enables us to be embraced with the unlimited resource of His Person! This is the structure of the Kingdom of Heaven. Rejoice in this state of grace. In constant response to our helplessness (mourning) we are filled with comfort from the Comforter (Matthew 5:4). What grace is bestowed upon us, rejoice! Jesus' nature flows through us producing meekness of life; it allows us to relate to our physical world as He originally intended (Matthew 5:5). Rejoice in such a measure of grace! We hunger and thirst for Him. We are filled (Matthew 5:6). His filling does not dissipate; we hunger and thirst for all He reveals; we are filled again only to hunger in that filling. We leap from one revelation to another; oh, rejoice in such a privilege of grace. Is there persecution? Will there be persecution? Do trouble and trials come our way? No doubt they do, but in light of all we experience in Jesus, are we not blessed? Rejoice! Do difficulties confront us because of this "righteousness?" They certainly do! Merger with Jesus is this state of grace. I am a Jesus pusher!!!

I am a Jesus pusher!!! ***"Rejoice and be exceedingly glad, for great is your reward in heaven, for so they persecuted the prophets who were before you"*** (Matthew 5:12). Jesus begins with the Greek word "chairo," translated **rejoice**. This is a "word group" coming from the rood word "char." "Chara" is a noun; it is the Greek word for "joy." "Chairo" is the verb for "rejoice." We must also note that "charis" is the Greek word for "grace." From this comes the verb "charizomai" meaning "to bestow favor." "Charisma" also comes from this root word. Therefore, there is a connection between "rejoicing" and "grace." We dwell in a state of grace! Mercy is consistently ours (Matthew 5:7). Moment by moment we receive and give mercy. It is a state of grace in which we rejoice. We are pure in heart for we embrace Him (Matthew 5:8). Oh, how He has given Himself to us. In the consistent vision of His presence, we rejoice; oh, what grace we receive! To live in peace and extend it to our troubled world is such a privilege (Matthew 5:9). It is reality because we belong to Him as "sons." He is our peace. Peace is not the removal of conflict, but the embrace of His person. Rejoice, Rejoice, Rejoice in His grace! Do difficulties confront us because of this "righteousness?" They certainly do! How can we not continue in joy? Does slander come against us for His sake? Yes, there is a spiritual war actively battling in our lives. However, that battle is minor in contrast to Jesus! Rejoice! Is there a cross at the heart of our experience in Him? After experiencing Him, how can we not eagerly participate in the "fellowship of His suffering?" I am a Jesus pusher!!!

I am a Jesus pusher!!! ***"Rejoice and be exceedingly glad, for great is your reward in heaven, for so they persecuted the prophets who were before you"*** (Matthew 5:12). The statement of Jesus is "***Rejoice*** (chairo) ***and be exceedingly glad*** (agalliao)!" These two Greek words are often used together in the New Testament. The Greek word "chairo," translated ***rejoice,*** expresses less intensity than the Greek word "agalliao." This combination heightens the expression of what is to be experienced. "Agalliao," translated ***be exceedingly glad,*** comes from the combination of two Greek words. The first is "agan" meaning "much." The second is "halomai" meaning "to leap." Sometimes it is translated "to be glad" (Acts 2:26). This places our rejoicing on a level of "dancing for joy." It is joy "over the top" and "off the charts." This is not a token joy but a genuine, soul-gripping, ever present, and abiding result of His presence. Persecution cannot eliminate or deaden it! Rejoice and dance for joy!

In this process, Jesus gives us reasons for such joy. We have been highlighting "**For the Sake of Jesus.**" In a real sense, Jesus becomes the cause of the persecution. It is a "declaration of His priority" in my life. I must allow Him to be who He is within me. This requires a cross. I must abandon all to live in His presence. Persecution becomes the privilege of having Him my high priority. Also, it is a "declaration of my personal linkage" with Him. Persecution for His sake comes from intimacy with Him. It is neither the church program nor its doctrine; it is Jesus. I want to suffer for His sake. I am a Jesus pusher!!!

Jesus PUSHER | **159**

I am a Jesus pusher!!! ***"Rejoice and be exceedingly glad, for great is your reward in heaven, for so they persecuted the prophets who were before you"*** (Matthew 5:12). Jesus places persecution in the context of eternity. This is such an important element in the Christian perspective. We must never confine ourselves to just the present moment. The long-range view must be our focus as Christians. Matthew proposes this repeatedly to his audience, the Jews. In the first four chapters of his book, almost every paragraph contains a prophecy. He points us to the plan of God; it is a plan, which moves us beyond this moment into the eternal dreams of God.

The long-range view of eternity forces us to look beyond the immediate moment. What will matter one hundred years from this moment? What will be the state of our existence at the end of these brief years on earth? For most of us, our concept of eternity formulates our view of Jesus' statement, ***"your reward in heaven,"*** (Matthew 5:12). Our question is the same as Peter's, ***"See, we have left all and followed You. Therefore what shall we have?"*** (Matthew 19:27). While this was an expression of Peter's selfish heart, there is an intense desire to know what is awaiting us in eternity. How will it benefit us? What do I need to do now in order to insure good things in eternity? Let us approach this from the view of our passage. The Sermon on the Mount is not proposing additional activities to be accomplished. It is a merger between my helplessness and His Divine nature. This new creature is planned for by God's eternal dreams. There is a plan that goes beyond the few years of this earth. With this understanding the pleasures or comforts of this earth will not determine the level of rejoicing in our hearts. Jesus is ours in eternal purpose! I am a Jesus pusher!!!

I am a Jesus pusher!!! ***"Rejoice and be exceedingly; glad, for great is your reward in heaven, for so they persecuted the prophets who were before you"*** (Matthew 5:12). One reason for rejoicing is THE INDICATED REWARD that is clearly in the Greek text. There is an article placed before the Greek word "misthos, "translated ***reward***. This is not just "any" reward or "a" reward: it is "the" reward! This ties the reward directly to the experience of persecution. If Jesus said there would be a specific reward for those who suffer with Him, then the reward is for every Christian. The impact of Jesus' statement is that every Christian will experience a consistency of persecution.

The picture of the ***reward in heaven*** taught throughout my days of growing up in the church seems to be generally accepted among evangelical Christians. It consists of a mansion, streets of gold, and servant angels. Everyone in heaven will experience these blessings; however, they are greatly improved or diminished determined by the material we provide for their production. If you desire a brick mansion you will need to render more service than for a vinyl sided mansion. The difficulty with this concept is the lack of biblical backing. This is a focus on the physical rewards of a materialistic mindset. This thought views comfort from the satisfaction of the physical needs, which is the opposite of rejoicing in the upset of your physical comfort. It places the joy in persecution in an endurance mode so you can get eternal comfort in heaven. In the context of our passage, ***the reward*** is the culmination of the Beatitudes. All the Beatitudes are focused on Jesus. Is Jesus really enough for you? I am a Jesus pusher!!!

Jesus PUSHER | 161

I am a Jesus pusher!!! ***"Rejoice and be exceedingly; glad, for great is your reward in heaven, for so they persecuted the prophets who were before you"*** (Matthew 5:12). Much of our evangelical view of *"**reward in heaven**"* is determined by what is not going to be present. We love the "no more" song about heaven. There will be no more sorrow, no more death, no more temptation, no more trials, no more tears, etc. When you finish the list, you wonder what will be left. This is a negative approach leaving us with negative feelings. It is an escapism approach; it does not create joy in the midst of persecution. It simply encourages me to endure to the end for "joy comes in the morning."

In the context of our passage, ***the reward*** is the culmination of the Beatitudes. All the Beatitudes are focused on Jesus. We are helpless but we are embraced by His unlimited resource. In the fullness of His presence we become the Kingdom. The Comforter, the Spirit of Jesus, envelops us in our mourning. His nature throbs within and through us resulting in meekness embracing our world. We constantly expand in the revelation of Jesus as our hunger is filled. Mercy, purity, and peace are intimately connected to seeing Him and being His son. When persecution results from the intimacy of His presence would we not rejoice? When everything contained in the opposite of who He is dislikes us, would we not dance for joy? Will this not create within us a tighter embrace? We will experience the expansion of His presence in greater ways. Is Jesus not our reward? Is Jesus enough for you? I am a Jesus pusher!!!

I am a Jesus pusher!!! *"Rejoice and be exceedingly; glad, for great is your reward in heaven, for so they persecuted the prophets who were before you"* (Matthew 5:12). How does this *reward* relate to *in heaven*? The Greek word "en," translated *in,* refers to a "fixed state." The Greek word "ouranos," translated *heaven,* is difficult to dogmatically define. Is Jesus referring to the actual place of eternal dwelling? Is He referring to the state of righteousness in which the individual experiences the reward of the Beatitude life? It probably does not matter. In either case, Jesus is the reward. In both situations the experience of persecution only massages the soul to see Jesus clearer and embrace Him tighter. Jesus is our *reward*; could we ask for anything more?

THE INDIVIDUAL REWARD is also clearly defined in this explanation. In the Greek text Jesus definitely says that this reward is "yours." It is a translation of the Greek word "humon." It is the second personal pronoun. It is in the genitive case, which describes relationship between substances. "Of, from, or concerning you, or in regard to you" are all an expression of the word.

This extends beyond simple possession. While this *"reward"* belongs to you the meaning of this possession is greater than ownership. Since you endured persecution, you along with thousands of others, will receive a reward. But this is not the meaning. Jesus is expressing distinctiveness in His statement. Each individual receiving a reward receives the only reward of its kind; the persecution experienced by each individual is different. Therefore, the reward received is different for each individual. All of the aspects tell us that God designed something unique and special for each one! If He is your reward, does not your unique relationship with Him design the reward? What a Jesus!!! I am a Jesus pusher!!!

Jesus PUSHER | 163

I am a Jesus pusher!!! ***"Rejoice and be exceedingly; glad, for great is your reward in heaven, for so they persecuted the prophets who were before you"*** (Matthew 5:12). THE INDIVIDUAL REWARD is also clearly defined in this explanation. In the Greek text Jesus definitely says that this reward is "yours." Consider for a moment the uniqueness of you! Your fingerprints are different from everyone else who exists or has ever existed. Your DNA may be similar to family members, but is not duplicated in any other person. Your experiences and how they affect you are completely different due to your unique qualities of character and personality. The call of God upon your life is so unique no one has ever had one like it. No one else can duplicate the way God wants to use you in your generation. He created you with a unique purpose in mind!

What does this concept mean? Jesus is our reward! His relationship with each of us is unique. No one can know Him or experience Him exactly as you do. The manner in which He reveals Himself to you is exclusive to only you. Since He created you different from all others, He knows exactly how to embrace you. Jesus meets your needs in exact proportions to what is best for you. This is not "one size fits all." In this kind of unique relationship, your life takes on the high quality only found in Jesus. The uniqueness of the intimacy between you and Jesus is the basis of your ability to ***rejoice and be exceedingly glad*** in the midst of persecution. No other kind of relationship is so powerful it can overshadow suffering. Even as I attempt to describe the ***reward*** of relationship I realize how inadequate it is. What a reward He is! I am a Jesus pusher!!

I am a Jesus pusher!!! ***"Rejoice and be exceedingly glad, for great is your reward in heaven"*** (Matthew 5:12). The uniqueness of the intimacy between you and Jesus is the basis of your ability to ***rejoice and be exceedingly glad*** in the midst of persecution. No other kind of relationship is so powerful it can overshadow suffering. Even as I attempt to describe the ***reward*** of relationship I realize how inadequate it is. This may be why Jesus used the Greek word "polus," translated ***great,*** to modify ***reward***. It is an INCREASED REWARD. This word is focused on amount and refers to "much abundance." The encompassing intimacy of your relationship with Jesus far surpasses all other relationships. He is your personal, unlike any other, intimate, and abundant ***reward***.

There are great expressions of this reality in the Scriptures. Paul spoke of preaching such a message. He was amazed that God gave him the grace to preach to the Gentiles the ***unsearchable riches of Christ*** (Ephesians 3:8). The Greek word "anexichriastos" is translated ***unsearchable***. It only appears in the Scripture in two places. Paul wrote a great passage describing the mercies of God. He was captured by ***the depth of the riches both of the wisdom and knowledge of God! How unsearchable are His judgments and His ways past finding out!*** (Romans 11:33). This Greek word "anexichriastos" means "untraceable." It cannot be detected. If you expect to "master the material," you will be greatly disappointed. In experiencing Jesus, we find no end to the expansion of His presence. It is the Beatitude of "hungering and thirsting after righteousness." We will be filled! However the filling creates new hunger for what we see in Him. He fills us again, only to create a new hunger driving us to seek Him more and more. It is the "increased reward" of the revelation of His person.

Will you allow Him to reveal Himself to you? Will you set aside all other priorities for this one driving hunger? He is your reward! I am a Jesus pusher!!!

I am a Jesus pusher!!! ***"Rejoice and be exceedingly glad, for great is your reward in heaven, for so they persecuted the prophets who were before you"*** (Matthew 5:12). Jesus stretches my mind beyond its limits with the Beatitudes. I realize it is only the "prologue" to the Sermon on the Mount, but will I ever be able to live in the reality of such an experience? The answer is firmly and clearly proclaimed in the Beatitudes. He is the answer. The Kingdom is formed in His embrace; comfort is found in the fullness of His Spirit. Meekness becomes my nature through Him. The filling of all life is experienced in His revelation. He is my purity; I see God in Jesus. Peace is known in His embrace. Everything I need is found in Him. It is no less true with persecution. If I must choose between Jesus and personal safety, then I choose Jesus. He is more important and valuable to me than I am to me. How can this be? It is because I am not "me" without Him. Jesus is not an option; He is not one choice among many others. I cry with the Apostle Paul, ***"For to me, to live is Christ, and to die is gain"*** (Philippians 1:21). Do my lungs fight for oxygen? Indeed, they cannot survive without this life-giving resource. In starvation does not my body cry for food? In dehydration does not my flesh scream for water? My life cries for Jesus in the extreme measure. In this passion, everything else shrinks in importance. Anything that distracts me from Him must be eliminated. There is nothing more valuable to me than Jesus! I am a Jesus pusher!!!

I am a Jesus pusher!!! ***"Rejoice and be exceedingly glad, for great is your reward in heaven, for so they persecuted the prophets who were before you"*** (Matthew 5:12). Could I be so foolish as to stand and proclaim my sacrifices and suffering for Jesus? I must declare there are no sacrifices. There are only benefits. Anything set aside for His sake is overshadowed by His abundance. In Peter's second epistle, he wrote of a group of people who knew Christ and turned aside. It was so shocking to him that he quoted an old proverb, ***"A dog returns to his own vomit,"*** and, ***"a sow, having washed, to her wallowing in the mire"*** (2 Peter 2:22). Whatever risk I have taken, whatever safety I have refused is no sacrifice at all! I would not return.

We are blessed, congratulated, and in a fortunate place in the midst of persecution. Therefore, you and I should ***rejoice and be exceedingly glad***. Jesus presents three fundamental reasons for this perspective. One is FOR THE SAKE OF JESUS. Persecution becomes a sign of my intimacy with Him. Any thought that "Jesus died for me and I get off scot free" is gone. I have the mind of Christ. I have joined Him in such oneness that the power of His life is sourcing me. Inevitably I will embrace His suffering as well. I cannot join Him in His life without joining Him in His death. Our self-sourcing desires to utilize all the provisions of Jesus without identifying with His nature, which sources the provisions. It cannot be! The health and wealth so-called gospel has been present in every generation. The core of sin, self-sourcing, generates it. His involvement in persecution and sacrifice to redeem the world will become mine. What a privilege to suffer for Jesus' sake! I am a Jesus pusher!!!

I am a Jesus pusher!!! ***"Rejoice and be exceedingly glad, for great is your reward in heaven, for so they persecuted the prophets who were before you"*** (Matthew 5:12). Jesus proposes a second reason for rejoicing in the midst of persecution. It is FOR THE SECURITY OF HEAVEN. Our eyesight must never be for the present moment. Every circumstance of the present moment must be viewed in light of eternity. Self-sourcing always focuses on our present comfort. Evangelical Christians have no dispute with the concept of "rewards." But their perspective becomes one of endure, tolerate, count to ten, or white-knuckle it through in order to obtain the opposite in heaven. In heaven we will experience everything we think we do not have here. I am convinced this is not the reward of the Spirit-sourced individual. His reward is Jesus. In the embrace of His heart I experience a unique relationship with Him that no one else has had or can have. Persecution seems to be a part of the uniqueness. I experience Him not only in the superficial blessings of physical benefits, but I experience Him in the depth of His suffering nature. Intimacy is amazingly tight when two individuals share their hearts. Jesus allows me into His cross, the expression of His heart! Embracing His heart is the reward I desire.

The intimacy of relationship with Jesus gives me the strength and tone of ***rejoicing and being exceedingly glad*****.**" The core of ***rejoicing*** is "joy." This is not as strong as the emphasis of "***be exceedingly glad*****.**" This is a compound Greek word, which means "much" and "to leap." This combined with "joy" places our response on the highest level. If my celebration is on this level, my intimacy with Jesus must be beyond description. Any suffering called persecution becomes a minor irritation. I am a Jesus pusher!!!

I am a Jesus pusher!!! ***"Rejoice and be exceedingly glad, for great is your reward in heaven, for so they persecuted the prophets who were before you"*** (Matthew 5:12). The last phrase regarding the prophets begins with the Greek word "gar." It is a causative particle; it assigns a reason for what has been done. This is not another argument you should consider in your response to persecution. This is a further explanation of the status and context of your persecution, which should automatically produce ***rejoice and be exceedingly glad***. Jesus is saying, "You are in very good company. You are not only intimate with Me, but you have a link with all those who are intimate with Me!"

Jesus will expand this idea throughout His ministry. In contrasting the Old Covenant with the New Covenant, He highlighted John the Baptist. While John the Baptist was the greatest in the Old Covenant, He does not measure up to the "least" in the Kingdom of Heaven. John was a prophet ***"and more than a prophet"*** (Matthew 11:9). He was actually one who was the subject of prophecy (Matthew 11:10). If they persecuted the greatest in the Old Testament and are now persecuting you, you have a link with your heritage.

"The company of the prophets" must be understood from the viewpoint of the Jews to whom Jesus spoke. They highly honored the prophets. In His last public message, Jesus said, ***"Woe to you, scribes and Pharisees, hypocrites! Because you build the tombs of the prophets and adorn the monuments of the righteous, and say, 'If we had lived in the days of our fathers, we would not have been partakers with them in the blood of the prophets'"*** (Matthew 23:29-30). For Jesus to include anyone in this group was a high honor. In persecution you have become like your heroes! I want to be like Jesus who leads the parade! I am a Jesus pusher!!!

I am a Jesus pusher!!! *"Rejoice and be exceedingly glad, for great is your reward in heaven, for so they persecuted the prophets who were before you"* (Matthew 5:12). In the Old Covenant system the prophets were the only individuals who interacted directly with God. They were uniquely different from the priests. The priests were of the tribe of Levi. They were in their position because of their ancestry. Their role was the same as their father's role before them. They performed the routine duties of the temple regarding all the daily requirements. They maintained the Jewish system established by God from the beginning days of their nation. While this was important it was neither distinct nor unique.

The prophet was a CHOSEN individual. His father was not a prophet; he was not a product of a school or special training. He did not seem to have any qualities or talents qualifying him to be a prophet. He did not submit a resume or request the position. Much of the time these individuals were stunned at their selection; many times they attempted to be excused from their role. It was never their choice. Some were from the north; some were from the south. Many were educated but many were not. Wealth did not seem to be a factor; poverty did not qualify them. They were simply chosen by God. From the start, they had direct contact with God. It was the nature of their calling. God came to them! They did not study or produce a message. They were told the message and simply repeated it to the people. *"Rejoice and be exceedingly glad"* is based on being in this category. We may not be prophets but we are chosen! We belong to Jesus! I am a Jesus pusher!!!

I am a Jesus pusher!!! ***"Rejoice and be exceedingly glad, for great is your reward in heaven, for so they persecuted the prophets who were before you"*** (Matthew 5:12). God CHOSE the prophet. The message of God became his message. Often they themselves did not fully understand the total implications of the message. There was an intimacy between the prophet and God that no one else had. They were so tightly connected that God's message was their message. When the people responded to the message, they were not responding to the prophet; they were responding to God. Whatever they did to the prophets, they were doing to God.

If this was true of a unique, small group of people in the Old Covenant, the new individual of the Kingdom of Heaven is beyond belief. In his helplessness he is embraced by the unlimited resource of God. Thus, the Kingdom is formed. This individual is such an intricate part of the Kingdom; he is the Kingdom in intimacy with God. The Comforter comforts him. The nature of God flows through him; he lives in an expanded filling which causes him to dwell in a state of mercy, purity and peace. He sees God and is called a son of God. If the persecution of the prophets was actually a persecution of God, how much more it is true of those of the Kingdom. ***Rejoice and be exceedingly glad*** for your unity with Jesus! No persecution could overshadow the reality of His presence! I am a Jesus pusher!!!

Jesus PUSHER | 171

I am a Jesus pusher!!! ***"Rejoice and be exceedingly glad, for great is your reward in heaven, for so they persecuted the prophets who were before you"*** (Matthew 5:12). Once God chose the prophet, He COMMISSIONED him. This commissioning consisted of the "filling of the Spirit of God." It was task oriented. It was not for the purpose of intimacy or purifying of the inner heart. It was to accomplish a purpose or task. The prophet was empowered to stand before the nation of Israel in confidence and boldness. They dealt with kings and the threats of those who had powerful armies at their command. Many of them did miracles, participated in defeating the enemies of God, and boldly proclaimed God's message. The prophet dared not claim this power as his own. His power was the power of God who filled him.

It was this power which enabled the prophet to bravely endure persecution. The writer of the Book of Hebrews thunders forth this message. These individuals lived by faith. "Faith" is invoking the activity of the second party. In other words, their lives were a product of the Spirit of God who was using them as they responded to Him. ***And what more shall I say? For the time would fail me to tell of Gideon and Barak and Samson and Jephthah, also of David and Samuel and the prophets: who through faith subdued kingdoms, worked righteousness, obtained promises, stopped the mouths of lions, quenched the violence of fire, escaped the edge of the sword, out of weakness were made strong, became valiant in battle, turned to flight the armies of the aliens. Women received their dead raised to life again. Others were tortured, not accepting deliverance,*** *that they might obtain a better resurrection. Still others had trial of mockings and scourgings, yes, and of chains and imprisonment* (Hebrews 11:32-36). Think of the privilege of joining this great group! Think of being filled with the Spirit of God for intimacy and cleansing. You will not experience persecution for Him; you will experience it with Him. I am a Jesus pusher!!!

I am a Jesus Pusher!!! As we begin our study on **salt** and **light** following the Beatitudes, we must view it in the flow of the chapter. The chapter is formulated into four sections: The Formation of the Kingdom (Matthew 5:3-12), The Function of the Kingdom (Matthew 5:13-16), The Fulfillment of the Kingdom (Matthew 5:17-48). The Beatitudes are "The Formation of the Kingdom." They are statements of "congratulations!" All other moral systems of the world promote working, striving, and trying. Through faithful endeavoring one may hope to reach the goal. Jesus begins with congratulations for your arrival. In other words, what all other moral systems require you to earn, Jesus give you!

How could this be? Jesus is the answer! Every section of the Sermon on the Mount is found true because of Jesus. All Beatitudes, from the first to the last, become true because of intimacy with Jesus. Jesus said, ***"Blessed are the poor in spirit. For theirs is the kingdom of heaven"*** (Matthew 5:3). He just congratulated us for being ***"poor in spirit."*** The Greek word "ptochos," translated ***"poor,"*** means to be absolutely destitute. It is "begging poor" without any resources. This condition enables Jesus to be our total resource! When we become an individual sourced by Jesus, the Kingdom of Heaven is formed. We do not get there by discipline, earning, or meriting; we must ***"mourn"*** (Matthew 5:4). In accepting who we are, we enable Jesus to come. We become the Kingdom in Him. The Kingdom of Heaven is a state of existence, which is relationship with Him. All the Beatitudes are ours in this relationship. Each is a state of being in Him. He is all in all; so, I am a Jesus pusher!!!

I am a Jesus pusher!!! Is the Kingdom of Heaven a personal thing for my own benefit? The second section, "The Function of the Kingdom" (Matthew 5:13-16) describes how the uniting of the Spirit of Jesus and our spirits will affect our world. He uses the imagery of **salt** and **light**. This imagery is pronounced because it naturally highlights a state of being. In other words, the Kingdom of Heaven does not need to worry about performance or accomplishment. This function is a by-product of who He is in us, the Kingdom.

Therefore, our concern is not about accomplishing the task of **salt**, it is about being one with Jesus. We do not concern ourselves with functioning as **light**; we simply focus on Jesus. Both of these imageries seem to focus on influence. Paul expressed it, *"Now thanks be to God who always leads us to triumph in Christ, and through us diffuses the fragrance of His knowledge in every place. For we are to God the fragrance of Christ among those who are being saved and among those who are perishing. To the one we are the aroma of death leading to death, and to the other the aroma of life leading to life. And who is sufficient for these things?"* (2 Corinthians 2:14-16). In the next verse, he exclaims that we are not salesmen selling our wares. We do not market a program, promote a gimmick, or create a commercial. We simply abide in Jesus and His fragrance changes our world. How can I not be a Jesus pusher!!!

I am a Jesus pusher!!! David Livingston was a Scottish physician who left a promising practice in his homeland to become a medical missionary in Africa. News of his ministry and sacrifice soon made its way to America. Henry Stanley, a reporter, was given the opportunity to spend time with the missionary to capture his story for America. He traveled by boat for several weeks; upon his arrival he became the constant companion of Dr. Livingston. Arriving back in America, Henry's friends held a welcoming party for him. They quizzed him about his time in Africa. Questions such as "What was David Livingston like?" were asked. He seemed to have nothing to tell them. When they pressed him further, he answered, "If I had been with him any longer, he would have compelled me to be a Christian." He paused and then added, "Though he never spoke to me about it at all."

Jesus did not proclaim a working, meriting, or doing religion, but an abiding, experiencing, and embracing relationship. This is the Kingdom of Heaven. You are not the Kingdom; Jesus is not the Kingdom. You and Him in embrace and relationship form the Kingdom of Heaven. The depth of this relationship produces an influence that cannot be stopped. We are *salt* and *light* in our world (Matthew 5:13-17). It is a state of being, filled with Him. We are not isolated from but influential in our world. I am a Jesus pusher!!!

I am a Jesus pusher!!! Each teaching in the Sermon on the Mount flows from the instruction preceding it. Each beatitude logically follows the one before it, giving it content and meaning. In the Beatitudes, we are instructed on "The Formation of the Kingdom" (Matthew 5:3-12). In an intimate relationship with Jesus' abiding presence, we become the Kingdom. This Kingdom of relationship influences the world around it. It is "The Function of the Kingdom" (Matthew 5:13-16). If we do not experience being the Kingdom, we do not experience this function. The function is an influence derived from His presence. All of this rests on a foundation, "The Foundation of the Kingdom" (Matthew 5:17-20).

"The Foundation of the Kingdom" is the heart of the Beatitudes' inner qualities. These qualities derive from the relationship with Jesus. "The Function of the Kingdom," **salt** and **light**, rests upon this foundation. The qualities are a flow of His Spirit through us; the influence in our world is because Jesus sources us. One would think that the foundation would be the person of Jesus! But in this next section, the Function of the Kingdom, the focus is on the Word of God. But Jesus is the Word of God! He is the Living Word demonstrating the Written Word. In fact, as He fills us in merger, we become shaped by His Written Word. Jesus lived by the presence of the Spirit within Him; but that Presence used the Written Word to shape everything Jesus did. It is the interaction of the Living and Written Word that fulfills our lives. The Scripture is fulfilled in the living of the Kingdom person. Jesus living in us is speaking to us through His Word. What a relationship! I am a Jesus pusher!!!

I am a Jesus pusher!!! This is such a marvel! Jesus uses words like *"The Law or the Prophets"* (Matthew 5:17) and *"the least of these commandments"* (Matthew 5:19). He does not refer to the oral traditions, 613 in number. The Pharisees gauged their righteousness by these traditions. They took the pure Word of God and interpreted it to a lower standard, which they could accomplish. Jesus said, *"For I say to you, that unless your righteousness exceeds the righteousness of the scribes and Pharisees, you will by no means enter the kingdom of heaven"* (Matthew 5:20). But everyone knows you can never match the laws of God. Who can fulfill all the requirements of the Mosaic Law? Even man-made traditions cannot be maintained consistently. The Jews expected a Messiah who would bring God's standards down to a level they could manage. But Jesus came to raise the standard not lower it! He said, *"Do not think that I came to destroy the Law or the Prophets, I did not come to destroy but to fulfill"* (Matthew 5:17).

When Jesus fulfilled the Scriptures, He did not remove or eliminate them, but He elevated them to compete their intended purpose. This happens when the Living Word and the Written Word interact intimately in our lives. Jesus wants to merge with our inner nature and reveal Himself through His Written Word. He becomes the full Word of God in our lives! I am a Jesus pusher!!!

I am a Jesus pusher!!! Is the foundation of the Kingdom of Heaven Jesus or is it the Word of God? What if they are the same? It is wonderful how often Jesus is referred to as the Word. ***In the beginning was the Word, and the Word was with God and the Word was God*** (John 1:1). John refers to this ***Word*** as ***life*** and ***light*** (John 1:4), which is the Bible, but it is also the Person of Jesus! Are they the same? No! We worship Jesus; we do not worship a book. Jesus is the Second Member of the Trinity who became flesh. The Bible is not a member of the Trinity. Jesus is my Savior; the Bible is not my Savior. Jesus defeats the enemy in my life and joins me in becoming the Kingdom of God. It is not a book that accomplishes this.

However, there is a connection between Jesus and His Word. The Bible is an extension of His Person. We have consistently used the example of "your hand." You are not a hand; yet, you have a hand. Your hand is a vital part of who you are and how you function; yet, you could cut off your hand and you would still be you. Jesus is not a book; yet, the words of this Book flow from His mouth and give instruction and life to me. This Book becomes a revelation of who He is, what He thinks, and His heart. I cannot know Him in intimacy without the truth of this Book. He speaks to me through prevenient grace, through nature, and through others. But those messages pale in light of the intimacy found in Jesus through His Word. His Word is pillow talk at night; it is the personal revealing of all He is. I want to know Him! I am a Jesus pusher!!!

I am a Jesus pusher!!! Jesus takes the hard-fast rule of the Old Testament and makes it an invitation to join Him in the revelation of His person. God told us of His holiness; ***"You shall therefore be holy, for I am holy"*** (Leviticus 11:45). God is holy; what does that mean? I have no way of putting content to this holiness. I do not live in God's world, think His thoughts, or know His structure. God communicated this holiness to us through ***The Law***. He said, "If I were a man, living in your world, here is how I would act." ***The Law***, His Word, became an expression of His heart. Now He has gone beyond this; He became man and lived among us. Now God's holiness is in the person of Jesus. But even then, Jesus is still someone I read about or look on. No! He comes to indwell me in intimacy. The "living out of God" takes place in and through me as He interacts with me through the Scriptures. His Word, the Scriptures, become a revelation, a foundation, for my relationship with Him. The Living Word, Jesus, communicates to me through His Written Word, the Bible.

Jesus did this for His disciples; ***"These are the words which I spoke to you while I was still with you, that all things must be fulfilled which were written in the Law of Moses and the Prophets and the Psalms concerning Me"*** (Luke 24:44). Then Luke wrote, ***"And He opened their understanding, that they might comprehend the Scriptures"*** (Luke 24:45). If He could do this for His disciples in His physical presence, what can He do when He indwells me with His Spirit? This is the fulfillment of His promise, ***"But the Helper, the Holy Spirit, whom the Father will send in My name, He will teach you all things, and bring to your remembrance all things that I said to you"*** (John 14:26). What a wonder! I am a Jesus pusher!!!

I am a Jesus pusher!!! The Formation of the Kingdom (Matthew 5:3-12) is to be lived out in the Function of the Kingdom (Matthew 5:13-16). What will this look like? What are the details of the action of such intimacy with Jesus? Jesus marched directly into the bulk of this chapter. He gave us "The Fulfillment of the Kingdom" (Matthew 5:17-48) highlighting it in every section of this chapter. He focused on attitude, which is a state of being. The *righteousness of the scribes and Pharisees* focused on the external; Jesus focused on the internal. The fulfillment of the Law and the Prophets is to move each from the external action to the internal. Jesus intensified, heightened, or deepened the Law with this focus.

There appears to be basic principles expressed in all of the applications Jesus gave regarding the Law. The first one is "The Spirit of the Law." The letter of the Law is content with doing the bear minimum. If the Law is to be internalized in the person, the spirit of man must participate. It is here we know what God really wanted by the Law. This was the consistent theme of the Old Testament prophets concerning this New Covenant. The laws of God were to be written on the inner tablet of our hearts (Jeremiah 31:31). Religion can be content with ceremonies and curbed behavior, but Christianity cannot! Christianity demands the reality of God's presence in the human nature. The Spirit of the law is a Person. Merger between Jesus' heart and mine must take place. I must know Jesus in intimacy! I am a Jesus pusher!!!

I am a Jesus pusher!!! There appear to be some basic principles expressed in the applications Jesus gave regarding the Law. The first one is "The Spirit of the Law." Jesus is the Spirit of the law. The second principle is "The Support of the Law." The Law speaking of an outward action is doing so to focus on the inner attitude. A good outward act is validated before God only when it honestly represents what is on the inside. Jehovah said, *"I, the Lord, search the heart, I test the mind, even to give every man according to his ways, according to the fruit of his doings"* (Jeremiah 17:10). In the Sermon on the Mount, Jesus did not modify the Law of Moses, the teaching of the Psalms, the standards of the prophets, or any other part of Scripture. Everything He taught was in agreement with every truth, every word, of the Old Testament. He revealed that the Jewish oral traditions did not meet this criterion.

The third principle is "The Subject of the Law." The subject of the Law is deeper than the law itself. In other words, the Law is not an end itself. The real subject is not just the righteousness of human being. The ultimate subject and purpose of the Law is to glorify God Himself. In other words, the law of God is an expression of God's heart. The heart of God is the essence of who He is. In merging with Him, we think like He thinks, want what He wants, and act like He acts. Jesus is seen through us and thus glorified. I must experience the fullness of Jesus to accomplish this. I am a Jesus pusher!!!

I am a Jesus pusher!!! The fourth principle is proposed by Jesus regarding the Scriptures. It is "The Singular Judge of the Law." It is foolish for any man to judge another man regarding the keeping of the Law. Perhaps a man might on occasion be qualified to judge regarding the accomplishment of an outward deed. But, if the Law requires the knowledge of the internal motive and spirit of man, no man is qualified. We must leave such judgment to God! My focus must be on Jesus not on comparing myself to others.

The fifth principle is "The Standard of the Law." What does Jesus present as the standard for man's living? Jesus does not excuse, rationalize, or compromise the standard. We are required to live up to the perfect Divine standard to which the Law points. However, the human heart cries, "This is impossible!" Therefore, God Himself provides fulfillment through Jesus! The One who demands righteousness is also the One who gives righteousness. The One who presents the Law is also the Source of redemption.

We come full circle in this first chapter of the Sermon on the Mount! We began *"poor in spirit."* There is no hope in us; we can do nothing but *"mourn."* But Jesus comes to embrace us; it is in the intimacy of His presence we become the Kingdom. The unobtainable righteousness of the Kingdom is found in us. Jesus is our righteousness. Jesus is all in all! I am a Jesus pusher!!!

I am a Jesus pusher!!! The "Formation of the Kingdom" is strongly established for us in the Beatitudes, the opening directives of the Sermon on the Mount. In many ways, they are foundational; everything Jesus states after them will be found in them and come from them. The Beatitudes do not make sense unless they are clearly seen in Jesus. He is the solution to the mystery of the Beatitudes. No doubt this will be stated repeatedly in every study. The Sermon on the Mount is not an instructional manual for godly living. It describes a relationship with Jesus changing the very level of one's living. Our position is *"poor in spirit."* In this helpless, destitute estate, He finds us! When my helplessness and His resource come together, the Kingdom is formed. We become the Kingdom and the remaining Beatitudes happen in this relationship.

It is quite natural to be enamored with this new life, the Kingdom of Heaven. We might naturally become fixated on the personal benefits we experience in His embrace. But He will not allow this. All Jesus does in us is focused. We are not to experience the Beatitudes in isolation or just among fellow believers. In the Sermon on the Mount, Jesus attaches four strong verses on the "Function of the Kingdom" (Matthew 5:13-16). He does not emphasize a good program at the church. He does not highlight spiritual disciplines, charitable deeds, or prayer and fasting. He does not present a set of rules for the activities resulting from intimacy with Him. From the beginning the view is worldwide! Jesus is the answer for my world. I am a Jesus pusher!!!

I am a Jesus pusher!!! Consider this statement, *"You are the salt of the earth"* (Matthew 5:13). The Greek word "ge," translated *"earth,"* means the solid part of the whole of the terrene globe including the occupants. In the context of our passage, it refers to a location where the Kingdom is lived; it takes place on earth, which refers chiefly to humans. This is a broad view! Jesus continued, *"You are the light of the world"* (Matthew 5:14). The Greek word "kosmos," translated *"world,"* is tied to the concept of the universe. The heart of the word describes an order or arrangement. Thus, it came to mean an order or standard by which things of the world are held together. In other words, the interaction of the human race is the platform for the manifestation of the light. This is highlighted further by the imagery of *"a city set on a hill,"* a light placed *"on a lamp stand,"* and *"before men."*

As one saturates in these four verses, it becomes evident the main function of this Kingdom relationship is "influence." Jesus points to the superior impact this Kingdom relationship will have on the world population. But it is not so broad that you and I are not intricately included; we play a key role. This is not accomplished by masses, but by individuals. Notice *"salt"* and *"light"* are both singular. The imagery of *"light a lamp and put it under a basket"* is singular. Jesus instructs us to *"Let your light so shine before men."* This points to the individual. These four verses call us as individuals to allow the Kingdom (merger with Jesus) to influence our world. I am a Jesus pusher!!!

I am a Jesus pusher!!! Let us begin by discussing THE ASPECT of this Kingdom. An aspect is a particular part or feature of something. The main aspect of the Kingdom of Heaven is "a state of being." Let us look again at the description of the Kingdom of Heaven as portrayed in the Beatitudes. The Kingdom is not a location to which we travel. You do not earn the right to relocate to this location. This is not a moral system of merits; eventually you will make it to the goal, the Kingdom of Heaven. The Kingdom of Heaven is established in the link between you and Jesus. You and I are poverty stricken; He is powerful and resourceful. He made me this way. I mourn my state, because, I have desperately attempted to resource myself. I mourn all those attempts and come in simple response to His fullness. The Kingdom is formed in relationship! What a privilege to be His!

All beatitudes become reality in this embrace. We experience meekness because He is "meek and lowly in heart" (Matthew 11:29). Filling and hungering are both discovered in His presence. He gives us mercy and we give mercy to others. Purity of heart and peace are all a part of Jesus. Even persecution is not a result of one's own doing; it is "for My sake" (Matthew 5:11). In each case, we are congratulated for who we are in Him, not what we do for Him! If we were adequate within ourselves Jesus would not discuss a "state of being" but a "state of doing." The Kingdom person dwells consistently in a state of dependency and intimacy with Jesus. I am a Jesus pusher!!!

I am a Jesus pusher!!! Jesus discusses with us how we function in our world. In regard to influence is it "doing" or "being?" He explains it in the imagery of **"salt"** and **"light."** It is clear that neither one of these comes about in what we do. They are both natural states of being. There is no list of rules for being salt. There are no disciplines for producing light. We do not develop into salt; we do not gradually become light. Neither is what one does; both are who you are! Salt and light are the imagery of "being."

This is certainly verified by the grammar of Jesus' statements. Jesus said, **"You are the salt of the earth"** (Matthew 5:13). He continues, **"You are the light of the world"** (Matthew 5:14). Each sentence begins with the Greek word "humeis;" it is a personal pronoun, second person, and in the nominative case making it the subject of the sentence. The next Greek word is the verb of the sentence. It is "eimi," the second person, present, active, indicative. It is the verb translated "I am." It is a state of being. The next two words are "ho halas" (**the salt**) and "ho phos" (**the light**). They are both nominative nouns used as subjective compliments. This means the salt and light are the same as the personal pronoun. They are equal! If one asks, "I am not salt nor light so what should I do?" The answer is not in doing more religious activities. Being salt and light are byproducts of intimacy with Jesus. It is what He makes you! You must focus on surrendering to Him, responding to Him, and embracing Him. This should not be difficult once you recognize your helplessness, **"poor in spirit."** You do not accomplish salt and light; it is who you are in Him! I am a Jesus pusher!!!

Jesus PUSHER | 186

I am a Jesus pusher!!! We must understand the proper use
of "affect" and "effect." "Affect" is a verb declaring the action of
the state bringing about the result. "Effect" is a noun stating the
result or consequence. Let us discuss the AFFECT of the state of
being in light and salt (Matthew 5:13-16). We do not do anything
to become salt or light; but once this state is accomplished there
is an "affect" flowing from this state. Should the focus of my life
become the accomplishment of this "affect?" Absolutely not! All
activities ascribed to the state of salt and light are natural and
automatic from the state. In the context of Jesus' use of the terms,
the action is in the mystical, spiritual world. Something spiritual
occurs beyond the calculation of any human effort.

Woodrow Wilson told the story of being in a barbershop.
"I was sitting in a barber chair when I became aware that
a powerful personality had entered the room. A man had come
quietly in upon the same errand as myself to have his hair cut.
Every word the man uttered, though it was not in the least
didactic, showed a personal interest in the man who was serving
him. And before I got through with what was being done to me
I was aware I had attended an evangelistic service, because Mr.
D. L. Moody was in that chair. I purposely lingered in the room
after he had left and noted the singular effect that his visit had
brought upon the barbershop. They talked in undertones. They
did not know his name, but they knew something had elevated
their thoughts, and I felt that I left that place as I should have
left a place of worship." (The MacArthur New Testament
Commentary, Copyright © Moody Press and John MacArthur,
Jr., 1983-2005.) It is Jesus. I am a Jesus pusher!!!

I am a Jesus pusher!!! The imagery of salt and light describes a mystical occurrence that cannot be manufactured (Matthew 5:13-16). In order to help our understanding, let us view it three different ways. One is "accomplishment." Since this cannot be done, therefore one does not know if it has been accomplished. This makes it difficult. We may never be aware of the "effect" of the "affect" of this merger with Jesus. There was no pride in accomplishment; we do not pat ourselves on the back at the marvelous words we spoke or activities we accomplished. It is simply an expression of who He is! This is the mystical element of the wonder of the presence of Jesus!

There are some extreme examples of this in the New Testament. Regarding Peter, Luke writes, *"And believers were increasingly added to the Lord, multitudes of both men and women, so that they brought the sick out into the streets and laid them on beds and couches, that at least the shadow of Peter passing by might fall on some of them"* (Acts 5:14, 15). This same kind of mystical flow took place from Jesus. *"And suddenly, a woman who had a flow of blood for twelve years came from behind and touched the hem of His garment"* (Matthew 9:20). Luke gives us more details in his account (Luke 8:43-48). The mystical power of God flowed from Jesus to this woman without will or choice. Someone was affected by the power of the Holy Spirit through Jesus. I am willing to simply belong (merge) to Him and allow Him to do and be in me what He desires. I am a Jesus pusher!!!

I am a Jesus pusher!!! Perhaps you think the illustrations given for the effect of being salt and light (Matthew 5:13-16) in previous studies is extreme. It is easy to say these situations have never happened to me. But let it be known to us all that this is happening through and to each of us. There is a mystical flow of spiritual life influencing everyone around us. We are consistently changing our world. Oh, to be filled with Jesus, intimate with His presence, until such powerful movements of His presence are felt by everyone around us. We tend to live our daily lives going through our routine of existence without awareness of what we leave behind us. We march into our local stores dedicated to securing an item. We leave totally unaware of what happened to the spiritual realm of that store. How were the eternal destinies of people affected? This is the consideration of "accomplishment." Oh, to be in Christ and become *salt* and *light*!

A second factor for consideration is "assessment." Since we cannot do this, we do not know what is accomplished. Since we cannot know what is accomplished, we cannot measure it; therefore, we do not know how well we accomplished our mission. Again, this eliminates all pride of a job well done. Self-centeredness is focused on self-assessment. We derive our value from what we accomplish. Everything changes when we are filled with His presence. Our value and worth are derived from Him. Each person within our reach must be brought into His presence. How will it affect them? What will be the long-range results? This is all unknown to us! I am willing just to be His! I am a Jesus pusher!!!

I am a Jesus pusher!!! Paul instructed us, *"Let nothing be done through selfish ambition or conceit, but in lowliness of mind let each esteem others better than himself"* (Philippians 2:3). This is the influence of **salt** and **light** (Matthew 5:13-16). This is a state of being. We do not earn or accomplish such a state. The results cannot be measured; therefore, results are not given consideration. Success is not determined by results; it is determined by intimacy. Any attempt to manufacture the results of **salt** and **light** leave us either broken or living in false allusion. This allusion will ultimately be exposed and crushed in its loss. We again are driven to Jesus. We must embrace that we are *"poor in spirit."* Accrediting ourselves with any other attribute will destroy the state of being, **salt** and **light**. This is the consideration of "assessment."

A third factor is "acknowledgement." If the above is true, we cannot and must not take credit for our state of being and its results. We never receive the glory for anything. The closing verse of our study reveals this truth, *"Let your light so shine before men, that they may see your good works and glorify your Father in heaven"* (Matthew 5:16). Who can resist the temptation of glory, praise, and being acknowledged? Only the person who is fully convinced he is *"poor in spirit."* This is what drives us to continually **mourn** before Jesus allowing His presence to unite with us. The Kingdom of God is formed in that union. We become **salt** and **light**. It is merger with Jesus! I am a Jesus pusher!!!

I am a Jesus pusher!!! We have viewed the "affect" of our state of being. It is a verb describing the action of the state of being, which brings about the results. The results are called "EFFECT." This word is a noun describing the consequence of the action of the Spirit flowing from us. As hard as it is to describe the mystical flow of the Spirit that makes us *salt* and *light* (Matthew5:13-16), so it is hard to describe the "effect." There is no way to fully know the extent or scope of the results. However, there is a definite concrete aspect to this mystical flow of Jesus through our lives.

The one thing plainly described in our passage is the focus of the results. It is always about others. The "effect" is never for one's personal benefit. There is no mention of rewards in the future. There is nothing we can do to earn our eternal home. It is simple; this is the way you are. You are *"poor in spirit."* You are embraced with the greatness of His Spirit. In this intimacy, you become the Kingdom of God. Within and without you are filled and flow with mercy and peace. This produces a state of being with influence. A parable of this state is *salt* and *light*. The result of this state is always for the benefit of others. The heart of Jesus was always for others; I want His mind and heart. I am a Jesus pusher!!!

I am a Jesus pusher!!! The focus of our passage is the "effects" of the state of being (Matthew 5:13-16). Jesus demonstrated the state of being through the imagery of *salt* and *light*. The "effects" are always about others. *"Salt"* does not exist for itself nor does *"light"* shine for its own benefit. The intent of its being is others. Jesus asks us to consider this statement: *"You are the salt of the earth, but if the salt loses its flavor, how shall it be seasoned? It is then good for nothing but to be thrown out and trampled underfoot by men"* (Matthew 5:13).

The negative of salt is to lose *its flavor*. If this happens, how can it preserve anything? The influence of salt is lost! Salt has no benefit but to that which it preserves. *"You are the light of the world."* Obviously, the light is not the light of the light. Its effect is to the world. *"It gives light to all who are in the house." "Let your light so shine before men, that they may see your good works and glorify your Father in heaven."* This should not be difficult to understand. The life of Jesus is a pure demonstration of such. His heart is a redemptive heart! Now the same Spirit that filled Him and caused His state of existence has come to fill us. Let us be *salt* and *light*! I want to be one with Him. The nature of God indwelling, and sourcing Jesus must be merged with me. I want the fullness of Jesus. I am a Jesus pusher!!!

I am a Jesus pusher!!! There is a significant shift in language related to our study. The eight Beatitudes are specifically addressed in the third person plural. Jesus used the pronouns "they, theirs, and those consistently. The language he used described the people of the Kingdom. They are individuals who are in intimate oneness with Jesus. They become the Kingdom through Jesus sourcing their lives. This beginning section of the Sermon on the Mount introduces the Kingdom concept to anyone who would hear and respond. It is the "Formation of the Kingdom" (Matthew 5:3-12).

Now the language changes to the second person plural. This means the pronouns are "you and yours." This shift happens in verse eleven. The last beatitude is one of persecution. ***"Blessed are those who are persecuted for righteousness' sake, for theirs is the kingdom of heaven"*** (Matthew 5:10). This is a strong beatitude, radical in our view. Jesus gives it more attention. As He moves into this special instruction, His language shifts to the second person plural pronouns. It is no longer an announcement that all can experience Jesus and be the Kingdom. But now, since you are the Kingdom, let me discuss some intimate details with you. Merging with Jesus is not for your comfort, but for the fulfillment of the Kingdom you have become. It is the expression of the nature of Jesus to your world. I am a Jesus pusher!!!

I am a Jesus pusher!!! The change in pronouns bears directly on the interpretation and understanding of our passage (Matthew 5:11). We must understand our passage not in light of the entirety of the Beatitudes, but also in light of persecution. The thrust of the first seven beatitudes is positive. Even the first beatitude reminding us that we are ***"poor in spirit"*** is positive in light of His presence sourcing us! We inherit the land (Matthew 5:5); we hunger and are filled (Matthew 5:6). We live in mercy (Matthew 5:7); we are pure in heart and see God (Matthew 5:8). We dwell in peace (Matthew 5:9). This becomes positive instruction giving us courage to be ***salt*** and ***light*** is our society. Our passage (Matthew 5:13-16) is about how we, the Kingdom people, function in the world.

A negative is definitely injected with the last beatitude on persecution (Matthew 5:10). Jesus gives further instruction to eliminate any confusion or oversight. He said, "I am really talking about persecution. I am not saying they will experience it; I am saying you will experience it." Everything He is says about being ***salt*** and ***light*** must be experienced and expressed in a world persecuting ***you; and saying all kinds of evil against you falsely for My sake"*** (Matthew 5:11). This is not a call to comfort, solutions to all your problems, or elimination of all difficulties. This is not a call to happiness, good feelings, or emotional highs. This is a call to the fulfillment of God's plan, which is your destiny. He has uniquely created you to merge with you. As a Kingdom person you will give demonstration to who He is in the uniqueness of your own identity. This will happen in the context of persecution. It is a privilege to be an expression of who He is! I am a Jesus pusher!!!

I am a Jesus pusher!!! After giving the last beatitude, Jesus explains the element of persecution. This is not casually mentioned but forcibly spoken. It is in the emphatic *"you,"* beginning the passage (Matthew 5:13-14). The pronoun is stated in the Greek verb "eimi," and as the opening word and subject of the statement, "humeis." Thus, it is stated twice making the emphasis of "you yourselves." The contrasting conjunction *"but"* (de) verifies this (Matthew 5:13). If you do not influence your world as *salt*, you are not a Kingdom person. This is an imperative for all Kingdom people. You cannot live for yourself and be a Kingdom person! Jesus presents this without justification, answering "why?" No explanation is offered; no verification is presented! This is stated without interpretation, explaining "how." No instruction is forthcoming; no rules or steps to take are listed.

This *"you"* is also plural; this suggests it is a corporate action of a united Kingdom. No doubt in our passage, Jesus addressed His disciples from this point forward in the Sermon on the Mount. We are to come together as the body of Christ to influence our world. We do not hide in the upper room of our sanctuary; we march in bold ways into our world. It is a contrast. Here is how the world treats us, persecution; here is how we treat our world, *salt* and *light*. This is achieved through our merger with His presence and the sourcing of His Person. I am a Jesus pusher!!!

I am a Jesus pusher!!! The ***salt*** imagery is strong in this opening statement concerning "influence" (Matthew 5:13). There are dozens of Bible commentaries we can read that highlight the various uses of salt in the Scriptures. Usually the elements of "purity," "preservation," and "flavor" are emphasized. These issues are proposed because they immediately come to mind with this imagery. However, is this what Jesus suggested with this statement? Although these issues may be true results of the use of salt, do they properly portray the passage?

"You are the salt of the earth" (Matthew 5:13). If we limit our discussion to the passage itself, our first consideration is that salt is identified as ***"of the earth."*** In the Greek language the statement is ***"the earth"*** (ho ge). There is a definite article "the" connected to "earth," in the genitive case showing relationship between ***"salt"*** and ***"earth."*** The Greek word (ge) translated ***earth*** comes from the primary Greek word for "soil." This presents a puzzle regarding the influence of salt. ***"Salt"*** does not do well with soil. All of the Jews were aware of the Dead Sea known as the "Salt Sea." It was five times higher in salt content than our oceans. Nothing lived in this sea. Fish, vegetation, or shells could not survive. The shores of this sea were barren. Salt renders all soil lifeless. Why would Jesus connect ***"salt"*** with the soil? One idea is that ***"earth"*** (ge) refers to people. The salt imagery is focused on how we influence people! The nature of God is passionate about "others." If we merge with Him, He will express His nature through us with this same passion. We are the demonstration of who is He to our ***"earth."*** They will see the life of Jesus. I am a Jesus pusher!!!

I am a Jesus pusher!!! The nature of God expressed through us is verified with the imagery of *"light."* Jesus said, *"You are the light of the world"* (Matthew 5:14). *"World"* is a translation of the Greek word "kosmos," referring to "an orderly arrangement." "Kosmos" seems to refer to the inhabitants of the earth. Jesus indicates this as He says, *"Let your light so shine before men"* (Matthew 5:16). There is no purpose to refute or deny this possible meaning.

However, let us consider the context of the statement of Jesus. As already noted, He forcibly states the "Formation of the Kingdom" (Matthew 5:3-12). The Beatitudes are true only in the context of the Kingdom. The Kingdom is a relationship between Jesus, a state of resource, and humanity, a state of helplessness. The Kingdom is in relationship! In the intimacy of His presence and flow of His person the Kingdom exists. His qualities are demonstrated in and through my humanity. I exist in a state of "meekness" (Matthew 5:5). It is in this state that I *"inherit the earth"* (Matthew 5:5). This is a translation of the same Greek word "ge" as in our passage. In a previous study of this passage, we discovered this did not refer to the inhabitants of the earth. It has to do with the "land!" There is a strong reference in creation, in the covenants, and now in the Kingdom of Heaven regarding the "land." It seems to refer to the physical aspect of man's life. Mankind is to have dominion over all physical life (Genesis 1:28). This physical world is to be the platform for God to demonstrate His nature through us. We get to be Jesus pushers!!!

I am a Jesus pusher!!! From a logical point of view, we decide to be a Christian. It is in intimacy with Jesus, we work hand in hand with the physical universe. Our health is better; our finances are more stable. Our relationship with our environment prospers. Carefully read and experience the story of sin. The physical earth came under the domination and cruse of sin. Weeds began to grow; production of crops became harder. The physical body began to die. Physical relationships crumbled; murder was committed. Kingdom people, those who live in the flow of His sourcing, are the essence of physical health. Christianity is the answer to the problems of ecology. Let all humanity bow at the feet of Jesus and see how quickly our world is restored to health. Let all greed and selfish financial gain be destroyed; let generosity and love prevail. You will be startled at how quickly the financial dilemma of our world comes to order.

Jesus made this promise to those in the Kingdom of Heaven. ***"But seek first the kingdom of God and His righteousness, and all these things shall be added to you"*** (Matthew 6:33). Jesus just finished encouraging us ***"do not worry."*** He says we worry about "life," "eating," "drinking," "clothing," and "tomorrow." He proclaims the truth that ***"your heavenly Father knows that you need all these things"*** (Matthew 6:32). These are the things that are contained in ***"the earth."*** Kingdom people are the ***"salt"*** of all these things! Jesus demonstrates Himself through us; our physical lives are the platform for the demonstration. I am a Jesus pusher!!!

Jesus PUSHER | 198

I am a Jesus pusher!!! We must understand this passion through the element of persecution. We are to be *"salt"* in the physical world that looks to destroy us! When the enemy persecutes us, both spiritually and physically, he does so in the physical realm. Think of the early Church's persecution, *"tortured," "trial of mockings and scourgings, yes, and of chains and imprisonment," "stoned," "sawn in two," "tempted," slain with the sword," "wandered about in sheepskins and goatskins," "being destitute," "afflicted,"* and *"tormented"* (Hebrews 11:35-37). What was their response to all the physical persecutions? They *"obtained a good testimony through faith."* They were *"salt!"* They never allowed their circumstances to dictate to them; they, the Kingdom people, dictated to their circumstances. Instead of being shaped by what was happening in their physical world, they became the influence of change in their physical circumstances.

This influence is called "cross style!" Whatever the effect of salt, it always seems to act according to this basic principle. For instance, when salt is applied properly to food, one does not taste the salt. The purpose of salt is not to make everything taste like salt. Salt is to intermingle with the ingredients to enhance the flavor of the food. This is why Jesus could without hesitation call each disciple to *"take up his cross, and follow Me. For whoever desires to save his life will lose it, but whoever loses his life for My sake will find it"* (Matthew 16:24-25).

I am a Jesus pusher!!! Does the basic premise of Christianity repulse you? Losing your life is the opposite thought process of the world of persecution. But there is a reasonable attraction to the style of the cross. One would think in losing our lives we become the same, all simply tasting like salt. However, in losing my life to Jesus He so saturates me with His presence that I finally become who I was really meant to be. Instead of diminishing, I flourish. Instead of dying, I live; instead of losing, I win! How can it be? It is the principle of *"salt."* Without hesitation, we call every individual to the cross. There is no compromise, soft peddling, or pampering in this Gospel. There is no "trying," "experimentation," or "let us see how it works out." This is an unconditional call of the cross to become *"salt."*

Although this is true about becoming *"salt,"* our passage is about being *"salt."* We cannot fathom how we could experience becoming *"salt"* and then hesitate in being *"salt."* We dwell in a state of death where life is found. Paul expounded this truth when he said, ***"But we have this treasure in earthen vessels, that the excellence of the power may be of God and not of us"*** (2 Corinthians 4:7). This is another description of the Kingdom of Heaven; my earthen vessel helplessness is filled with the treasure of ***"the light of the knowledge of the glory of God in the face of Jesus Christ"*** (2 Corinthians 4:6). The purpose of this treasure is not so my earthen vessel can be glorified, but that everyone around me will experience ***"the excellence of the power"*** of God. I am to become *"salt"* that He might be seen. I am a Jesus pusher!!!

I am a Jesus pusher!!! *"But we have this treasure in earthen vessels, that the excellence of the power may be of God and not of us"* (2 Corinthians 4:7). What does this mean? Paul said, *"We are hard-pressed on every side, yet not crushed; we are perplexed, but not in despair; persecuted, but not forsaken, struck down, but not destroyed"* (2 Corinthians 4:7-9). Does this not sound like the Beatitudes ending on a note of persecution? God uses the platform of persecution to display *"this treasure in earth vessels."* The Kingdom of Heaven influences my world through the persecution. My helplessness is filled with His all-surpassing resource creating the Kingdom of Heaven. The Kingdom of Heaven loses its life in the world of persecution. A self-centered, self-focused, self-sourcing world pounds its own chest, demands its own rights, and exerts its own desires. We live the cross style in the midst of such a world; we are *"salt."* We bring authenticity to life; the tasteless world of drab existence sees what it is to live.

Paul said the secret to such a display is, *"Always carrying about in the body the dying of the Lord Jesus, that the life of Jesus also may be manifested in our body. For we who live are always delivered to death for Jesus' sake, that the life of Jesus also may be manifested in our mortal flesh. So then death is working in us, but life in you"* (2 Corinthians 4:10-12). What makes us *"salt"* causes us to be *"salt."* In a world of persecution, driven by self-centered, self-sourced people, we live the dying of Jesus. We refuse to live out of ourselves; we will not respond from our rights; we cannot react out of our needs. Jesus must be seen in us. I am a Jesus pusher!!!

I am a Jesus pusher!!! The Kingdom person does not want to be seen or tasted; we redeem every situation by filling it with His life. The seemingly evil circumstance becomes an opportunity for good, the demonstration of His life. Those of the persecuting world flow with hate; Kingdom people respond with His love. Those who would destroy everything around them experience the creative life of the Kingdom of Heaven. The constant negative is saturated with the constant positive. The low and debase is always elevated to the high and lofty. Revenge and lack of forgiveness are overshadowed by grace and mercy. Congratulations! The Beatitudes are a manifested in our physical world. We *"are the salt of the earth."*

All Jesus invades all we are. In this oneness of His presence we become the Kingdom of Heaven, not contained in performance or accomplishments, but in His presence. We have profound influence on our physical world. Our physical world is under the curse of sin and is dominated by the self-centeredness of men under the curse of sin. In Jesus, we have come to death; it is death to all we are in self-focus. We are not self-sourced, but Christ-sourced. Our physical world with all of its circumstances experiences the death of Christ in us and manifests the life of Christ to them. Our purpose is not self-centered. We do not design that everyone will taste like salt. We are used to bring every physical circumstance to the display of His glory. We lose our lives that He might live. We participate in the redemption of our world. What a privilege! We *"are the salt of the earth!"* I am a Jesus pusher!!!

I am a Jesus pusher!!! Salt was of extreme value in Jesus' day. There was no lack of supply. The Jebel Usdum, to the south of the Dead Sea, is a mountain of rock salt about seven miles long and from two to three miles wide and some hundreds of feet high. The Dead Sea, also called Sea of Salt, is located at the southern end of the Jordan River. It is one thousand three hundred feet below sea level making it the lowest point on the earth. The deepest point of the sea is the northeast corner. The size of this sea varies but it averages fifty miles in length and nine to ten miles in width. Its water contains twenty-five percent salt; our oceans are six percent. Due to extreme heat there is a rapid evaporation of water. Thus, the marshes around the sea have an abundant supply of salt. Salt was used in man's food (Job 6:6) and added to fodder for the animals (Isaiah 30:24). Newborn babies were rubbed with salt (Ezekiel 16:4). The grain and burnt offerings were sprinkled with salt (Leviticus 2:13; Ezra 16:4). This does not include the use in food for preservation in a hot climate and for flavor in cooking.

Jesus used the imagery of **salt** to highlight the spiritual reality of the Kingdom of Heaven (Matthew 5:13). The content of **salt** is the content of the Kingdom of Heaven; the content of the Kingdom is the content of the Beatitudes. It is not a location but a relationship of intimacy with Him. The relationship is called the Kingdom of Heaven. It includes comfort, inheritance, filling, mercy, purity, and peace. He places equal to these qualities the wonder of suffering for His sake. **Salt** affects and influences every aspect of life. Jesus influences the Kingdom person and through them to their world. I am a Jesus pusher!!!

I am a Jesus pusher!!!

Jesus used **salt** as a parable (Matthew 5:13). Being **salt** is being the beatitudes. As the beatitudes give content to **salt**, so **salt** gives content to the beatitudes. It there was any tendency to think of working, earning, or meriting the Kingdom of Heaven, the **salt** imagery eliminates it. **Salt** and **light** dwell in a state of being. **Mercy** is not something we attempt to merit or extend; **mercy** is a natural result of the embrace of Jesus. "Peacemaking" is not a skill we master; it is an inner condition of the soul resulting from Jesus' presence. We are not really salt; we are the presence of Jesus, the sourcing of Christ, manifested in and influencing our world. We must not view our verse physiologically but spiritually.

Jesus begins with a proposition. ***"You are the salt of the earth."*** Then He reveals to us the content of this statement. As with all parables, it is tempting to add our own thinking and understanding to what Jesus said. We can easily go way beyond what Jesus intended. We must come under the discipline of the Spirit and stay in the limits of the passage. The Trinity God's focus is that we merge with Jesus. Therefore, in the merger with Jesus we know the fulfillment of God's dreams for us. Our focus has to be on Jesus. We must live within the boundaries of His presence, be filled with the fullness of His nature, and allow Him to source our expressions. "Be in Jesus" is His message. I am a Jesus pusher!!!

I am a Jesus pusher!!! ***"You are the salt of the earth; but if the salt loses its flavor, how shall it be seasoned"*** (Matthew 5:13)? There are several indications in the passage of the permanency of the Kingdom call. This is not a statement by Jesus proving we can never lose our salvation. That particular issue is not being discussed in this passage. Even a suggestion of that subject is a violation of the passage. However, Jesus is calling His disciples to remain steadfast in a state of being, the Kingdom of Heaven, ***"the salt of the earth."*** Do not waver from such a state!

Jesus opens with, ***"You are the salt of the earth."*** The verb is in the present tense and the indicative mood. The present tense in the Greek language points to the present moment with continuous action in every present moment as it approaches. This speaks to consistently maintaining the condition of being ***salt***. The indicative mood of the verb forms the basis of an imperative. In fact, both statements, ***"You are the salt of the earth"*** and ***"You are the light of the world"*** are thrust upon the disciples without justification as to "why" or "how." He simply says, "This is how you are to be!" We must not ask, "How can I do this?" You and I are helpless (Matthew 5:3). Jesus does not propose something you are to achieve. He describes the result of the merger of our helplessness and His nature! I must have Him! I am a Jesus pusher!!!

Jesus PUSHER | 205

I am a Jesus pusher!!! ***"You are the salt of the earth; but if the salt loses its flavor, how shall it be seasoned"*** (Matthew 5:13)? The present tense verb in the indicative mood indicates permanency. But permanency is also in the genitive clause, ***"of the earth."*** You are salt, yes, but for the earth, not for yourselves. The same is true for ***light***. "You are light, but for the whole world, not for a closed fellowship of disciples." This statement gives us the sense of permanency. This is not a task we accomplish or a duty we perform. There is a call, a permanency, contained within Jesus' statement, which points to an eternal view. There is no end in view or termination point to anticipate. This is who we are as Kingdom people and it will never change.

Another indicator of the principle of permanency is in the statement, ***"but if the salt loses its flavor."*** This statement provides a problem in the passage. Sodium chloride (salt) does not lose its taste. In other words, the statement in the passage when applied to salt is chemically impossible. At the end of the first century a rabbi was asked, "How could one make saltless salt salty again?" He replied, "One should salt it with the afterbirth of a mule." Being sterile, mules have no afterbirth; he was simply saying that a stupid question deserves a stupid answer. My helpless state embraced by God's sovereign Person creates a new creature called the Kingdom of Heaven. There is a permanency to this resource. I do not need to worry about exhausting His resources. Questions such as these are meaningless: What if He grows weak? What do I do when He is not adequate? How do I regain Kingdom status when He is no longer available? What if He grows tired of my weakness? These are foolish questions. Jesus is adequate forever! I am a Jesus pusher!!!

I am a Jesus pusher!!! Jesus is the permanent provision for the Kingdom. There is never a hint of lack or inability contained in the Gospel account. Jesus is always adequate. No excuse is made for failure, falling, or backsliding. We are consistently encouraged to be more than conquers. Words like "abundant" (1 Timothy 1:14), "unsearchable" (Romans 11:33), "exceeding" (Ephesians 1:19), "greatness" (Ephesians 1:19), "riches" (Ephesians 2:7), "glory" (Jude 24), "faithful" (1 Corinthians 1:9), "power of God" (1 Corinthians 1:24), "wisdom of God" (1 Corinthians 1:24), "ordained" (1 Corinthians 2:7), and others fill the New Testament. This is only the beginning of the list!

Jesus introduced the Sermon on the Mount with a series of eight statements known as the Beatitudes (Matthew 5:3-12). Each begins with **"Blessed!"** It means "Congratulations," a statement of assurance. Now Jesus follows this with a definite statement of fact, the indicative! *"You are the salt of the earth!"* We lack nothing in Him! The final beatitude is, *"Blessed are those who are persecuted for righteousness' sake, for theirs is the kingdom of heaven"* (Matthew 5:10). We must see our circumstances in light of the permanency of Kingdom power and grace. Jesus does not speak of victory on good days, or when we are inheriting the land (Matthew 5:5), or being filled (Matthew 5:6), or seeing God (Matthew 5:8). The Kingdom is unshakable even *"when they revile and persecute you, and say all kinds of evil against you falsely for My sake"* (Matthew 5:11). The Kingdom, intimacy with Jesus, is beyond all circumstances? We lack nothing in Him! I am a Jesus pusher!!!

I am a Jesus pusher!!! Jesus ascribed limited boundaries for His view of the Kingdom of Heaven. The elements of which the Kingdom consists are few. This does not allow us to require additional elements He did not include; it does not allow us to eliminate or treat lightly elements He does include. The perimeters are strong! They are set forth in the Beatitudes. There are only two interacting ingredients forming the Kingdom. Man is present in his absolute helplessness; Jesus is present in His magnificent resource. There is no attempt to go beyond these two elements. It is in the surrendering and uniting of man and God that the Kingdom is formed. The prototype of this reality is Jesus! He is the beginning of the Kingdom; He is the first man to experience the fullness of the Spirit.

Flee from the danger of adding any ingredients to the mix. If we propose "meekness" is an essential element of the Kingdom, we are wrong. We are not the Kingdom because we are meek; we are meek because Jesus who has this quality sources us. Purity of heart is not a building block of the Kingdom. No one is pure in heart unless he is the Kingdom. The righteousness of Christ invades his life and purity is demonstrated. If you are a peacemaker you will be allowed to be the Kingdom. NO! You are embraced by the Prince of Peace and experience His sourcing in all your relationships. The qualities in the Beatitudes are not pieces that form the Kingdom. We must see all the Beatitudes in the light of the shaping of the Kingdom, the joining of man and God, helplessness and Divine resource! The Kingdom is merger with Jesus. I am a Jesus pusher!!!

I am a Jesus pusher!!! ***"You are the salt of the earth."*** Next Jesus proposed a contrast represented by the conjunction ***"but"*** (de) ***if the salt loses its flavor, how shall it be seasoned?"*** (Matthew 5:13). When the ***"poor in spirit"*** unite with Jesus in intimacy, they form the Kingdom. We will call this unit ***"salt."*** What would happen if salt is not salty? It is chemically impossible for salt not to be salty, but let us imagine it for the sake of illustration. Many Bible scholars suggest ***"if"*** introduces a conditional statement. If the condition of salt loses its flavor, then how will the salt be re-salted? However, this is not the case. When conditional, the word ***"if"*** is a translation of the Greek word "ei." Jesus uses the Greek word "ean," making it suppositional. To understand this clearly we must grasp the significance of the Greek word "halizo," translated ***"shall it be seasoned?"*** It is the basic word for ***"salt"*** (halas), which is a noun. Jesus turns this noun into a verb, which means, "to salt something or sprinkle with salt."

Here is a substance that may look like ***salt,*** but it does not have the flavor of ***salt,*** nor does it season like ***salt***. It simply is not ***salt***. You cannot re-salt it; it must be discarded from all functions of ***salt***. Saltless salt is a substance that appears to be ***salt*** without the flavor of ***salt***, therefore it is not ***salt***. This is not a conditional statement where Jesus suggests that if ***salt*** loses its flavor we should try to put the flavor back in the ***salt***. He wants us to see that if we are not ***salt*** we will not influence our world. We are not ***salt*** or the Kingdom. Merging with Jesus is the state of being called ***salt***, the Kingdom. I am a Jesus pusher!!!

I am a Jesus pusher!!! ***"You are the salt of the earth; but if the salt loses its flavor, how shall it be seasoned"*** (Matthew 5:13)? This is a parable or metaphor concerning the disciples, which we must apply to our lives. I am poverty stricken and helpless; Jesus is the resource for my life. The Kingdom of Heaven is formed through the uniting of my helplessness and Jesus' resource. Who I am and who He is! The result is that we influence my world. I can never develop enough skills or techniques to achieve influence in my world. I do not need training seminars on "how to do it," or motivation to stimulate me. I am simply not the Kingdom! The Kingdom does not need to put the Kingdom back into the Kingdom. As you cannot enable ***salt*** to be ***salt***, so you cannot enable Kingdom people to be Kingdom people. It is simply who they are!

The focus is my helplessness being embraced by His nature. In this merger we become a new creature called the Kingdom. As ***salt*** naturally effects its surroundings so the Kingdom person naturally alters his environment. The early Church in the Book of Acts saw the world converted to Christianity within seventy years. It is significant Luke does not write in this book about talent or personality types. He down-plays education by showing us situations in which the apostles are referred to as ***"uneducated and untrained men"*** (Acts 4:13). However, he says that the presence of Jesus was responsible for the demonstration. The explanation in the Book of Acts is never focused on the disciples but is always focused on their lives being filled with the Spirit of Jesus. This is the single factor. I am a Jesus pusher!!!

I am a Jesus pusher!!! "Pea-brain!" What are you doing? Have you stooped so low as to begin name-calling? NO! It is a part of our verse. Remember Jesus begins with a great proposition, *"You are the salt of the earth."* In giving us content to this statement, He breaks with the contrast, *"but."* The contrast is *"if the salt loses its flavor, how shall it be seasoned?"* The Greek word "moraino," translated *"loses its flavor"* determines the meaning of the phrase. It is used four times as a verb and twelve times as an adjective. "Moraino" is translated "fool" or "foolish" in every instance except in this statement on **salt** (Matthew 5:13; Luke 14:34). Some other possible translations are "idiot, blockhead, dunce, ignoramus, imbecile, dullard, simpleton, moron, clod, nitwit, dope, ninny, nincompoop, chump, dimwit, dingbat, dipstick, dumbo, dummy dumdum, fathead, numbskull, thickhead, airhead, flake, jughead, jerk, donkey, twit, dork, bozo, turkey, goofball, meatball."

How can this be right? Jesus would never call anyone such names. At the close of the Sermon on the Mount, He gave a parable. There was a wise man that built his house upon a rock. When the storms came, his house stood firm. There was a *"foolish man"* (moros) that built his house upon the sand. When the storms came, his house was destroyed (Matthew 7:26). The Greek word "moros" is the noun form of our verb "moraino." It means, "stupid, silly, or foolish." It is the word from which we derive the English word "moron." Jesus relates this to a person who looks like salt, or tries to do what salt does, but is simply not salt. It is the picture of a helpless person not merged with Jesus, but acting as if he is not helpless. Nothing makes sense outside of Jesus. I am a Jesus pusher!!!

I am a Jesus pusher!!! Jesus says, ***"But if the salt loses its flavor*** (moraino)*"* (Matthew 5:13). A translation would be: "But if the salt is foolish, stupid, or silly." The question for translators is "how do you translate what Jesus is intending." The translator allowed the translation to be influenced by the application of the parable or metaphor of ***salt***. They translated it ***"loses its flavor."*** But what if this disturbs the imagery to which Jesus refers? After all, Jesus is not speaking about ***salt*** but is referring to disciples. In the opening statement of the Sermon on the Mount, the Beatitudes, He clearly congratulates us for being Kingdom people. We are helpless individuals who are united with Him; He sources us. Now we influence our world something like ***salt*** and ***light*** do!

If Jesus sourcing us causes us to lose our sense of helplessness, we become fools. If we cease to ***"mourn"*** (Matthew 5:4), we become morons, silly, stupid, and foolish. If we for one moment rely on our own effort or self-sourcing, we have moved from the Kingdom of Heaven, to the category of a "pea-brain, idiot, blockhead (view the list in previous study). Jesus calls us to influence our world, but only in the framework of His sourcing. Any thought of self-performance, self-control, or self-production would be ludicrous. Only Jesus makes sense! Let us focus on the person of Jesus. We must embrace Him in a deeper way. Let us open our lives to be captured by Him in a new way. We must be submerged in His nature. I am a Jesus pusher!!!

I am a Jesus pusher!!! ***"It is then good for nothing but to be thrown out and trampled underfoot by men"*** (Matthew 5:13b). The interpretation of this statement is determined by the opening remarks of Jesus. ***"You are the salt of the earth, but if the salt loses its flavor, how shall it be seasoned?"*** (Matthew 5:13a). Jesus refers to us as ***"the salt of the earth."*** The Greek word "ge," translated ***earth,*** comes from the root word for "soil." Soil becomes barren when sprinkled with salt. We discovered a definite tie between this statement and the third beatitude. The person who embraces his helplessness can be filled with the resource of Jesus. A by-product of Jesus' presence is ***"they shall inherit the earth."*** In the Old Testament covenant "land" was an important part of the promises. The last beatitude is focused on persecution. This seems to involve destruction the physical being. Life is in the midst of this destruction. We are not sourced by the decaying physical world around us; we are sourced by the intimacy of His presence making us ***"salt."*** The answer to everything wrong in the physical is in this intimate embrace with Jesus.

Paul said, ***"For I consider that the sufferings of this present time are not worthy to be compared with the glory which shall be revealed in us"*** (Romans 8:18). ***"For we know that the whole creation groans and labors with birth pangs together until now. Not only that, but we also who have the firstfruits of the Spirit, even we ourselves groan within ourselves, eagerly waiting for the adoption, the redemption of our body"*** (Romans 8:22-23). We are the ***"salt"*** of all physical things! Hope comes when we unite with the resource of Jesus, the Kingdom of Heaven. I am a Jesus pusher!!!

I am a Jesus pusher!!! Jesus said, *"But if the salt loses its flavor"* (Matthew 5:13). This is chemically impossible. Therefore, this discussion is not about *"salt"* but disciples. The Greek word "moraino," translated *"loses its flavor"* here is translated everywhere else "fool" or "foolish." It is the Greek word from which we get the English word "moron." Jesus continues, *"But if the salt loses its flavor, how shall it be seasoned?"* The Greek word "halizo," translated *"shall it be seasoned,"* is the same root word as *"salt."* Jesus took the noun and turned it into a verb. It could be translated, "How shall it be salting?" When salt isn't salting, then it is not salt! This statement is not a conditional clause but suppositional. Jesus says when a Kingdom person does not influence his world, he is not a Christian. There is never a time when we can put salt back into salt, nor put the Kingdom back into the Kingdom. You either are or you are not! Therefore, if salt is not salt, *"It is then good for nothing but to be thrown out and trampled underfoot by men"* (Matthew 5:13). Jesus gives us an emphatic statement, saying there is no compromise or room for adjustment. We must understand this statement in light of what He just said.

Let me summarize. When salt is not salting (seasoning), it is not salt, but is playing the fool. Let us focus this statement on the disciples to whom He is speaking. When a Christian is not influencing his world, he is not Christian! The secret of being a disciple is oneness with Jesus! I am a Jesus pusher!!!

I am a Jesus pusher!!! *"You are the salt of the earth, but if the salt loses its flavor, how shall it be seasoned? It is then good for nothing"* (Matthew 5:13). In the Greek language the first word in the statement (*It is good for nothing*) is the Greek word "eis," translated *"for."* It is a movement term (into) indicating a change in location. When a helpless person is filled with the resource of the Spirit of Jesus, the Kingdom of Heaven is formed. All the benefits and flow of His presence aggressively influences the believer's world. However, Jesus begins to describe a disciple who moves into the realm of non-influence. In the imagery of light, he is under a basket (Matthew 5:15). In the imagery of salt, he is not salting (seasoning) his world. What does this mean?

"Nothing" is a translation of the Greek word "oudeis." It means, "not even one, not the least." This describes the state of helplessness in which we dwell. In the beatitudes, the *"poor in spirit"* is the picture of complete helplessness. The Greek word "ptochos," translated *"poor,"* is the strongest Greek word available. There is no resource. We often hide our helplessness with a superficial ability to perform a certain act. James Dobson reported that a teenager's self-esteem is based on one of three things: talent, good looks, or money. However, none of these three things have anything to do with the inner spirit of the person. They become ways to hide our helplessness. Jesus addressed the leaders of Israel as hypocrites. *"For you cleanse the outside of the cup and dish, but inside they are full of extortion and self-indulgence"* (Matthew 23:25). We are successful in business, careers, or performance of skills; in reality we are covering our helplessness. We must find our value in Jesus. I am a Jesus pusher!!!

Jesus PUSHER | 215

I am a Jesus pusher!!! Jesus said that when salt is no longer capable of seasoning *"it is then good for nothing"* (Matthew 5:13). The Greek word "ischuo," translated *"it is good,"* gives us the subject and verb of the statement. It means, "strong, powerful, mighty, or able to do." It is a part of the word group from "ischus." This word is focused on the resource itself, not the action or performance of the resource. In other words, in Jesus' statement, the emphasis is not on the person who cannot do anything, action, performance, or duty; therefore, they have no value. He highlights the "state of being" at the base of His presentation. The person who does not influence His world with the presence of Jesus is like *"salt"* that is not "salty."

This person is self-sourced; therefore, he has no resource. There is not any, not even one, amount of resource within him. Even with the parade of good deeds or successful performances acclaiming his fame, he is helpless. This testifies to the shallow, impractical, and hypocritical state of the Kingdom of Satan. It is a kingdom source by demonic nature, self. He is a substance attempting to be salt when he is not! He is a person trying to be the Kingdom of God, when he is not! When a person is helpless he manipulates every situation for his benefit. He must guard and protest. It is the best he can do because he is helpless. What a tragic position when the resource of the Trinity God wants to fill our helplessness with Himself. Jesus wants to indwell us! I am a Jesus pusher!!!

I am a Jesus pusher!!! In our verse, Jesus said, *"It is then good for nothing but . . .."* (Matthew 5:13). The Greek word commonly translated *"but"* is "de." However, Jesus states, "ei me." It is a combination of "if" (ei) and "not" (me) often translated "except, if not, or unless." It marks a contrast by designating an exception. Jesus forcibly said that a person filled with the Spirit, a Kingdom person, is going to influence their world. It will not be by their performance or doing, but by the flow of the Spirit of God through them. If this is not happening, they are not Kingdom people. They are *"salt"* that is not "salty;" therefore, it is not *"salt."* They are in the condition of being helpless without any resource at all. They are useless, without value.

Jesus says, "Let me correct my statement." There is an exception of the absolute helpless, useless, and without value. The one value they now have is *"to be thrown out and trampled underfoot by men"* (Matthew 5:13). There are several parallel illustrations of this same idea given by Jesus, who spoke of the holy and sacred things given to dogs. These dogs have no comprehension of this truth's value and the eternal significance of its impartation. A dog treats a book of pornography and the Holy Scriptures the same. A person sits under the exposition of the Holy Word of God and misses it all because of a cobweb hanging from the sanctuary light enamors them. Jesus described it, *"Do not give what is holy to dogs; nor cast your pearls before swine, lest they trample them under their feet, and turn and tear you in pieces"* (Matthew 7:6). We only discover proper value through intimacy with Jesus. I am a Jesus pusher!!!

Jesus PUSHER | 217

I am a Jesus pusher!!! ***"You are the salt of the earth, but if the salt loses its flavor, how shall it be seasoned? It is then good for nothing but to be thrown out and trampled underfoot by men"*** (Matthew 5:13). A direct parallel to our verse is the Parable of the Vine and Branches. Jesus said, ***"If anyone does not abide in Me, he is cast out as a branch and is withered; and they gather them and throw them into the fire, and they are burned"*** (John 15:6). A branch that does not abide in the life of the vine is fruitless. He is ***"cast out"*** and "gathered" like firewood. He is no longer a branch; he has become dead, lifeless wood.

Jesus' statement, ***"to be thrown out"*** (Matthew 5:13), is an infinitive indicating purpose. An infinitive depends upon the main verb and the main subject, which are ***"It is good."*** It is a focus on "uselessness, lacking value." Therefore, there is only one thing left. It is not an expression of meanness; it does not indicate anger, condemnation, or even judgment. It is only a matter of fact, the final determination. The focus is not using what is leftover, or all that remains. It has "no use, except," referring to the fate of the useless; it can only ***"be thrown out."*** ***Uselessness*** is the picture of a helpless individual who does not embrace his destiny, which is to be filled with the nature of Jesus. Our only value is in Him! Who I am and who He is must merge into the union of a new creature, the Kingdom person. My full potential, value, and identity are in this relationship of intimacy with Jesus. I am a Jesus pusher!!!

I am a Jesus pusher!!! ***"You are the salt of the earth, but if the salt loses its flavor, how shall it be seasoned? It is then good for nothing but to be thrown out and trampled underfoot by men"*** (Matthew 5:13). The Greek word "ballo," translated ***"to be thrown out,"*** is in the present tense. In the Greek language, it means now with continual action. There is a consistency to this action. Every time the writer uses this Greek word in the New Testament, it has the tone of impulsive. In other words, there is no plan or thought process involved. No one is plotting against us. It is a simple reaction to something that has no value. The Greek word "exo," translated ***"out,"*** is equally impressive. It is not just "out" but contrasted to being "in." It does not merely describe a location of where one is, but we must see the position of "out" in light of being "in." There is an emphasis on separation. He is ***"out,"*** which means, separated from all that is in the Beatitudes.

The Greek word "katapateo," translated ***"and trampled underfoot,"*** is powerful. "Kata" is added to the main word for intensity. "Pateo" means "to tread." However, it is trampling with intention and indicates scorn or to despise. There was no anger, condemnation, or even judgment regarding the Greek word "ballo," translated ***"to be thrown out."*** Jesus is merely saying He fills the helpless one with His Spirit; he becomes the Kingdom in linkage with Him. This person will influence his world, but if he is not, then he is not a Kingdom person. The value of one who is helpless and is only sourced by his helplessness is nothing. His casting out is the only value he has; he will live among those who feel contempt for themselves. They bring destruction upon their own lives. Jesus must fill me. I am a Jesus pusher!!!

Jesus PUSHER | 219

I am a Jesus pusher!!! ***"You are the salt of the earth, but if the salt loses its flavor, how shall it be seasoned? It is then good for nothing but to be thrown out and trampled underfoot by me,"*** (Matthew 5:13). We are back to the state in which we started, helplessness. We are ***"poor in spirit"*** (Matthew 5:3). We will admit and ***"mourn"*** this, opening us to the filling of His resource. He will come in the wonder of His presence and source us. With His embrace, God will form the Kingdom. Or we will attempt to source ourselves, those who are in a state of helplessness, poverty-stricken to the worst degree, trying to give themselves all they need. This group will be driven to recognize their helplessness. They have ***"nothing"*** (oudeis), not even one, not the least. ***"It is good"*** (ischyo) is lacking, meaning there is no resource sourcing them. This helplessness without adequate resource drives them to uselessness, leaving them to one fate. They are ***"thrown out and trampled underfoot by men."***

Helplessness is our intended state, the glory of humanity; it makes him unique among the creation. God created us individually to be helpless so He can fill us with Jesus! There is no shame in this reality; the shame is in the denial of such a state. We are the ***salt of the earth***. In His embrace with us, God forms the Kingdom; in His embrace, we influence our world. The alternative is to have no resource, not even one. The only thing that can happen is separation, ***"thrown out and trampled underfoot by men."*** Our value is in Jesus! I am a Jesus pusher!!!

I am a Jesus pusher!!! ***"You are the light of the world"*** (Matthew 5:14). We must approach this statement with fear and trembling. At first glance, the responsibility is enough to break the spirit of any man. The claim Jesus made concerning Himself is the imagery of ***"light!"*** ***"Then Jesus spoke to them again, saying, 'I am the light of the world. He who follows Me shall not walk in darkness, but have the light of life"*** (John 8:12). In another setting Jesus said, ***"As long as I am in the world, I am the light of the world"*** (John 9:5). Old Testament prophecy pointed to Jesus as the light, ***"The people who sat in darkness have seen a great light, and upon those who sat in the region and shadow of death Light has dawned"*** (Matthew 4:16; Isaiah 9:2). We must note that Jesus is never refer to as ***"salt."*** Neither He nor any New Testament writer used this imagery regarding Jesus, which is all the more reason to tremble as we move into this verse.

The moment the subject of light appears we are drawn to John's Gospel because ***"light"*** is a key word in his account. In his prologue he said, ***"In Him was life, and the life was the light of men"*** (John 1:4). The Word (Logos) means God joined the created. Jesus' manifested ***"life"*** is the essence of the ***"light."*** This "life/light" came into our world; its brilliance penetrated the darkness (John 1:5). Is God, the expression of light, becoming one with humanity? Is this the new covenant, the fullness of the Spirit? Can I be filled with Jesus as He was filled with His Father? I am a Jesus pusher!!!

I am a Jesus pusher!!! ***"You are the light of the world"*** (Matthew 5:14). Legalistic scribes and Pharisees brought to Jesus a woman caught in adultery. The Law said they should stone her. They wanted Jesus to state His opinion on the matter. He proposed the only person who qualified to throw the first stone would be one who had never sinned. Jesus waited, the scribes and the Pharisees slipped off one by one, convicted by their conscience. No one but Jesus could throw a stone and He would not! Jesus did not condemn her but urged her to go and sin no more. Then Jesus made the statement, ***"I am the light of the world. He who follows Me shall not walk in darkness, but have the light of life"*** (John 8:12). The Pharisees continued to argue with Him about His witness. He proposed to them that His witness and judgments were not His own, ***"for I am not alone, but I am with the Father who sent Me"*** (John 8:16).

Notice the progression of this situation carefully. The life and witness of Jesus were powerful, giving ***"light"*** to the Jews and the woman. She left without sin and sinned no more; the scribes and Pharisees remained condemned and guilty. They attempted to undermine His witness only to discover a fantastic truth. His ***"light"*** or witness was not His but was a result of the Father who sent Him and was with Him. Their relationship was so close that Jesus answered, ***"You know neither Me nor My Father. If you had known Me, you would have known My Father also"*** (John 8:19). I can only know ***"light"*** within the context of my helplessness merged with His nature. It is intimacy with Jesus! I am a Jesus pusher!!!

I am a Jesus pusher!!! *"You are the light of the world"* (Matthew 5:14). Jesus was walking with His disciples as they passed a man who was born blind. The disciples asked a question, which was the traditional concept of their day. They wanted to know who was guilty of the sin that caused this man to be born blind. Jesus quickly corrected their false thinking. This condition of blindness was not the result of anyone's particular sin; this man's blindness was for the purpose *"that the works of God should be revealed in him"* (John 9:3). Then Jesus began to highlight the need for them to carry out all activities in the *"day"* or "light." Activities done in light are distinctly tied to the phrase, *"the works of Him who sent Me"* (John 9:4). In other words, the Father is intimately involved in the works, and when the Father works through the Son, it is *"light."* Jesus concluded, *"As long as I am in the world, I am the light of the world"* (John 9:5). Jesus is the *"light of the world"* because the Father filled Him; His life and His activities demonstrate the presence, the *"light,"* of the Father.

Now in the Sermon on the Mount, Jesus informed the disciples of the Kingdom to which He calls them. God forms Kingdom people from their helpless state and fills them with His nature. In this uniting, they will be the *"light of the world"* precisely as He is the *"light of the world."* Jesus fulfilled the destiny of the Father within Him, so this was not a challenge to the deeds Jesus did; He fulfilled the destiny of the Father within Him. To what has He called you? In the expression of His nature through you, you will be *"light."* I am a Jesus pusher!!!

I am a Jesus pusher!!! ***"You are the light of the world"*** (Matthew 5:14). Jesus was ministering in Judea alongside John the Baptist. Suddenly John was put in prison; upon hearing this news Jesus left Judea to begin a new ministry in Galilee. Galilee, a mixture of Gentiles and Jews, had little connection with the temple and the strict order of the scribes and Pharisees. This area was often called the "Galilee of the Gentiles." Isaiah prophesied concerning this moment, describing this region as ***"people who walked in darkness"*** (Isaiah 9:2). Hundreds of years later, Matthew quoted this passage about Jesus (Matthew 4:15-16). He took liberty with the quote saying, ***"The people who sat in darkness,"*** indicating they are worse than those who walked in darkness. Darkness overwhelmed them, and in their comfort they no longer knew they were in such a state. They were content sitting in their sin. But the good news is that they ***"have seen a great light."***

Jesus came to Galilee; He did most of his mighty works in the three major cities of Galilee (Matthew 11:20). He chose eleven of His disciples from the citizens of this area. According to Matthew, this happened shortly after the Father filled Jesus with the Holy Spirit (Matthew 3:16). ***"Light"*** came to a darkened area because a Man sourced by God walked among them. His messages and His activities were all a demonstration of the power of the Spirit within Him. He could not control the ***"light"*** contained within Him. He pushed back the demonic forces and penetrated the darkness. Jesus is ***"the light of the world!"*** Now Jesus proclaims this same reality for us. We must be filled with Him as He was filled with the Father. He is the prototype of this reality. I can know Jesus as Jesus knew His Father. I am a Jesus pusher!!!

I am a Jesus pusher!!! ***"You are the light of the world"*** (Matthew 5:14). John highlights Jesus as ***"the light of men"*** in his Gospel account, and he contrasts Jesus with John the Baptist. Both Jesus and John the Baptist had miraculous birth. Jesus was born of a virgin; John was born of a barren woman, which should have been impossible births. Even though it was an Old Testament filling, John was filled with the Holy Spirit from his birth. Jesus was filled with the Holy Spirit (Matthew 3:16) as the first man of the New Covenant. John was the forerunner; Jesus was the Messiah! Both men were called and sent by God. Jesus held John the Baptist in high esteem. He proclaimed John as the greatest ever been born of man (Matthew 11:11).

Jesus recognized a very important distinction between John and Himself. John, as great as he was, did not compare to the least in the Kingdom of Heaven (Matthew 11:11). What is more remarkable, John recognized his position as well. The Jews sent priest and Levites from Jerusalem to ask him, ***"Who are you?"*** (John 1:19). He strongly denied that he was the Messiah. ***"It is He who, coming, after me, is preferred before me, whose sandal strap I am not worthy to loose"*** (John 1:27). In preaching to the Pharisees and Sadducees, John said, ***"I indeed baptize you with water unto repentance, but He who is coming after me is mightier than I, whose sandals I am not worthy to carry. He will baptize you with the Holy Spirit and fire"*** (Matthew 3:11). We can receive the same Spirit of Jesus making us ***"the light of the world."*** I am a Jesus pusher!!!

I am a Jesus pusher!!! *"You are the light of the world"* (Matthew 5:14). John, the Gospel writer, recognized the distinction between Jesus and John the Baptist. He proclaimed the mission of John to be *"a witness, to bear witness of the Light, that all through him might believe. He was not that Light, but was sent to bear witness of that Light"* (John 1:7-8). While both Jesus and John the Baptist were filled with the Spirit, there was something in Jesus that John did not have. The New Covenant was born when the Spirit of God joined, linked with Jesus, in intimacy and oneness. John the Baptist was filled with the Spirit to do a task, but did not know the same intimacy Jesus knew with the Father. He could point to the Light, but he was not the light. Jesus was filled with the Spirit in intimacy and became the demonstration of the light; He was the light! All who believe the Gospel believe that Jesus is *"the Light of the world!"*

What shall we say of this statement, *"You are the light of the world"* (Matthew 5:14)? Jesus was not empowered by the Spirit merely for a task, and we are not called just to activities. The essence of Christianity is not the performance of duties or rules. Christianity is a state of being, having intimacy of relationship with Jesus. There must be a merger between the mind of Christ and our mind where His emotions and our emotions become one. What Jesus desires and what we desire become the same. This oneness only happens when I embrace my helplessness and experience His fullness. A new creature emerges through this merger producing our state of existence. *"You are the light of the world"* (Matthew 5:14). What a privilege! I am a Jesus pusher!!!

Jesus PUSHER | 226

I am a Jesus pusher!!! ***"You are the light of the world"*** (Matthew 5:14). Jesus brings us into the imagery He used for Himself. He begins with the second person pronoun, "humeis." The verb also contains the second person pronoun, giving a double emphasis. One translator said it as, "You and you alone." There seems to be an imperative in the undertone of this statement. The tone is not casual, indicating being the light is not something we can take or leave. ***"The light of the world"*** is a bold declaration of the Kingdom person. Jesus did not indicate that fifty or seventy-five percent of Kingdom people will be light. NO! One hundred percent of the Kingdom people ***"are the light of the world."*** We cannot adjust, compromise, or rationalize what Jesus says. Jesus statement is emphatic!

We see the effects of ***"the light"*** in the following verse giving further explanation (Matthew 5:15). How ridiculous to light a lamp and place it under a bushel! The purpose of a lamp is to give light to the house. When we put the lamp on a lamp stand we help the lamp fulfill its purpose. There is no logical way to refute these statements. We dare not adjust, rationalize, or compromise Jesus statement that our position is ***"the light."*** Do not ask, "How can I do light?" It is not the achievement of performance; it is the experience of a relationship! Jesus wants to fill me with His light. The same light expressed through Him will now be expressed through me, as I dwell in Him and He in me. I am a Jesus pusher!!!

I am a Jesus pusher!!! Jesus commanded, ***"Let your light so shine before men, that they may see your good works and glorify your Father in heaven"*** (Matthew 5:16). The Greek word "houto," translated ***"so,"*** is a demonstrative adverb giving content and describing the verb ***"shine,"*** meaning "this one," "in this manner," "on this wise," or "thus." "Houto" is the first word in the sentence in the Greek text. This Greek word takes all the content of the preceding verse and places it into the ***"shine"*** to which Jesus calls us. The verb of the sentence is ***"shine"*** and is an imperative. Jesus commands us to shine in the exact same manner as the lamp on a lamp stand. The lamp on the lamp stand fulfills the purpose to light the house. Our purpose is to answer God's call to be the ***"light of the world."***

Jesus emphatically calls us to be ***"the light of the world,"*** which is a call to be who Jesus is. The challenge to be Christ-like has always been somewhat uncomfortable for Christians. His standard of living, manner of loving, and flow of learning is so high; who could come close to such achievement? But this reaction only highlights our misunderstanding of His call. Jesus Himself called us to this level of ***"light!"*** The call is unrealistic unless the pattern by which God accomplished it in Jesus' life becomes mine. He embraced His helplessness in humanity and was filled with the nature of God. He did not do what He did because He is God, but did what He did because He was a helpless man filled with God. Now He calls me to this same state of existence. I can be filled with the Spirit of Jesus. What a privilege! I am a Jesus pusher!!!

I am a Jesus pusher!!! ***"You are the light of the world"*** (Matthew 5:14). Let's turn to some of the great statements of Jesus. He said, ***"I am the light of the world. He who follows Me shall not walk in darkness, but have the light of life"*** (John 8:12). The Greek word "echo," translated ***"have,"*** means to hold as a possession, implying continued possession. Engrained in the "following" of Jesus is the possession of who He is; He is the light of the world. We are coming back to the awareness that as He was the light of the world, so in the same manner we are the light of the world. Jesus was filled with the Father and radiated with the light of His presence, and we are filled with Jesus and radiate the light of His presence. The Father source Jesus and now Jesus is sourcing us, giving us what He has! He brings us to His level in the fullness of the New Covenant.

Jesus said, ***"While you have the light, believe in the light, that you may become sons of light"*** (John 12:36). In the preceding paragraph we told you the Greek word "echo," translated ***"have,"*** means to hold as a possession, implying continued possession. Through faith (invoking the activity of the second party) will they become this same light? Paul said, ***"The night is far spent, the day is at hand. Therefore let us cast off the works of darkness, and let us put on the armor of light"*** (Romans 13:12). We are to ***"cast off"*** (apotithemi), meaning "to put aside, lay aside, or eliminate and ***"put on"*** (enduo), means "to sink down into as a garment." The Greek word "hoplon," translated ***"armor,"*** means an instrument, a tool, an implement, or a weapon of war. We are to run from anything that slightly resembles darkness and run into everything that is light. Sinking down into the light is your weapon for defeating everything the darkness. You are the weapon! ***"You are the light of the world."*** Sink into Jesus! I am a Jesus pusher!!!

I am a Jesus pusher!!! *"You are the light of the world"* (Matthew 5:14). As Jesus lived in the fullness of the Spirit and was light to His world, so we are filled with the same light and are the light of the world. Would you let Him shine through you? Would you allow the radiation of His presence to bring illumination to your surroundings? Think of your home! Your family must live in the presence of the light, being constantly exposed to the presence of Jesus. Your fellow employees speak of Jesus working at their job, because you, a fellow employee bring Him to work with you. Matthew proposes a strong force in this verse. Jesus said, *"A city that is set on a hill cannot be hidden"* (Matthew 5:14). This statement is in the negative, expressing an inability. A city on the hill does not try to be seen; a city on a hill is simply incapable of not being seen.

Letting Jesus shine through you brings us back to "being!" You are "being" light; you are not "doing" light. There is contained within the nature of light the inability of not being seen. The moment a match flames in a dark room, we see its light. A helpless person filled with the resource of Jesus' light becomes the Kingdom of God, influencing his world. It has nothing to do with personality types, training, or talents. It is innate within the nature of the person filled with Jesus. It is not about our resources because we are helpless. It is about the linkage between Jesus and humanity. Our responsibility, role, or response must be to seek Him. I am a Jesus pusher!!!

I am a Jesus pusher!!! We must see this section (Matthew 5:13-16) from the perspective of the Beatitudes (Matthew 5:3-12). This view allows for no misinterpretation of meaning or approach. The Beatitudes declare the "Formation of the Kingdom." It becomes evident from the opening statement of the Sermon on the Mount that you and I are not responsible for this development. We do not build the Kingdom of God; we do not grow into the Kingdom of God. We are helpless! Our carnal pride of self-centeredness hinders our admission of such a state. God created us to live dependent on Jesus. When we link with Jesus, depend on Him, and live in the resource of His Person, the Kingdom of God is formed.

The nature of God and man's merger, the Kingdom of God, has a purpose. Jesus immediately moves to propose the "Function of the Kingdom" (Matthew 5:13-16). In the Kingdom of God, we cannot live in isolation. It demands community; however, it is not just a community in their private group's isolation. We already discovered this section is intimately attached to the beatitude discussing "persecution." The Kingdom of God must influence a world that reacts adversely to the link forming the Kingdom. The fact that there is persecution loudly proclaims the influence. The world persecutes the Christian because of the power generated from the link we have with Jesus. He is a Jesus pusher!!!

I am a Jesus pusher!!! Jesus states the imagery of **"salt"** and **"light."** Many Bible scholars make a strong comparison between these two. Salt is negative; light is positive. Salt works in a hidden way; light opens and reveals. While these factors are true, there is no indication in the passage Jesus intended this emphasis. We must note that only one verse deals with salt, while three verses explain light's influence, possibly due to the imageries' focus. "**Salt**" is focused on **"the earth." "Light"** is focused on **"the world."** In previous studies, we discovered **"the earth"** (ho eg) is really "the land," relating to the third beatitude (Matthew 5:5). How we relate to physical circumstances is determined by our involvement in Jesus, forming the Kingdom of God. "**Light**" is focused on **"the world,"** which is the Greek word "kosmos," making a more direct reference to the people of the world.

The idea of "visibility" permeates the imagery of **"light."** This visibility appears to have two aspects throughout these verses. Light makes things visible. Others will see the flow of Jesus' resource within and through (Matthew 5:16). The purpose is that we demonstrate the link between Jesus and us. When Jesus sources a helpless person with His resource, those who witness it will **"glorify your Father in heaven"** (Matthew 5:16). They will recognize the cooperation between God and man, which consistently took place in the Book of Acts. God demonstrates Himself through believers. The world asks how this demonstration happens, allowing the Holy Spirit to minister in sermon or testimony through a key person. They were Jesus pushers!!!

I am a Jesus pusher!!! In using the imagery of *"light"* (Matthew 5:14-16), Jesus stressed the idea of "visibility." This visibility appears to have two aspects in these verses. One is the reality of making things visible. However, the Kingdom link between God and man becomes visible, but the light exposes their lives. Jesus pointed to this in the imagery of the lamp placed on a lampstand. *"It gives light to all who are in the house"* (Matthew 5:15). In another place, Jesus said, *"And this is the condemnation that the light has come into the world, and men loved darkness rather than light, because their deeds were evil. For everyone practicing evil hates the light and does not come to the light, lest his deeds should be exposed. But he who does the truth comes to the light that his deeds may be clearly seen, that they have been done in God"* (John 3:19-21).

When the light of Jesus shines on a person's life, that light reveals his deeds and spiritual condition. Jesus ends the Beatitudes with the note of persecution (Matthew 5:10-12). While God reveals His loving heart through the Jesus pusher, the inner life of the one receiving the revelation is exposed, which is irritating for the ungodly to live in such a brilliant examination. It is not that the Jesus pusher is judges or condemns, but it is the consequence of being the Kingdom person. Light exposes sin. I want to be a Jesus pusher!!!

I am a Jesus pusher!!! Jesus increases the issue of "visibility" by saying, ***"A city that is set on a hill cannot be hidden"*** (Matthew 5:14). All three verses in this section use the imagery of ***"light"*** (Matthew 5:14-16). Jesus presented the lamp and the lampstand as part of this imagery, giving the picture of a city. What was His purpose? The keyword seems to be "design." In Jesus' day, the people built their cities on top of a hill, not by accident but for visibility. The best clue for interpreting our phrase is in the next verse's beginning Greek word (Matthew 5:15). ***"Nor"*** is a translation of the Greek word "oude," a conjunction linking two clauses, which represent parallel "impossibilities." No one can hide a city on a hilltop; you do not light a lamp and put it under a bushel. Building a city on a hill is assertive, expressing absolute confidence and claim to importance, telling us that the inhabitants desire to play a broader role in human affairs. People who want to live a quiet and secluded life build their cities out of sight, hoping others will not notice. Our statement focuses on the ridiculous image of trying to hide a city by design made for prominence.

Jesus used this imagery to highlight the truth about the Kingdom of Heaven's function. Man is helpless; God fills him with the Holy Spirit, which gives him a new level of living. There is design involved in this linking of God and man. God did not fill you for seclusion and isolation. No one can hide the Kingdom of God because that violates the design or nature of its being. The hidden or concealed Kingdom of God is an oxymoron. It is as unimaginable as dry water. The Jesus pusher is designed by God to reveal Himself to our world. We are Jesus pushers!!!

I am a Jesus pusher!!! God created us to be the visibility of Himself as He indwells us. Paul described Jesus as *"the image of the invisible God, the firstborn over all creation"* (Colossians 1:15). It is an unbelievable truth. Jesus was the first man of the New Covenant, a helpless man filled with the essence of God's Spirit. In this combination and linkage, He demonstrated the image of God, making God visible through Him. It was God's design of man's creation from the beginning. Jesus restores what we lost in the fall of Adam.

God boldly declared Jesus' restoration in the creation of man! Before the fall, Adam and Eve lived in the fullness of the Kingdom of God. Their sin was their refusal and admission of their helplessness without the Spirit of God. They denied their dependency on God. In the fullness of the Spirit, God had given them prominence in the created world. *Then God said, "Let Us make man in Our image, according to Our likeness; let them have dominion over the fish of the sea, over the birds of the air, and over the cattle, over all the earth and over every creeping thing that creeps on the earth"* (Genesis 1:26). Notice that being created in His image is linked with dominating all creation. In other words, man is created by and filled with God; he only rules through God's sourcing; he is the invisible God's visible image. Contained in his ruling is the demonstration of all that God is, the demonstration of the Kingdom. Visibility is at the heart of his design. I am a Jesus pusher!!!

I am a Jesus pusher!!! Job is the oldest book in the Bible. The opening chapter reveals a gathering of all *"the sons of God."* They *"came to present themselves before the Lord, and Satan also came among them"* (Job 1:6). In God's discussion with Satan on the condition of the earth, God mentioned Job. *"There is none like him on the earth, a blameless and upright man, one who fears God and shuns evil"* (Job 1:8). Satan challenged Job's loyalty and faithfulness to God. God established limits beyond which Satan was not allowed. Job became the visible display of a man filled with God. The spiritual realm watched as God highlighted Job.

Job's story parallels our passage. *"You are the light of the world. A city that is set on a hill cannot be hidden"* (Matthew 5:14). We must see the function of the Kingdom of God in the context of persecution. God set Job on a stage of persecution, adverse circumstances, and terrible criticism. In this context, Job displayed the design of his nature. He demonstrated the righteousness of God. He was a city set upon a hill, the design of the new creature we are in Christ. We are the display of His image amid suffering and persecution. The difficulties of our lives become the stage for the highlighting of His image. People must see Jesus in us; it is the purpose of the design. We are Jesus pushers!!!

I am a Jesus pusher!!! ***"You are the light of the world. A city that is set upon a hill cannot be hidden"*** (Matthew 5:14). The verb of our statement is startling. There are two Greek words translated ***"cannot,"*** which form the main verb. These two words are "ou dunamai." The Greek word "ou" is the word "not," placing the negative statement. The main part of the verb is "dunamai," which is a part of the word group containing "dunamis," from which our English word "dynamite" comes. It is explosive in nature, often translated "mighty deeds." "Dunamis" not a focus on the power of the resource; it focuses on the action of the resource as it accomplishes something. If Jesus had positively stated this, it would say, "The nature of a city set on a hill reveals itself." The people painted their city buildings with white limestone, consistently whitewashing them. The white limestone gleamed in the sun and even shone in the moonlight. Each home had a lamp or candle in its window. The moving power of light reflected and radiated from this city, giving it strong visibility. The resource and power residing in the town moved to make it known.

This verb, "dunamai," is in the passive voice. The subject is not responsible for this visibility. It is not the city or its building that made them visible, but the location's power. Jesus described the Kingdom of God. I am helpless. When His Person's strength contains my helplessness, an action takes place that is far beyond me. I am not responsible for it; I do not produce it. My responsibility is to respond to Him. When His resource flows through me, the Kingdom of God is made visible. I am a Jesus pusher!!!

Jesus PUSHER | 237

I am a Jesus pusher!!! Throughout the Sermon on the Mount, Jesus highlighted one truth. In the Beatitudes, we discovered it. We do not merit, work, or accomplish the Kingdom; it is not a discipline we achieve. God congratulates us for having arrived. We are helpless. How can we claim the Kingdom as ours? Jesus, the deciding factor, came to us. Our helplessness becomes the platform for the display of His Person. We respond to Him, and He moves our world. We do not influence our world to get into the Kingdom; we impact our world because we are the Kingdom people, our purpose, our design, as we depend upon His power. He establishes us on the hill for the display of His Person. We become the visible image of the invisible God as He flows through our lives.

People see God in us through the light of persecution. Our self-sourcing screams for us to hide. Self-sourcing will always run away, escape, or to deny in some manner. If one church is difficult, why not go to another church? If my wife gives me problems, why not escape and go to another marriage? If I work with people I do not like, why not move to another job? Jesus ends the Beatitudes with the note of persecution. After seven beautiful descriptions of God's glory sourced by His presence, He thrusts us into suffering (Matthew 5:10-12). It is absolute; people will persecute us. Persecution produces and displays the greatness of the Kingdom's linkage. Jesus views this truth as one that sets our hearts on fire. "***Rejoice "and be*** Kingdom's ***exceedingly glad'"*** is His exhortation (Matthew 5:12). I am a Jesus pusher!!!

I am a Jesus pusher!!! Why would Jesus link **"You are the light of the world"** with persecution? The logic is straightforward. When circumstances are blessed, you remain steadfast. Everything is working out, giving you no difficulty, and you remain faithful. This ease does not cause the power within you to become visible. Your world is not in awe at your spiritual linkage with Jesus. The world around you can do as well. In the story of Job, it was not until the difficulties came that the test came. Everyone can praise when they are blessed. What happens when you are not blessed?

What an opportunity we have during persecution! This setting becomes the stage on which God reveals His power through the believer's helplessness. The world looks on and knows that self-sourcing cannot produce singing with a bleeding back in the Philippi jail. The Kingdom of God is verified, glorified, and magnified in persecution. What an opportunity we have amid persecution!

Will we influence our world? If we are Kingdom people, we will! It is a natural result of our helplessness linked with His great Person. We will be like a city set on a hill, not hidden. We are Jesus pushers!!!

I am a Jesus pusher!!! Jesus distinctly states the "Function of the Kingdom of Heaven" through the imagery of *"salt"* and *"light"* (Matthew 5:13-16). There is a distinction in the three verses focused on *"light."* OUR POSITION (Matthew 5:14) is a definite statement about our existence or essence, not an instruction of how to be light; it is a recognition of who we are! When my helplessness is filled and sourced by Jesus, the Kingdom of Heaven is formed. In this sense, I do not master the Kingdom; it masters me! Then Jesus proposes OUR PURPOSE (Matthew 5:15). The influence of *"light"* is best-described as invisibility. There are two aspects of visibility indicated in this section. The Kingdom of Heaven, my helplessness filled with His Person, is seen. It is parallel to *"A city that is set on a hill cannot be hidden."* However, this visibility produces persecution where the light exposes and pressures what is going on around it. When persecution results, it only heightens and increases the opportunity for the light! Our response is to *"Rejoice and be exceedingly glad"* (Matthew 5:12).

Step by step, Jesus brings us to a firm conclusion. If this final statement about *"light"* is ignored, all is lost. It is not just lost but becomes damaging. It is a statement about OUR PRESENTATION (Matthew 5:16). The focus of our visibility is on Him. What we are as light is to be visible *"that* (purpose) *they may see your good works and glorify your Father in heaven."* Our self-sourcing naturally demonstrates and glorifies self. We present ourselves in the best light; we promote ourselves. It is only helpless people filled with the Father whom God continuously uses to glorify the Father. Any exalting of self nullifies the glory of the Father. It is in God's call to continually recognize "our position" that "our presentation" would shine bright, fulfilling "our purpose." I am a Jesus pusher!!!

I am a Jesus pusher!!! Understanding "our purpose" becomes very important in revealing the Kingdom of God. Jesus makes it clear that visibility is essential. There is no chance that the Kingdom people can hide or be secretive. There are places in our world and times in our history when the world drove the church underground. Doesn't this contradict this reality? It does not! The church always is the strongest and expands the most during the time of great persecution. Even when driven underground, the Kingdom cannot hide in secret. The light continues to shine.

Let's look at the LOGIC OF THE STATEMENT. Jesus begins with a powerful statement of fact, ***"You are the light of the world"*** (Matthew 5:14). It is so strong it carries with it the weight of an imperative. The imperative will follow in the last verse of this section, ***"Let your light so shine before men"*** (Matthew 5:16). After this opening declaration of "our position" as ***"light,"*** Jesus injects this statement about a city, ***"A city that is set on a hill cannot be hidden"*** (Matthew 5:14). As we discovered in a previous study, this statement's strength is not illuminated or shining but is invisible. Jesus quickly reverts to the imagery of light in the next statement, ***"Nor do they light a lamp and put it under a basket, but on a lampstand, and it gives light to all who are in the house"*** (Matthew 5:15). Everything Jesus states about ***"a city"*** becomes more vital in this statement about the ***"lamp."*** He does not attempt to change the imagery from ***"light"*** to ***"a city."*** He gives additional emphasis to the issue of visibility. We must see Jesus! We are Jesus pushers!!!

I am a Jesus pusher!!! One does not set a city on a hilltop to hide it; one does not light a lamp and put it under a bushel. It is a decisive action to build a city on a hill. It expresses absolute confidence and a claim of importance. It tells us that the inhabitants desire to play a broader role in human affairs. People who want to live a quiet and secluded life build their cities out of sight, hoping no one will notice. Our statement focuses on the ridiculous image of trying to hide a city by design made for prominence. It is a statement concerning visibility.

Once this reference to a city is complete, Jesus moves immediately back to the imagery of *"light." "Nor do they light a lamp and put it under a basket, but upon a lamp stand, and it gives light to all who are in the household"* (Matthew 5:15). The Greek word "modios," translated **basket,** refers to a Roman measuring basket of various sizes to measure dry things. This basket was a common household item present in every home. The prospect of placing a lamp under this measuring basket would be ridiculous unless there were some evil intent. Some ancient writers pictured those who had malicious intent hiding a candle under a bushel. When all were asleep, they would rise with light at hand to help them carry out their evil plot. Evil is hidden and deceptive. But we are the light of the world, making Jesus visible for all to see. We are Jesus pushers!!!

I am a Jesus pusher!!! *"Nor do they light a lamp and put it under a basket, but on a lamp stand, and it gives light to all who are in the house"* (Matthew 5:15). The Greek word 'luchnos," translated *"a lamp,"* refers to a portable lamp or illuminator rather than a candle. The New Testament period's typical lamp was a small clay vessel, popularly called a Herodian lamp. It was about three inches long, two and one half inches wide, and one and one half inches deep, made to hold olive oil, which was poured into the lamp's central opening. Small flax, cotton, or hemp wick was placed in the spout. When the wick became soaked with oil, the user would light it, and the lamp produced a tiny flame. The lamps placed on lamp stands throughout the home gave sufficient light.

There is no need for argument or proof of Jesus' statement. The logic of the statement is clear. No one would purchase a lamp, fill it with oil, and maintain its light to hide it under a measuring basket. Such an action would defeat the purpose for which the lamp existed, and the owner of the lamp wasted his time in the preparation. The purpose of the lit lamp was visibility. The application to our lives is unmistakable. We are lamps, destined and designed by God to give off light, placed on lamp stands for visibility, not so people can see us, but that our visibility might extend throughout the house. We give visibility to the presence of Jesus. We are Jesus pushers!!!

I am a Jesus pusher!!! *"**Nor do they light a lamp and put it under a basket, but on a lamp stand, and it gives light to all who are in the house**"* (Matthew 5:15). This imagery indeed links with our condition of helplessness (Matthew 5:3). The oil within the lamp is not mentioned by Jesus and is not a part of the image He suggested. However, He highlighted this factor in the Parable of the Virgins (Matthew 25:1-13). The issue of this parable is not one of visibility but of readiness. Jesus ended the parable with this statement, *"**Watch therefore, for you know neither the day nor the hour in which the Son of Man is coming**"* (Matthew 25:13). In this parable, there is no possibility of being ready for His coming without the oil. The parable points to the lack of oil for the foolish virgins and the abundance of oil for the wise virgins. The only difference between the two groups was oil. This parable is a description of the *"**kingdom of heaven**"* (Matthew 25:1). The lamp needs oil, or its destiny is not fulfilled. The lamp is helpless; it is to be filled and sourced with the oil. It is in this linkage that light is produced.

In our passage, the helplessness of who we are without Him is the context. It is because of our linkage with Jesus that the Kingdom of Heaven is formed. Grasp the logic of His proposal. The need for light is present. The lamp is purchased and carefully filled with oil. The wick is trimmed and soaked with the oil. All of this is for one purpose and destiny; it is to give forth light! To hide such a lamp under the measuring basket would violate the purpose for which the lamp existed. We must see Jesus! We are Jesus pushers!!!

I am a Jesus pusher!!! ***"Nor do they light a lamp and put it under a basket, but on a lamp stand, and it gives light to all who are in the house"*** (Matthew 5:15). We can easily apply this to our lives. Congratulations! You are the Kingdom of Heaven. Your poverty-stricken life is filled with the wonder of His presence and resource. In Him, you are a new creature. Will you influence your world? How could you not? The design of who you are in Him bespeaks the purpose of making Him visible before your world. If you hide in secret, you work against the destiny of your existence. The focus of Jesus' discussion does not regard how to produce light, or even on the necessary oil. It is about visibility. We must display the Kingdom of God in our lives.

We could give a lengthy discourse on the baskets in our lives used to hide the light, going from materialism to sexual addictions, including hobbies or careers. The essence of all is self-sourcing. Only one thing stands in the way of Christ revealed to our world; it is self. But if self is present to cover the light, how will there be light? If we are not helpless, how will we embrace His presence? How will He shine through our lives? The destiny and purpose of our lives are defeated by self-sourcing. Anyone desiring fulfillment in their lives must embrace their helplessness. It is in our helplessness Jesus shines forth. Any debris of self-sourcing produces baskets to destroy visibility. We are Jesus pushers!!!

I am a Jesus pusher!!! *"Nor do they light a lamp and put it under a basket, but on a lamp stand, and it gives light to all who are in the house"* (Matthew 5:15). The entire purpose of the *"light"* imagery is visibility. The lamp is to be placed on the lamp stand to shine throughout the home. However, every heart's carnal self-sourcing readily embraces this because self wants to be visible—many of our battles with each other flow from not being adequately recognized and appreciated. We leave the church, quit our jobs, and divorce our wives because we are not elevated to our choice's proper lamp stand. It is annoying and offensive when the applause for our performance is not loud enough; indeed, we deserve better.

But the discussion of Jesus does not have the tone of self-promotion. How could it? It begins with *"poor in spirit"* (Matthew 5:3). The Greek word "ptochos," translated *"poor,"* is the most important Greek word for poverty-stricken. It comes from the idea of cringing in shame with one hand covering your face; the other hand is extended to receive. Tremendous desperation is involved. It is *"Blessed are those who mourn"* (Matthew 5:4). In this condition, one receives the fullness of Christ; in this embrace, God forms the Kingdom of Heaven. Who would want their helplessness placed on a lamp stand for all to see? It could only be the person who embraces this helplessness and becomes captured by Jesus. He recognizes the light is not a reflection of himself but of Jesus, who is within him. We desire to be visible, so we can be invisible, making Him visible. Everyone must see Jesus! We are Jesus pushers!!!

I am a Jesus pusher!!! There is an intriguing verse describing John the Baptist. Jesus uses this same imagery for John, ***"He was the burning and shining lamp, and you were willing for a time to rejoice in his light"*** (John 5:35). In the Greek language, the statement reads in order of the words, «*He* (ekeinos) *was* (en) the (ho) *lamp* (luchnos),» describing a state of being. It is not a description of what John did, but who John was. The Greek text then gives two participles: verbs acting as adjectives and modifying ***"lamp."*** They are ***"burning*** (kaiomenos) ***and*** (kai) ***shining*** (phainon).»

The root word for ***"burning"*** means "to set on fire, kindle, or consume," a natural part of the imagery of ***"light."*** We are not only to be light but also to be consumed as we burn. It is in being consumed that we radiate light to make Him visible in our world. The very idea or suggestion of being consumed is opposed to all self-centeredness. Self is about gaining, getting, and achieving. It is never about giving, sharing, and dying, the strange logic of the Kingdom of Heaven. It is in losing that I win; it is in dying that I live. It is in being consumed that others see the ***"light"*** of His presence in us. Would you be willing to give your entire life as the vessel through which He could demonstrate Himself? Would you be willing to never think about yourself and be consumed for His glory to shine? In the imagery of "life," this is called "death." In the imagery of "resurrection," this is called "crucifixion." In the imagery of "freedom," this is called "slavery." In the imagery of "forgiveness," this is called "repentance." In the imagery of "grace," this is called "sacrifice." In the imagery of "love," this is called "laying down one's life." Others must see Jesus in me! I am a Jesus pusher!

I am a Jesus pusher!!! ***"Nor do they light a lamp and put it under a basket, but on a lamp stand, and it gives light to all who are in the house"*** (Matthew 5:15). There are several dilemmas in the passage we need to address. They might be called assumptions. The verses concerning "light" leave one with great-unanswered questions, which the author assumes you can answer with an understanding of Jewish culture and tradition. The Old Testament gives a significant background for the presentation. In our verses, there is no attempt to tell us from where the light comes. What is the exact source of the light? How is the light maintained? The presentation is so focused on the physical, and yet this is not the discussion at all!

In searching the Scriptures, we can discover light's imagery from the beginning to the end, where the writers use it both literally and figuratively. The very beginning of creation in the Biblical narrative demonstrates the importance of "light." Physical light springs forth as the first created thing (Genesis 1:3-4). At the other end of the Biblical account, the light of God obliterates all traces of darkness. ***"There shall be no night there. They need no lamp nor light of the sun, for the Lord God gives them light"*** (Revelation 22:5). There are nearly two hundred references too light between these two references at the beginning and end of the Scriptures. "Light" is seen as powerful and complex imagery in the Scriptures. Jesus is the source of the light!! I am a Jesus pusher!!!

Jesus PUSHER | 248

I am a Jesus pusher!!! The first appearance of *"light"* (phos) in the Scriptures is physical. The very basis of all physical life on earth is *"light."* How important was *"light"* to the created physical world? It is the first recorded event! ***Then God said, "Let there be light"; and there was light. And God saw the light, that it was good; and God divided the light from the darkness*** (Genesis 1:3-4). This event is the power of existence springing from nonexistence! Suddenly there is a powerful illuminating, life-giving thing called *"light."*

Biblical writers are meticulous in highlighting that God makes physical light consistently. The pagan religions deify the heavenly bodies because of their light-giving properties. However, in the Scriptures, physical light is always separated from its Creator. It is an indicator, measure, or sign of the Divine Creator instead of the Creator Himself. The psalmist demanded the sun, moon, stars, and the heavens of the heavens must praise our God. The reason is quite simple: ***"For He commanded and they were created"*** (Psalms 148:5). God is the source and creator of *"light."* How can I be the *"light of the world?"* The answer is the premise of Jesus' sermon. Jesus must fill our helplessness with Himself! Others must see Jesus in us! Any attempt to be the source of the light is to destroy the light itself. We must be Jesus pushers!!!

I am a Jesus pusher!!! In the spiritual realm, God does not separate Himself from light. Spiritual light is not created but is who He is! In other words, He is the source of the light. The Old Testament boldly presents God as the source of light for daily living. David wrote, *"Thy word is a lamp to my feet and a light to my path"* (Psalms 119:105). However, He is the source of all light for our lives is the gigantic truth that He is light. Again, David wrote, *"For with You is the fountain of life; in Your light we see light"* (Psalms 36:9). The New Testament writers were distinct and transparent in their statements of this truth, *"This is the message which we have heard from Him and declare to you, that God is light and in Him is no darkness at all"* (1 John 1:5). *"God"* and *"light"* are both singular, nominative nouns. They are connected with a form of the Greek verb "eimi," translated as *"is,"* which is the Greek verb for the great "I am" statements. *«God»* and *"light"* are equal; they are words for the same thing.

"And in Him is no darkness at all" strengthens the reality of light. *"At all"* is a translation of the Greek word "oudemia." It means "not even one." John has given a double negative to convince us of the complete absence of darkness in God. Paul writes to Timothy, *"Who alone has immortality, dwelling in unapproachable light, whom no man has seen or can see, to whom be honor and everlasting power. Amen"* (1 Timothy 6:16). God's dwelling place is a state of *"unapproachable light." "Unapproachable"* is a translation of the Greek word "aprositon." It is a combination of "a" meaning "without" and "proseimi." "Proseimi" is a combination of "pros" meaning "unto" and "eimi," meaning "to be."

*"**unapproachable**"* is the inability to come into a state of being God is an *"**unapproachable light.**"* In my helplessness, He has come to me! I am His, and He is mine! I am an expression of who He is! I am a Jesus pusher!!!

I am a Jesus pusher!!! We must picture God sitting on His throne. From the very core of His inner nature and being flows light. The light is not the product of fire burning and consuming God's material because that would make fire greater than God and responsible for the production of the light. God is not a light bulb through which great electricity flows, producing light. That would mean that God is a mere instrument in the hands of something bigger than Himself. At His core is the essence of light. He is not making or producing light; He is light. His nature is shining. He is *"light."* How does one picture such brilliant light at the core of spiritual life? We can speak of truth, righteousness, or holiness in which there is no deception, darkness, or sin. But it does not give the imagery of brilliancy, as does light. The Scriptures attempted to capture this in the word "glory." It is brilliancy, light, shining, radiance, and perspective all in one word. At the core of God's essence is light, the dynamic of spiritual truth!

The Scriptures refer to the physical being like a shadow or copy of the real, which exists in the spiritual. Paul wrote, *"So let no one judge you in food or in drink, or regarding a festival or a new moon or Sabbaths, which are a shadow of things to come, but the substance is of Christ"* (Colossians 2:16-17). The author of the Book of Hebrews contrasts the priesthood of Jesus with the priesthood produced by the Law. The priests of Levi's tribe *"serve the copy and shadow of the heavenly things"* (Hebrews 8:5). The imagery of physical light offers us a profound insight into the essence of God. If the physical light is a copy or shadow of God who is light, how does that look? We are distributors of that light. We are Jesus pushers!!!

I am a Jesus pusher!!! ***"Nor do they light a lamp*** (luchnos) ***and put it under a basket, but on a lampstand*** (luchnia)***, and it gives light to all who are in the house"*** (Matthews 5:15). The Greek word "luchnos" refers to a portable lamp fed with oil, not a candle as commonly translated. Lamps were made of clay or metal, had a wick, and were fueled with oil. "Luchnos" gives content and becomes an explanation for the statement, ***"You are the light of the world."*** When analyzed, this becomes the same form used for Jesus' statement, ***"I am the light of the world"*** (John 8:12). In both cases, the statement begins with a pronoun in the nominative case. The Greek word (phos) translated ***"light"*** is also a noun in the nominative case and connected with a form of the Greek verb "eimi," translated ***"am"*** and ***"are."*** "Eimi" is the Greek verb for the great "I am" statements. In other words, ***"You / I"*** and ***"light"*** are equal; they are words for the same thing.

Jesus is God who set aside everything that made Him different from us; He became a total man. He contained the nature and person of God who is ***"Light."*** He became a lamp from which God displayed His light. ***"He is the image of the invisible God"*** (Colossians 1:15). Jesus is the light of the world because the Light of the world filled Him! Jesus is a prototype of what we are to be; He was the first member of the Kingdom of God. As He became a lamp for the display of light, we are also lamps for the same display. God is light; the nature of God comes to indwell us, causing the display of who He is, ***"Light."*** We are lamps! We are Jesus pushers!!!

Jesus PUSHER | 252

I am a Jesus pusher!!! *"Nor do they light a lamp* (luchnos) *and put it under a basket, but on a lampstand* (luchnia)"* (Matthew 5:15). The Greek word (oude) translated *"Nor"* is a combination of "ou" meaning "not" and "de," meaning "but," used in a continuative sense as in our passage. Jesus began with the remarkable statement, *"You are the light of the world."* He interjected information about a city, *"A city that is set on a hill cannot be hidden"* (Matthew 5:14). The purpose of a city placed on a hill is for visibility because the intention was not to hide. This verse is a negative statement. Now Jesus continues with the imagery of light. In the same negative sense, as a city not hidden but set on a hill, a lamp giving forth light is not intended to be under a basket but on a lampstand.

Paul captured the essence of this truth when he said, *"For it is the God who commanded light to shine out of darkness, who has shone in our hearts to give the light of the knowledge of the glory of God in the face of Jesus Christ"* (2 Corinthians 4:6). God created physical light; this is the imagery to give us the courage to believe that He took the essence of who He is (*Light*) and placed it in the face of Jesus, giving us the additional courage to believe God will shine the same light of who He is in our hearts! Take special note of the emphasis in Paul's statement on the light. He yells, *"light," "to shine," "has shone," "the light,"* and *"glory of God."* The God who created light in the physical took His being, which is light, and placed it in our hearts. In the next verse, he proclaims, *"But we have this treasure in earthen vessels, that the excellence of the power may be of God and not of us"* (2 Corinthians 4:7). The *"treasure"* is light. We are Jesus pushers!!!

Jesus PUSHER | 253

I am a Jesus pusher!!! ***"You are the light of the world"*** (Matthew 5:**14),** the destiny of a lifetime. Materialistic gain, fame, position, and all other accomplishments pale in light of this one great possibility for life. Everything feels right about this; it is like coming home. God created man for this purpose. What more tremendous privilege could we desire? Being the lamp through which others see the light of His Person is worthy of our entire focus. We must sacrifice everything else for this one pearl of great price (Matthew 13:45, 46). Jesus said, ***"Nor do they light*** (kaio) ***a lamp and put it under a basket"*** (Matthew 5:15). "Kaio" is only used once in our passage. It is used eleven times in the New Testament. The word's emphasis is not on the lighting of the candle but the "burning" of the light. It carries with it the focus of being consumed. Two men who walked with Jesus on the Emmaus road said, ***"Did not our heart burn*** (kaio) ***within us while He talked with us on the road, and while He opened the Scriptures to us?"*** (Luke 24:32).

In the lamp's use, the oil-soaked into the wick, consuming it to produce the light. The flame producing light consumed a substance (the oil) to continue giving light. We must take this imagery into the spiritual realm. This physical example is a copy or shadow of the real in the spiritual world. Are we willing to be consumed to be light for God? We must be Jesus pushers!!!

I am a Jesus pusher!!! *"You are the light of the world"* (Matthew 5:13). It is a mystery! Jesus presented this wonder to us in the Beatitudes. It is the *"poor in spirit"* that are enabled to participate in the Kingdom's forming. We have absolute poverty and are destitute. When Jesus, who is my total resource, fills my helplessness, that filling forms the Kingdom of Heaven. Because of our helplessness, we live in a state of mourning. The mourning is as severe as the helplessness. It is a constant and deep recognition of our state. Could it be this is the fuel allowing Him to consume us? The moment the slightest self-sufficiency appears in our relationship with Him, our burning ceases. It is in our consistent embracing of death that we live. In the constant recognition of our weakness, we are made strong. In our moment-by-moment embracing of dependency, we are set free!

Jesus went on to explain, *"Blessed are those who hunger and thirst for righteousness, for they shall be filled"* (Matthew 5:6). It is in our hunger that Jesus fills us, and in our thirst, He satisfies us. The amazing factor is the continuation of such! I am so hungry, yet He fills me. But the very filling gives me an increased hunger for more, yet He fills me. The satisfaction is within the hunger itself. What a mystery! Jesus consumes me, yet I live. I constantly lose myself to Him, yet I find myself. I am continually decreasing, yet He is always increasing within me. I am not disappearing but finding my fulfillment and destiny. In Him, I become the *"light of the world."* I am burned and consumed by His presence! I am a Jesus pusher!!!

I am a Jesus pusher!!! ***"Let your light so shine before men, that they may see your good works and glorify your Father in heaven"*** (Matthew 5:16). This verse stands as the climax to this section. We see the "Formation of the Kingdom" clearly stated in the Beatitudes (Matthew 5:3-12). Jesus fills our helplessness with His greatness; this intimate combination forms the Kingdom. Immediately Jesus presents the "Function of the Kingdom!" The critical emphasis seems to be "influence." We are ***"salt"*** and ***"light."*** It is a state of being through which our world is changed. One of the most striking truths of our verse is the use of the word ***"yours"*** (humon), which appears three times in the verse. Our attention is drawn to it immediately due to its repetitive appearance. The Greek word "humon" is not used primarily in the sense of "ownership." It is in the genitive case, which establishes the relationship.

However, this relationship can be in a variety of forms. It is typically used "in regard to yourself" or "concerning oneself," true in each of the three appearances of this word. ***"Let your light"*** is not a statement indicating you own the light. However, it is the light concerning your life; it is the light that you have become. ***"That they may see your good works"*** does not mean they are your works because you produced them. It is the works concerning your life coming from the Resource invading your helplessness. ***"Your Father"*** is not ownership, but the relationship. The Kingdom person is a new creature consisting of the merger of our helplessness and Divine resource. It is within this intimate, saturating relationship that we are light! We reflect Jesus! We are Jesus pushers!!!

I am a Jesus pusher!!! The Scriptures' cross-style message is continuously calling for death to self-sourcing; we must carefully give guidance to this death. "Death to self-sourcing" must never be seen as "death to self." While we might often use this phrase, we must understand it in light of the carnal context, the being of sin. "Self" is not evil within itself. God made you and me a "self." He called it "good!" Jesus did not die to eliminate "self" but to save "self!" He wants to save us from ourselves. "Self" elevated itself to the position of God. It is not "self" that is evil; it is the nature of self-promotion or self-exaltation that is destructive. We are *"poor in spirit."* The moment we discard the reality of our helplessness and promote self as adequate, destruction takes place. Our helplessness united with His sufficiency experiences the full potential of our existence. Jesus does not want to destroy "self;" He wants to save "self" from "itself."

Often we have confused self-sourcing with human nature. We see the expression of self-centeredness and say, "It is human nature." No! It is not human nature; it is carnal, sinful nature. God did not create Adam with the carnal, self-centered nature. However, he did have human nature, which God never intended to be sinful. Sin is a parasite that attaches itself to human nature. We do not need it; it is not natural to us; it is destroying us. As we investigate the use of *"your"* in our verse (Matthew 5:16), we understand Jesus did not speak concerning ownership as in what belongs to us. He said God made our person's uniqueness without self-sourcing, which is "self" embracing its state of helplessness. In constant acknowledgment of this aspect, the self responds to Jesus. *"You are the light of the world,"* a Jesus pusher!!!

I am a Jesus pusher!!! *"Let your light so shine before men"* (Matthew 5:16). Accepting our helplessness and responding to His resource allows His presence to invade our flesh. We become the Kingdom of God. Jesus describes this as *"light."* We do not produce the light or even offer a resource for the existence of the light. The light simple comes to us, and we embrace it. It is not ours in the sense of ownership or in being the creator of it. We are attached to the source of the light! Matthew's account of the Mount of Transfiguration gives us an excellent example of what Jesus is describing. Jesus is *"transfigured before them, His face shone like the sun, and His clothes became as white as the light"* (Matthew 17:2). The heart of the description is in the Greek word "metamorphoo," translated as *"transfigured."* It is two words forming one emphasis. "Meta" denotes a change of place or condition; "morphoe" relates to the form. Jesus' nature did not change; however, we can see the true nature of Jesus. Jesus is the beginning of the New Covenant.

God transfigured Jesus before the disciples. In a brief moment, God revealed the Holy Spirit's fullness as experienced in the New Covenant. Jesus said, "Here is what I want you to experience." The indwelling Holy Spirit, the "Light," begins to radiate through the life of Jesus. It is not an outside light shining upon Him but is the light of God within Him shining through Him. His clothes began to shine, like a flashlight covered with a cloth. His face shone like the sun. We must have a shining face! We are Jesus pushers!!!

Jesus PUSHER | 258

I am a Jesus pusher!!! ***"Let your light so shine before men, that they may see your good works and glorify your Father in heaven"*** (Matthew 5:16). It is ***"your light!"*** However, there is no claim of ownership; we did not create it. The light is master over us. The light captures us; He uses us for His manifestation. However, there is a sense in which we are essential to the light. Let me caution us. We must see this discussion in light of our helplessness. The light is the light! We do nothing to contribute to it. Yet, the One who is the source of light decided to shine through us but not produce pride or ownership. It only causes us to rejoice in our helplessness.

In the previous discussion of the Mount of Transfiguration, the three disciples saw the inner light through the face and clothes of Jesus. His physical being became the instrument of the radiation of the inner Light. His personality, facial features, hair, clothing, height, and entire physical being became the inner Light expression. If you experienced the Mount of Transfiguration, the Light would be the same, but the expression would be through a different instrument. Your height, hair, clothing, and personality would demonstrate the light differently. It becomes ***"your"*** light. Do you recognize the staggering opportunity of living daily in this experience? Jesus' light in you is contrasted with the strain and stress of self-sourcing, always insecure. What an opportunity we have to be Jesus pushers!!!

I am a Jesus pusher!!! *"Let your light so shine before men, that they may see your good works and glorify your Father in heaven"* (Matthew 5:16). Christianity is the only world religion that is called "a having religion!" It is most amazing! Strong indications and actual statements inform us that we have God, the Light. Listen to this verse, *"Whoever transgresses and does not abide in the doctrine of Christ does not have God. He who abides in the doctrine of Christ has both the Father and the Son"* (2 John 9). The Greek word "echo," translated as *"have"* or *"has,"* is significant. It implies continual possession. It refers to something you have in your possession over which you have charge, control, or power. John also said, *"He who has the Son has life: he who does not have the Son of God does not have life"* (1 John 5:12). We all concur that God has us, but it is excellent to think of having Him!

On the other side, the Scriptures reveal the Devil has us. However, the Scriptures never indicate that we have him. He possesses us; we never possess him. Why is it different with Jesus? It is because He gives Himself to us! We must understand the concept of having Jesus in light of our helplessness. He comes to infiltrate, merge, saturate, soak, permeate, weld, encompass, mix, and fuse Himself with us. What is the right word to use? We become one with Him. We give ourselves to Him, and He gives Himself to us! It is *"your light."* It is not yours because you produce or create it, but because Jesus saturates you. You become the shape and expression of the light! We are Jesus pushers!!!

I am a Jesus pusher!!! ***"Let your light so shine before men, that they may see your good works and glorify your Father in heaven"*** (Matthew 5:16). We must view ***"your good works"*** in light of the context of the Beatitudes. We are helpless; how could we possibly produce one single "good work?" There is no ownership of any good work. Therefore, the reference to ***"your"*** is not ownership but refers to works related to who we are. They refer to "works" demonstrated through us, although we are not the source of them. ***"Good"*** is a translation of the Greek word "kalos." This word portrays the idea of attractive or beautiful. ***"Good works"*** are constructive, not destructive; they are positive, not negative. They attract people, not repel people. The Greek word "ergon," translated as ***"works,"*** often refers to the result or object of employment. It is the performance and result of the activity. If we are helpless, there is a resource moving within us that is doing something through us that is simply beyond us.

The context of these ***"good works"*** is the Beatitudes. We demonstrate meekness within our lives. It affects the entire physical world around us (Matthew 5:5). We begin to experience fullness or completeness (Matthew 5:6). Mercy is both experienced and exchanged with others (Matthew 5:7). Holiness becomes the state of our existence, and it allows an intimacy with God (Matthew 5:8). Peace is both possession of our inner life and a by-product of our outward circumstances (Matthew 5:9). Even persecution cannot sidetrack us from what He provides in our lives (Matthew 5:10). These are the ***"good works"*** that have become ours! They are Him! We are Jesus pushers!!!

I am a Jesus pusher!!! ***"Let your light so shine before men, that they may see your good works and glorify your Father in heaven"*** (Matthew 5:16). The privilege of using such a phrase as ***"your Father"*** is overwhelming. Jesus' prayer was attractive to the disciples. They expressed a desire to learn its method and procedure. Jesus seemed to be involved in an intimate conversation with God. What was the technique? Jesus was going to introduce them to a new concept of intimacy, ***"Our Father in heaven, hallowed be Your name"*** (Matthew 6:9). Again, it is not ownership but intimacy of the relationship. It displays connection on the level of sourcing. The Spirit of the Father is producing us, fathering us! He brings about in us all that is characteristic of Him. His heart becomes ours; His mind penetrates ours. We begin to react like Him, not a technique, but a relationship. He is ***"your Father."***

He fills our helplessness with His greatness. He becomes ours, not because we own Him, but because He fills us with Himself. All of the beatitudes begin to be real in our lives because they are characteristic of Him. Will this not be seen through us? It is ***"your light"*** not because you own it, but because He fills you with it. They are ***"your good works"*** not because you own them, but because you are the vessel through which Jesus accomplished them. Indeed, He is ***"your Father"*** not because you own Him, but because you are His, and He gives Himself to you. All that Jesus displays through you glorifies Him. We become Jesus pushers!!!

Jesus PUSHER | 262

I am a Jesus pusher!!! Regularly, Jesus talks with me about my concentration. It seems to be a constant need in my walk in Him. Is it a flaw in my nature that I get distracted? However, in merging with Him, it is not as simple as focusing on Him. It appears in my relationship with Him, and I am to concentrate on what He concentrates on! His focus is to become my focus. When the major does not possess me, I will get involved in the minor. Someone said, "I simply do not have time!" It is not true. Everyone has the same amount of time. It is not a matter of the amount of time but the focus. We go where we want to go; we have time for what we want to do; we have money for what we want to buy. It is an issue of priority, concentration, or focus.

The Beatitudes present the truth. How easy it would be to concentrate on the various aspects given. ***"For they shall inherit the land"*** (Matthew 5:5). ***"For they shall be filled"*** (Matthew 5:6). ***"For they shall obtain mercy"*** (Matthew 5:7). ***"For they shall see God"*** (Matthew 5:8). ***"For they shall be called the Sons of God"*** (Matthew 5:9). Are not all of these factors great desires of our human life? However, they are not the focus of the Beatitudes, "The Formation of the Kingdom." These are mere by-products of what is present when God forms His Kingdom. They are the wrapping paper of the great gift of His presence. In my helplessness (***poor in spirit***), I experience the resource and embrace of Jesus! We become the Kingdom of Heaven together. He becomes my total focus. I am not to focus on forgiveness, gifts of the Spirit, rules, knowledge, power, etc. I allow Him to draw me into His focus. ***"You are the light of the world"*** (Matthew 5;13). We are Jesus pushers!!!

I am a Jesus pusher!!! The Sermon on the Mount moves from the "Formation of the Kingdom (Matthew 5:3-12)," a total concentration on Jesus," to the "Function of the Kingdom" (Matthew 5:13-16). We do not contain our relationship with Jesus in a vacuum of its own existence. Jesus does not isolate us from the rest of our world to use us for His benefit. In this section of *"Salt"* and *"Light,"* Jesus highlights this truth. It seems to be the passionate desire of His heart! *"Let your light so shine before men, that they may see your good works and glorify your Father in heaven"* (Matthew 5:16).

There is a clear-cut directive given in the statement, *"that they may see!"* The Greek word "eido," translated as *"they may see,"* is one of the several words for "know." It derives its meaning from two word groups. One group has the exclusive focus of "to see." There is a physical involvement of actually seeing something. The other focus is on "to know." It emphasizes "perceiving, grasping, or understanding." The Greek word "hopos" precedes the word "eido," translated as *"that."* It means "in such a manner, that, so that, to this end." When combined with a subjunctive verb (as in this case), it has to do with the final purpose. There is a distinct purpose; it is the act of *"shine."* It shouts of "motivation." The purpose of our light shining is that something might take place in others' lives, an awareness of the glory of the Father! We are Jesus pushers!!!

Jesus PUSHER | 264

I am a Jesus pusher!!! I have sat in judgment on the disciples only to discover I am as guilty. They consistently focused on the Kingdom for personal benefit. It was not a lack of belief in Jesus. They left all to follow Him. Their involvement in ministry activity was full-time. Jesus sent them out after giving *"them power over unclean spirits, to cast them out, and to heal all kinds of sickness and all kinds of disease"* (Matthew 10:1). On the surface, we could all applaud the ministry. However, there seemed to be a major flaw! Even while ministering to others, they continually focused on themselves. When Jesus suggested a ministry of "bleed, suffer and die," they were not receptive. The moment He injected the cross into the equation, *"Peter took Him aside and began to rebuke Him"* (Matthew 16:22). The whole concept of pouring your life out for others, never thinking about yourself, and embracing your world did not fit the focus for their lives.

E. Stanley Jones told of holding a chapel service in a mental institution for women. Upon viewing the facility, he noticed room after room well equipped with sewing machines. The ladies were making beautiful items for their personal use. Dr. Jones excitedly expressed the possibility of involving the ladies in repairing garments to give to homeless families. The director of the institution exclaimed, "Oh no! That is not possible. The ladies would not be interested in sewing for others." Dr. Jones inquired, "Why? They have the time, skill, and sewing equipment." The director replied, "You do not understand why they are here. If they could do something for someone else, they would not be in this place!" To the degree we are self-focused, to that degree we are insane! We must merge with Jesus and have His focus! I am a Jesus pusher!!!

I am a Jesus pusher!!! ***"Let your light so shine before men, that they may see your good works and glorify your Father in heaven"*** (Matthew 5:16). The total focus of shining the light is that others might come to understand the content of the Father's heart. The focus is not on accomplishing ***"good works,"*** a mere adjustment and form of self-centeredness. How easy it is to become "program centered." The focus of a church program becomes the production. The measure of its success is how many, how much, or how great! People are applauding. We find our value in how we are viewed instead of knowing the Father's heart. We must continually come back to revealing the Father's heart.

Let us put this in the perspective of the Beatitudes, "The Formation of the Kingdom." Jesus congratulates me on my condition of total helplessness. It is in the state of recognition and mourning that I am open to His infilling. In the embrace of my helplessness and the resource of His person, He forms the Kingdom of Heaven. In this relationship, we experience meekness, fullness, mercy, purity of heart, peace, and victory in persecution. But the focus is not that I would experience all of these benefits for myself. These are all aspects of the Father's heart now in me. I am to shine these aspects into the core of all my activities, attitudes, and mannerisms until it becomes apparent they are a product of His sourcing, a demonstration of the heart of Jesus. I am a Jesus pusher!!!

I am a Jesus pusher!!! *"Let your light so shine before men, that they may see your good works and glorify your Father in heaven"* (Matthew 5:16). In all of these studies, we highlight the helplessness of each of us. The Kingdom of Heaven is not something we achieve, manage, or accomplish. It is a result of recognizing our absolute need and the surrender to the resource of Jesus. The Kingdom is not what Jesus is or what I am. It is about "us!" "We" are the Kingdom in the intimacy of the relationship, Jesus and me. It is an unbelievable reality! We do not produce the light; we become an avenue for the shining of the light. We are not in control of the light.

Shining the light demands a consistency beyond what self-sourcing can produce. Self can be meek before certain people and at certain times. Self can experience a fullness of life for some moments in some circumstances. Self can extend mercy to certain people to some degree. Purity of the heart may be exhibited in some areas by self-control only to find the cancer of sin decaying the foundation of life. Peace may be a result of a controlling person filled with self. Many people have suffered at the hands of others with great endurance. But who can consistently flow with the heart of the Father? Who can day after day in all circumstances, in every attitude, and all moments spring forth with the loving heart of Christ? It could only be the helpless one filled with Jesus. Here is where the heart of the Father is clarified and becomes known. We must shine the heart of the Father and be a Jesus pusher!!!

I am a Jesus pusher!!! *"**Let your light so shine before men, that they may see your good works and glorify your Father in heaven**"* (Matthew 5:16). What is our role? Jesus gives us an imperative, a command, to *"**shine.**"* He indicates we affect the light and its manifestation through our lives, found in this section's imagery. Jesus speaks about "a lamp placed upon a lampstand." The size and shape of the lamp affect its ability to shine. It is challenging to talk about this area. The reason is that this discussion produces separatist language. We begin to separate Him for ourselves as we describe His part in the shining and my part in the shining. We cannot let that happen! There can be no separation or division between us. It is never what I do and what He does, His part and my part. It is our part. We must be woven together in the formation of the Kingdom through which the light is now shining.

Our minds become one. I am to have the mind of Christ! I must not have my ideas, and He has His ideas; they must be our ideas. It must not be that I love as best I can. Then He goes beyond my love to express His. I do not do all I can; then He takes over to carry me beyond what I can accomplish. I am helpless to the most extreme degree. I have no legitimate love. He so infiltrates my love that the nature of love in me becomes His. It is now my love because He gives it to me, yet it is never mine because I can never produce it. Yet Jesus is expressing it through me as if it is mine. We become one in the expression! Jesus expressing through me is the purpose of my person. I am destined to be His; He is destined to be mine, the intimacy of the Kingdom of Heaven. *"**You are the light of the world**"* *"**so shine.**"* We are Jesus pushers!!!

I am a Jesus pusher!!! *"**Let your light so shine before men, that they may see your good works and glorify your Father in heaven"*** (Matthew 5:16). This verse is Jesus' last statement in this section on the "Function of the Kingdom," making it the final word on the matter. One must view all of these according to the flow of the previous three verses. The key word in the ***salt*** and ***light*** imagery is "influence." The nature of these elements will make a difference wherever they appear. The Kingdom people are no different. It is not talent, education, nor connections of the individual that determines the influence. It is the nature of the Kingdom person, the nature of the Spirit of Jesus! The Kingdom person cannot keep from changing his world. One of the vital aspects of the imagery Jesus emphasizes is "visibility." He adds to the imagery of ***salt*** and ***light*** the picture of a city on a hill. People must see it; they cannot ignore it. The Kingdom person is confrontational and demands a decision.

There are several ideas contained in our verse; they appear for the first time. There is a strong ATTACHMENT of the Kingdom individual with the visibility. He does not own the ***light***. However, he is so intimately involved in its display He refers to it as ***"your light," "your good works,"*** and ***"your Father."*** This intimate linkage expresses itself in a deep concern for others. It is an expression of the Father's heart. The connection is not for personal gain or enjoyment but must create AWARENESS; it is for the purpose ***"that they may see."*** In our verse, the demonstration comes through the ATTRACTIVENESS of ***"your good works."*** This individual is a Jesus pusher!!!

I am a Jesus pusher!!! ***"Let your light so shine before men, that they may see your good works and glorify your Father in heaven"*** (Matthew 5:16). The message of the cross (cross style) is one of death. The death of Jesus becomes our death that His life might become our life. We do not live our lives for Him; He lives His life through us. Jesus living through us removes us from a religion of "doing" or "works" and plants us into a "state of being." However, the Bible never advocates a state of inactivity. The nature of Christ within the believer is always producing activity. In the imagery of Jesus, it is the influence of ***salt*** and ***light.*** There is a tension between being and doing or nature and works. It seems to confuse people, yet it is very simplistic. Anyone who advocates we did not believe in "works" proves he does not understand the cross style message. If you are living, you are breathing; if you are Kingdom people, you are acting. Faith never sits in the corner, hiding in inactivity. That is a lack of faith. When one lives in faith, he attacks the giant in the name of Jehovah, the message of Jesus. ***Light*** cannot abide under a basket; it demands a lampstand.

The "Formation of the Kingdom" presented in the Beatitudes is vital. Our helplessness is intimately linked to the person of Jesus. He becomes our total resource, and we depend on Him alone! That is a state of being. The phrase ***"your good works"*** does not have to be adjusted or explained away to maintain this state of being. Your life will be full of ***"your good works."*** Jesus demonstrates through the Kingdom Person, and the Kingdom Person is a Jesus pusher!!!

I am a Jesus pusher!!! ***"Let your light so shine before men, that they may see your good works and glorify your Father in heaven"*** (Matthew 5:16). ***"Your"*** is the Greek word "humon." In the Greek language, it does not necessarily mean ownership. It expresses the idea of "concerning." ***"Your"*** appears three times in our verse. ***"Let your light"*** is not a statement indicating you own the light. However, it is the light concerning your life or what you have become. ***"Your good works"*** does not mean you produce them. They are the works relating to your life coming from the Resource invading your helplessness. "***Your Father"*** is not ownership, but the relationship.

Jesus explained this in discourse to His disciples. He said, ***"He who has seen Me has seen the Father"*** (John 14:9). The reason this is true is simple. ***"The words that I speak to you I do not speak on My own authority; but the Father who dwells in Me does the works"*** (John 14:10). If the Father does the works through Jesus, then they are the Father's works! Jesus continued, ***"Believe Me that I am in the Father and the Father in Me, or else believe Me for the sake of the works themselves"*** (John 14:11). There are two strong bases for our belief in Jesus being a demonstration of the Father. One is that He is in the Father, and the Father is in Him. The second is that the Father demonstrates Himself through Jesus with the "works." Jesus gives a picture of the believer. The relationship Jesus has with the Father we now have! The expression of this relationship through Jesus is now ours! Jesus fills us with Himself as the Father filled Him. We are Jesus pushers!!!

I am a Jesus pusher!!! *"Let your light so shine before men, that they may see your good works and glorify your Father in heaven"* (Matthew 5:16). Jesus said to His disciples, *"Most assuredly, I say to you, he who believes in Me, the works that I do, he will do also; and greater works than these he will do, because I go to My Father"* (John 14:12). Jesus links the "works" with Himself and promises they will be ours also. The Greek word translated *"do"* is "poieo." It highlights the flow of the Father's nature within the individual. Jesus said that the "works" are His; at the same time, they are the Father's "works." Jesus is the avenue through which the Father demonstrates Himself! It will be true for us in the New Covenant.

Do you recognize the link between Jesus and the Father? They are so connected that the actions of One are the actions of the Other! We cannot consider them two, and yet they are! Jesus brings us into this relationship. In speaking about Pentecost, the New Covenant, He said, *"At that time you will know that I am in My Father, and you in Me, and I in you"* (John 14:20). It is an intimacy beyond knowing about or even knowing personally. It is a meshing of our being with His! It is welding as two pieces of metal mix their molecules. The Trinity has opened itself to draw us into their hearts. We become one with God. We are not God; we are weak (*poor in spirit*). Yet, Jesus comes in the intermixing of our being with His; we become a new creature together; it is the Kingdom! We *are the light of the world*. All we knew was darkness; now, we sit on a lampstand, giving light and visibility to our world. We participate in the "works" of God. We are Jesus pushers!!!

I am a Jesus pusher!!! ***"Let your light so shine before men, that they may see your good works and glorify your Father in heaven"*** (Matthew 5:16). ***"Good"*** is a translation of the Greek word "kalos." Since God is the source of the "works," they must be "kalos." This word does not so much emphasize quality, as it does attractiveness, beautiful appearance. There is only one other place in Matthew where he uses ***"good works."*** Jesus was in Bethany at the home of Simon, the leper. A woman with an alabaster flask of costly fragrant oil, valued as a year's wages, poured it on Jesus' head as He sat at the table. The disciples were indignant, considering it a waste. Jesus rebuked them, ***"Why do you trouble the woman? For she has done a good work for Me"*** (Matthew 26:10). The New International Version translates this verse: ***Aware of this, Jesus said to them, "Why are you bothering this woman? She has done a beautiful thing to Me."*** Jesus used the Greek word "ergon" twice, translated "work," used in the verb form, which says, ***"she has done,"*** meaning "she worked."

Also, Jesus used "ergon" as a noun describing the object of the action, a direct object, as a ***"work." "Good"*** (kalos) is an adjective describing the direct object, ***"work."*** Jesus was not expressing her generosity in terms of money. It was not the gracefulness seen in this physical activity. It had to do with the attractiveness, the beauty, of her intent and love. He went on to explain, ***"For in pouring this fragrant oil on My body, she did it for My burial"*** (Matthew 26:12). Jesus saw this fragrant oil as the burial preparation for His coming death! It was a beautiful act of a loving heart expressed in sacrificial giving. Our ***"good works"*** are an expression of the attractive, loving Jesus. We are Jesus pushers!!!

I am a Jesus pusher!!! ***"Let your light so shine before men, that they may see your good works and glorify your Father in heaven"*** (Matthew 5:16). Jesus' reference to ***"your good works"*** as expressions of the heart. He does not give a list of activities contained in this category. It is a description of the nature of the Kingdom of God expressed in every action. Luke highlights in the early church as they were ***"praising God and having favor with all the people"*** (Acts 2:47). Their activities had the sacrificial tone of the cross. God permeated their activities with the beauty of Christ's nature, not any specific activity but all the individual's actions, saturating the tone of their life with this element of Christ's beauty. Paul referred to this as ***"the fragrance of Christ among those who are being saved and among those who are perishing"*** (2 Corinthians 2:15).

The desired result of these beautiful displays of Jesus' nature is that everyone might ***"glorify your Father in heaven."*** We focus everything on the One who resources the goodness of our works. The Kingdom of God influences all the activities of the individual with attractiveness. It is because Jesus, the Source, is attractive. We become an expression of His person. Is there anything more significant than being in oneness with Jesus and allowing the beauty of His heart to be lived through us? We are Jesus pushers!!!

Jesus PUSHER | 274

I am a Jesus pusher!!! *"Let your light so shine before men, that they may see your good works and glorify your Father in heaven"* (Matthew 5:16). We must return to the Beatitudes, the context of our passage (Matthew 5:3-13). We begin with the most disgusting quality, weakness. Only Christianity proposes that that weakness is a virtue. Can you imagine the shock when Jesus congratulated those who are *"poor in spirit?"* When we embrace our helplessness and consistently respond in that state, something (Someone) transforming happens in our lives. Jesus embraces our helplessness and forms the Kingdom of God. We are new creatures created out of weakness in the embrace of great resource and strength.

This new creature is where you find the attractive, beautiful, and *good works*. "Meekness" begins to flow in all of the physical activities of our lives. We *"inherit the earth."* Instead of emanating death and destruction, meekness allows us to work with our physical world flow. Meekness is not a single activity but a flow of attitude from the mind of Christ united with the believer. There is a *"hunger and thirst for righteousness"* characterizing the entire life of the Kingdom person. It is an openness to growth, change, and correction. Instead of stubborn, narrow, and hardheaded, we are open, seeking, and responding. It is a beautiful and attractive attribute of our lives. It is not one activity we do, but a chief characteristic of all activities. *"Mercy"* flows from our lives. We obtain mercy from the Resource, indwelling our weakness, and purity comes from the heart. It is a flow of seeing God and expressing Him in every movement of our being. We demonstrate the beauty of holiness. Who wouldn't want that? It is a Jesus pusher!!!

I am a Jesus pusher!!! ***Let your light so shine before men, that they may see your good works and glorify your Father in heaven"*** (Matthew 5:16). The complete visibility of the light is to ***"glorify your Father in heaven."*** The Greek word "doxaz," translated as ***"glorify,"*** comes from the root word "doxa," meaning "to influence one's opinion about another, to enhance the latter's reputation," focusing on praise, honor, or extolling. We do not do ***"good works"*** to help those in need; we do them to manifest the love of the Father. The driving force behind every "good work" must be to make the Father visible.

Attitude saturates the activities flowing from the Kingdom person. An attitude is "a settled way of thinking or feeling about someone or something, reflected in a person's behavior." The way you feel or think about Jesus demonstrates itself in every activity of your life. For instance, I do not curse the name of Jesus; this is determined by how I feel about Jesus. There are places I do not go and activities in which I do not participate, choices determined by my relationship with Jesus. The satisfaction of my physical drives and appetites decides by my attitude about Jesus. My behavior reflects how I think and feel about Him. The determining fact is not about rules with the threat of punishment; it is a relationship! Due to my intimate relationship with Jesus, I want my entire life with all of its involvements and activities to ***"glorify"*** Him. That sounds like a Jesus pusher!!!

Jesus PUSHER | 276

I am a Jesus pusher!!! ***Let your light so shine before men, that they may see your good works and glorify your Father in heaven"*** (Matthew 5:16). The desire to ***"glorify"*** Jesus is not an obligation, although I do have a deep sense of indebtedness. Although I am entirely aware of the responsibility of being a Kingdom person, there is no duty involved. There is no fear of threat or doom pending if I do not glorify Him, although hell is real and eternity is long. There is a passion for glorifying His name burning within my bones. This passion captures me until it is the single driving motivation of my life. Every other drive and calling in my life are secondary. This passion rises to the top position in my life and brings every aspect of living into servanthood.

I do not have this passion because it is my career as a minister. However, realistically the call for ministry is partly formed by the passion, not financially driven. While materialism is a factor in everyone's life, materialism does not dominate nor control the passion. This passion for glorifying Jesus determines how I spend my money and invest my time and energy. Glorifying Jesus is not a con with hidden agendas seeking to glorify self. Far too often, we use His name for self-edification and self-glorification. Let Him be seen; let Him be glorified. I am ***"poor in spirit,"*** not just lacking in certain areas (Matthew 5:3). I am absolutely weak, destitute of all resources. The only answer is Jesus. He comes in His fullness to embrace me. He has destined me to be dependent on Him. He is not the Kingdom without me; I am not the Kingdom without Him. When He fills my weakness with His resourceful Person, WE are the Kingdom. He has included me! I glorify Him! I am a Jesus pusher!!!

Jesus PUSHER | 277

I am a Jesus pusher!!! ***Let your light so shine before men, that they may see your good works and glorify your Father in heaven***" (Matthew 5:16). Paul describes a great treasure planted within the life of an individual. It is ***"the light of the knowledge of the glory of God in the face of Jesus Christ"*** (2 Corinthians 4:6). He refers to all the wonder of the Father's presence indwelling the man called Jesus. It is this resource that caused the image of God to be seen through Jesus. He was the first man in the New Covenant to experience the sourcing of the Spirit. Paul continues, ***"But we have this treasure in earthen vessels, that the excellence of the power may be of God and not of us"*** (2 Corinthians 4:7). Paul describes the Kingdom person as an ***"earthen vessel."*** The Greek word "ostrakinos," translated as ***"earthen,"*** is an adjective modifying ***"vessel."*** It is an attempt to describe frailty.

The ***"earthen vessel"*** is a restatement of Jesus' definition of the Kingdom of God. God fills those ***"poor in spirit"*** with the Spirit of Jesus and creates a new creature, the Kingdom of God. Paul describes the purpose behind this combination, ***"that the power may be of God and not of us."*** He is my resource. Would you not be shocked if I did not burn with passion for glorifying Him? All that I am experiencing in and through Him compels me to worship Him. I want to spend all of my time glorifying and praising Him. He is my total focus, the center point of life, and the influential factor for life. I am a bride who is in love with the bridegroom. I am a Jesus pusher!

I am a Jesus pusher!!! *"Let your light so shine before men, that they may see your good works and glorify your Father in heaven"* (Matthew 5:16). Jesus captures me! There is a passion burning in the heart of my being to glorify Him. Anything and everything reflecting negative towards Him, I eliminate from my life. Any language I might speak that treats Him lightly must go. My only desire is to please Him! However, as I get into the heart of Jesus, I experience His focus, which is others. It soon becomes apparent that His passion is to redeem others. If I have a passion for Him, I will align with His passion. What drives Him drives me because a passion for Him drives me.

I find a deep desire to change your perspective concerning Jesus, a reality ingrained in the imagery of *"light."* Visibility is the focus of the light imagery. Jesus states it clearly by describing a city sitting upon a hill for visibility. Then Jesus returns to the imagery of light, *"Nor do they light a lamp and put it under a basket"* (Matthew 5:15). He establishes two parallel impossibilities. A city on a hill is placed there by design to be seen and cannot be hidden; in like manner, one lights a lamp for visibility and does not put it under a basket. If you put a lamp on a lampstand, *"it gives light to all who are in the house"* (Matthew 5:15). The purpose of the lamp placed on the lampstand is to influence and affect those in the household. What does it mean for them to see the light? *"Let your light so shine before men, that they may see your good works"* (Matthew 5:16). Its purpose is for "glorifying" (to influence one's opinion about another, to enhance the latter's reputation) *"your Father in heaven."* I am a Jesus pusher!!!

I am a Jesus pusher!!! *"Let your light so shine before men, that they may see your good works and glorify your Father in heaven"* (Matthew 5:16). I want you to see Him as He is. I want to convince you of how great, loving, and essential He is for your life. You must see Him without prejudice and in the *light.* The Apostle Paul describes the dilemma. *"But even if our gospel is veiled, it is veiled to those who are perishing, whose minds the god of this age has blinded, who do not believe, lest the light of the gospel of the glory of Christ, who is the image of God, should shine on them"* (2 Corinthians 4:3, 4). Paul boldly proclaims that the content of preaching is Jesus the Lord! If this is true, how is ministry ever going to exist? God caused *"light"* to shine in the person of Jesus; the glory of God was seen in His face. This same treasure is placed in us to shine the same light! *"The excellence of the power may be of God and not of us"* is the purpose of this shining light!

This motivation controls all of our activities. We are not attempting to improve society; we want everyone to see Jesus. Our passion is not to stop abortion; we want Jesus to be known, eliminating abortion. We do not provide programs to keep teenagers out of trouble; we want them to engage Jesus. We do not entertain great crowds; they must embrace Jesus. Our goal is not to educate children; Jesus must capture them. Everything we do, all of our energy expended, and the one passion that drives us is changing our perspective about Jesus. I am a Jesus pusher!!!

I am a Jesus pusher!!! *"Let your light so shine before men, that they may see your good works and glorify your Father in heaven"* (Matthew 5:16). If the light of Jesus shines in your life, you will want Him. If you see Him as He is, you will embrace Him. Love will grip your life, and you will not be able to resist Him. Jesus calls us to be a part of this process in your life. We participate in the prevenient grace of God, bringing revelation (shining) to your life. What a privilege! Revealing Jesus becomes the passion for our lives because it is the passion of God's heart! The above statements sound beautiful and spiritual. I feel much better after hearing them and thinking about them. But the reality is that I cannot conform to that kind of living all the time. I get distracted! Pressures come to my life that are beyond my control. I spend my energy on simple survival. I am exhausted at the close of my day. I spend my day fighting off the destruction of my life. Jesus and loving Him is a nice thing for those who have nothing to do but play shuffleboard in retirement.

Speak to your neighbor about the Christian faith. But when you invite them to come to church, they respond, "It is my only time to sleep in, and I am exhausted from working extra hours at my job." Invite them to donate to the work of the church; they respond, "I am scrapping to pay my bill and simply do not have anything left over." They view Christianity as an addition to an already busy life. Jesus is not an addition to my life's many activities; He is the source for those activities. He enhances my life! I am a Jesus pusher!!!

I am a Jesus pusher!!! *"Let your light so shine before men, that they may see your good works and glorify your Father in heaven"* (Matthew 5:16). Jesus began with the "Formation of the Kingdom" (Matthew 5:3-12). It started with the declaration of your poverty (Matthew 5:3). You are *"poor in spirit."* You are helpless, destitute, and without any resource. If you embrace your helplessness, He will embrace you. This unity forms the Kingdom of Heaven. His resource begins to source your life. You cease to live out of self; you live out of Him. That means all He is begins to shape who you are. You become like Him!

Jesus said that He was the light of the world; now He says that you and I are the light of the world. How can this be? What was in Him is now in us. He flows in and through my life, determining factor of all my living. He is the single controller of my attitudes and actions. He determines me. That is why I have His attitude and thought process. That is why I glorify Him! Let me define again for you the definition for the Greek word "doxazo," translated as *"glorify."* It means "to influence one's opinion about another to enhance the latter's reputation." I want to *"glorify"* Him in your sight. I want to be *"light."* The only possibility to influence your opinion about Jesus is for you to see Him. The only way you will see Him is through me. He must shape me; he must control me; He must express Himself through me! I must be filled with Him in every area of my life until He is evident through those areas to you. That is the Kingdom of Heaven. It is not "I" and "he." It is "we!" We become one! I am a Jesus pusher!!!

I am a Jesus pusher! The Greek word "pater," translated as *"Father"* in our passage (Matthew 5:16), is used four hundred and fourteen times in the New Testament. Two hundred and fifty times, it addresses God. We could fill pages discussing the various aspects of "God as our Father." There is the genealogical aspect; He is the source of our existence. Paul quoted from the Old Testament, *"I will be a Father to you, and you shall be My sons and daughters, says the Lord Almighty"* (2 Corinthians 6:18). However, with the proposal of this idea, we must recognize the protector, nourisher, and helper content. The content of *"Father"* carries us into the attitude and action of God towards us.

There is a distinction between God being the Father of Jesus and God as our Father. Jesus is the Eternal Son; He is the only begotten of the Father. John writes, *"And the Word became flesh and dwelt among us, and we beheld His glory, the glory as of the only begotten of the Father, full of grace and truth"* (John 1:14). We find the content of the perfect and infinite expression of the Father's love in Jesus. Peter said, *"Blessed be the God and Father of our Lord Jesus Christ, who according to His abundant mercy has begotten us again to a living hope through the resurrection of Jesus Christ from the dead"* (1 Peter 1:3). Everything existing between Jesus and the Father is now present in our relationship with Him! Live in the confidence of the love of the Father! I am a Jesus pusher!

I am a Jesus pusher! The author of the Book of Hebrews connects Jesus and the believer in the Fatherhood of God. He uses the phrase, *"all of one"* (Hebrews 2:11). They are three powerful words in their application to our lives. *"All"* (pas) refers to Jesus and the believer! *"Of"* (ek) denotes origin or source. *"One"* (heis) is the number pointing to the unity of Jesus and the believer. In other words, they are the same in life source. The origin of the believer (*"born from above,"* John 3:3) and the Man Jesus is God, the Father. The writer of the Book of Hebrews continues to state this, *"for which reason He is not ashamed to call them brethren"* (Hebrews 2:11). We are the brothers of Christ; we come from the same life source! God is our Father!

Jesus proposes this same reality in our passage (Matthew 5:16), which is the first time Matthew presents God as Father. Since we *"are the light of the world,"* it must be connected to *"your Father in heaven."* He is the source of the light, which is who we are! The expression of our beings displays *light* into the world. It glorifies, gives a perspective of honor to our Father. "The Father imagery" receives its content from the Beatitudes. We are helpless, *"poor in spirit."* His Divine Nature fills us; we become the Kingdom of Heaven. It is a picture of father and son. Allow this imagery to expand in your heart and mind! I am a four-year-old who is dependent upon my father. I know nothing about electric bills, food on the table, or transportation. He provides for me in ways I do not understand or know! I am helpless and loved by my Father! I am a Jesus pusher!

Jesus PUSHER | 284

I am a Jesus pusher! Don't forget the reaction of the crowds to the message of Jesus. They were "knocked out of their senses, "explesso" (Matthew 7:28). Everything the Old Covenant law proposed, Jesus fulfilled. The world's moral systems offered the goal of life to be gained by struggle, discipline, and merit. Jesus simply congratulated us on our arrival. Jesus gives us what other systems require us to earn. The Jews believed they could only achieve a relationship with God by strict adherence to the Old Testament law. Jesus changed the imagery of the relationship. We are not subjects desperately trying to appease a far-removed power to survive. He is our *"Father."* He embraces us in our helplessness; He created us this way. It was His design to cradle us moment by moment in His person, as a father cares for his newborn son.

In Jesus, He carries us into a whole new content for the word "father." The most exciting and vital term in the Gospels reflecting how Jesus thought about God is the simple word "Father." "Father" speaks of God's relationship to Israel as a people, not of His relationship to the individual. God is the Creator and Lord of His people; He can be called their Father. However, there are hints of God as the Father of the nation and individual believers. *"A father of the fatherless, a defender of widows is God in His holy habitation"* (Psalms 68:5). *"When my father and mother forsake me, then the Lord will take care of me"* (Psalms 27:10). But Jesus brings us into the New Covenant, a new relationship with the Trinity God as our Father! The wonder of security and confidence in the Old Testament as suddenly magnified beyond compare. Live in His love! I am a Jesus pusher!

I am a Jesus pusher! Whatever the level of God's fatherhood in the Old Testament, the New Covenant in Jesus far exceeds. It is not merely an expansion of the concept of God's fatherhood; it is the establishment of a relationship between God and man not known. The very expression of this in Jesus' preaching disturbed the leaders of Israel to the extent of plotting murder. Jesus said to them, *"My Father has been working until now, and I have been working"* (John 5:17). The reaction of the Jews demonstrates their understanding of the content of the Fatherhood of God. *"Therefore the Jews sought all the more to kill Him, because He not only broke the Sabbath, but also said that God was His Father, making Himself equal with God"* (John 5:18). Jesus used expressions relating to father and son that were offensive and foreign to the Jews. The name of God was so sacred it could not be pronounced even in reading the Old Testament Scriptures. The Holy of Holies contained God; He was behind a thick veil. Jesus used the language of familiarity. *"Most assuredly, I say to you, the Son can do nothing of Himself, but what He sees the Father do; for whatever He does the Son also does in like manner. For the Father loves the Son, and shows Him all things that He Himself does,* (John 5:19-20). The greatness of the Father fills the helpless man, supplying the resource needed for the life of the son! The change is unbelievable! I am a Jesus pusher!

I am a Jesus pusher! *"Your Father"* is a statement beyond imagination (Matthew 5:16).

This dynamic reality naturally flows into a life pattern. We often speak of it; it never grows old. It is so huge in its impact that it startles us each time we see it highlighted. In our everyday living, it is the most remarkable alteration. It is such intimacy with God that we cease to serve Him; He serves through us. We no longer live for Him; He lives through us. We do not act on His behalf; He demonstrates Himself through us. We do not shine for Him; He shines through us. The source of our lives moves from "us" to "Him," the impact of the Kingdom of Heaven found in the Beatitudes.

Jesus distinctly says, *"Your Father in heaven"* (Matthew 5:16). The actual Greek statement is revealing and instructive. Jesus said, *"The* (ton) *Father* (patera) *your* (humon) *the* (ton) *in* (en) *the* (tois) *heaven* (ouranois).*"* The article *"the"* stresses the definite fact of the case. It is *"the Father."* It is *"the in."* It is *"the heaven."* It is also essential to notice that *"heaven"* (ouranois) is plural in the Greek text. *"Heaven"* does not suggest a location where the throne of God dwells but indicates the spiritual world beyond our physical existence. He is transcendent! We are four-year-old children; our Father provides for us in ways beyond what we know. I am a Jesus pusher!

Jesus
PUSHER | **287**

I am a Jesus pusher! The remarkable reality of the sovereignty and existence of God in space is true. Our time zone or activities do not confine God. In understanding His dwelling place, we have a deeper appreciation for His embrace of our helplessness. The wonder of an infinite God indwelling a finite person is beyond comprehension. Even suggesting the possibility of this sovereign God embracing us, as a Father, is enough to "knock us out of our senses" (Matthew 7:28). The great expanse of the dwelling place of God becomes the context in which we discover the intimacy and fatherhood of God in our lives.

You will note in the Beatitudes, and throughout the rest of the sermon, Matthew records Jesus as using the phrase, ***"Kingdom of heaven"*** (5:3, 10, 19; 7:21; note also 3:2; 11:25; 13:1+; 18:1+). In Matthew, "heaven" is a substitute word designated for "God." Matthew follows the tradition of the Jews who considered God's name too sacred to pronounce. Therefore, we attribute all the qualities of God to "heaven." This statement of Jesus (in heaven) does not stress the remoteness of God's presence but establishes the wonder of His intimacy with us as our Father (Matthew 5;16)! "The Kingdom of heaven" is the intimate relationship of Father and son!

Congratulations, go to the ***"poor in spirit."*** We are the helpless ones. Our lives are destitute of all resources; it is the design of our creation. We can only exist in a relationship with the Father. The Sourcing One is not only the sovereign God of the heavens, and He is the sovereign Father of our individual lives. He is not just the sovereign God who controls universes and manages lightning bolts; He is the sovereign God who cares, loves, and tenderly embraces. He flows through our very being; produces all He is in and through us! He is the light shining through us! I am a Jesus pusher!

I am a Jesus pusher! ***"Let your light so shine before men, that they may see your good works and glorify your Father in heaven"*** (Matthew 5:16). Shining your light includes behavior, attitudes, thought processes, responses, and actions. The entire shape of one's life will be "fathered" by Jesus! The ***"light"*** that must ***"shine before men"*** is not contained in a deed but the tone, attitude, and shape of those deeds. We do not define sin in terms of a deed; we do not define ***"light"*** in terms of a deed. The act of giving a cup of cold water does not in itself shine the light of the Father, but giving it in the name and embrace of Jesus does (Matthew 10:42). It is not the activity of such a deed, but the flow of God's Spirit through the believer demonstrates the ***"light"*** to the little one.

The life of Jesus convinces us of this truth. While the Jews considered God their Father, Jesus put new content to it. He even used the word "Abba." In the Garden of Gethsemane, Jesus faced the greatest trial of His life. Facing His agony of suffering and death, He prayed, ***"Abba, Father, all things are possible for You. Take this cup away from Me; nevertheless, not what I will, but what You will"*** (Mark 14:36). The Greek word "Abba" is transliterated from the Aramaic language. In the New Testament, "Abba" addresses only God. It is always followed immediately by the translation, "Father" (Mark 14:36; Romans 8:15; Galatians 4:6). This double expression was common in the early church. Here is the tone of the ***"light"*** shining through the Kingdom child! I am a Jesus pusher!

I am a Jesus pusher! *"Abba"* is an intimate word used by children when addressing their father in the Aramaic language. Adults also use it in the intimacy of the family relationship. Jews avoided applying this word to God outside of prayer. There is no single example of God being addressed as *"Abba"* in Judaism except for Jesus in His prayers. Jesus taught His disciples to call God *"Abba, Father,"* a radical departure from Jewish traditions. Paul reflects the early Christian practice of prayer by using *"Abba, Father."* He wrote, *"For you did not receive the spirit of bondage again to fear, but you received the Spirit of adoption by whom we cry out, 'Abba, Father'"* (Romans 8:15). He continued, *"And because you are sons, God has sent forth the Spirit of His Son into your hearts, crying out, 'Abba Father!'"* (Galatians 4:6). In each of these verses, this attitude of openness, confidence, and affection as small children is prompted and produced by the Spirit of Jesus within the believer.

We *are the light of the world."* We are the avenues whereby the Father reveals His image. It is not because we follow a list of rules or accomplish certain religious activities. We are helpless yet filled with the Father. He is shaping our lives and fathers us in all our activities and expressions. We are small children who cling to Him; we want to be like Him in all manners. There is no resistance in us to His desires and patterns. He is giving us His mind, heart, and emotions. We are an expression of who He is! It is in this embrace that we become *"light."* I am a Jesus pusher!

Jesus PUSHER | **290**

I am a Jesus Pusher! The abruptness of Jesus' entrance into public ministry is easily recognized. For the first thirty years of His life on Earth, Jesus lived in privacy and obscurity. His fame soon escalated even into foreign countries bordering Palestine. The crowds followed Him everywhere, and thousands of miracles increased His popularity. However, His style of ministry was radically different from all others. He demonstrated the Beatitudes in ministry. His attitude of meekness and mercy distinguished Him from those who sought the praise of men. His proclamation of the Kingdom of Heaven demanded repentance (Matthew 4:17). This demand raised some pressing questions. Was He a revolutionary? Was He proposing an overthrow of the existing order of things?

His approach to the Holy Scriptures seemed radically different. The Pharisees and Sadducees based their proclamations on the Old Testament. Was Jesus undermining the Scriptures, attempting to substitute His own opinions? Jesus despised "the traditions of the elders," and it was plain. Therefore, the religious leaders supposed Him to be a deceiver attempting to destroy the foundations of Judaism. Jesus' concern was for the inner hearts of men rather than the ceremonial practices. Perhaps He was against the Levitical system of the Old Testament. He continually showed grace and mercy in His friendship with publicans and sinners. Was He opposed to the Law? In four verses, He established the relationship of the New Covenant with the Old Covenant, His ministry with the Law, and our lives with the Scriptures (Matthew 5:17-20). ***"Do not think that I came to destroy the Law or the Prophets*** (The Scriptures). Jesus based His life on the truth of the Scriptures! I am a Jesus pusher!

I am a Jesus Pusher! In a precise statement, Jesus proclaims His relationship to the Scriptures. Two contrasting statements are in this verse. The content of the first is, *"I came to destroy* (don't think this). *"* The Greek word "kataluo," translated ***destroy***, is a strong word. "Kata" is an intensive word, and "luo" means "to loose." It properly refers to travelers loosening their burdens or those of their animals when they stopped for rest on a journey. Our passage refers to dissolving, demolishing, canceling, or throwing down a building or its materials. Jesus relates that we are not to ***think*** (nomizo) this about His relationship to the Law or the Prophets. It projects the idea of "to assume, to suppose, or to regard as custom."

The second is *"I came to fulfill."* The Greek word "pleroo," translated ***to fulfill***, pictures someone placing content into a container until it is full. "Pleroo" is the word Matthew uses throughout his book in relationship to the fulfillment of prophecy. The prophecy of the Old Testament contains the event that he describes about Jesus. In this picture, *"The Law or the Prophets"* is completed; they are a container, and Jesus is the content making them full.

Understanding *"The Law or the Prophets"* is essential. They are what we now call the Old Testament. They were the only written Scriptures during Jesus' earthly time. Jesus continually called these Scriptures the foundation and context of His life (Matthew 7:12; 11:13; 22:40; Luke 24:27, 24:44-45). Everything Jesus taught in His ministry He based on the Old Testament. The Old Testament was the base for everything Jesus taught through the apostles, which validated the authenticity of the Scriptures. I am a Jesus Pusher!

Jesus PUSHER | 292

I am a Jesus Pusher! ***"Do not think that I came to destroy the Law or the Prophets. I did not come to destroy but to fulfill"*** (Matthew 5:17). The focus of His statement is an explanation of His relationship with the Scriptures. We do not worship a book called the Bible. We do not think it contains magical powers we can release by rubbing or waving it. Yet the Written Word, the Scriptures, when invaded and fulfilled (completed) by the Living Word, Jesus, becomes an organism. The Bible comes to life with His presence and becomes the speaking of God to us! This connection is essential in the relationship Jesus wants with us.

I am helpless (***poor in spirit***); He fills me with His presence. If this is all I have, how will I know Him? He will reveal Himself to me, but I will interpret His revelation through my helplessness. The flaws of my past and the scars of my life's failures shape Jesus into someone He is not. Some have gone to the extreme in their interpretation of Jesus. Others have reduced Him to their puppet. How can I keep this from happening in my life? I must embrace the Living Word through the Written Word. As Jesus completes the Scriptures in my life, I see Him as He really is! If I simply experience His presence without the Scriptures, I will create and shape Him as I desire. If I only have the Scriptures, I will develop a legalistic, academic Jesus of my own learning. I need Jesus fulfilling the Scriptures in my life. I am a Jesus Pusher!

I am a Jesus Pusher! The indwelling Jesus, the Living Word, will reveal who He is through the Written Word. This interaction between them saves me from my imagination of who Jesus is and being a legalistic snob. The leaders of Israel give us a perfect example of this. They developed a false picture of the Messiah because they did not embrace the Scriptures. Jesus said, ***"You search the Scriptures, for in them you think you have eternal life; and these are they which testify of Me. But you are not willing to come to Me that you may have life"*** (John 5:39-40). If we miss Jesus revealed in the Scriptures, we miss the real Jesus. If we embrace the real Jesus, we know the Jesus who completes the Scriptures.

You cannot read verse eighteen without knowing the permanence of the Scriptures. You cannot dismiss them as necessary only for the Jewish culture. A small religious movement cannot isolate the Scriptures, and it does not matter for the rest of the world. Something is all-inclusive about the Scriptures; they include all time and all nations. ***"For assuredly, I say to you, till heaven and earth pass away, one jot or one tittle will by no means pass from the law till all is fulfilled"*** (Matthew 5:18). Jesus introduces this statement with, ***"For assuredly, I say to you."*** He highlights the unique importance of His words. "I say this to you absolutely, without qualifications, and with the fullest authority." His authority is that He fulfills the Scriptures. The relationship of the inner presence of God and the written presence of God operates in His life. He yielded Himself to all that God places in the Scriptures, revealing it in His life. That is how a Kingdom person lives. The Scriptures reveal Jesus, who is within me. I know Him through the Scriptures. I am a Jesus Pusher!

I am a Jesus Pusher! In this context, Jesus uses this phrase, *"till heaven and earth pass away."* This phrase refers to the time in which the Earth exists. He refers to a *"jot"* (iota), the smallest letter of the Greek alphabet. He continues with reference to *"one tittle"* (keraia), a stroke, which means "little horn." A "keraia" is the small mark that helps distinguish one Hebrew letter from another. *"One jot or one title will by no means pass from the law till all is fulfilled"* (Matthew 5:18). As double emphasis, not only will the smallest letter not be erased, but also the smallest part of a letter will not be erased from the Scriptures. Knowing that Jesus equated His words sourced by the Holy Spirit with the Word of God is essential. Jesus said, *"Heaven and earth will pass away, but My words will by no means pass away"* (Matthew 24:35). What is true about the Old Testament Scriptures is true of Jesus' words!

The Living Word interacts timelessly with the Written Word. You and I must bring our lives into this interaction. Jesus reveals the principles forming the operation of the universes in the Written Word. You can discover the structure and proper maintenance for your life and relationships here. God dispels wisdom in this interaction, and the Written Word is all you need for decision-making. Allow God to fill your helplessness with the Living Word, who is speaking His Written Word in your life. I am a Jesus Pusher!

I am a Jesus Pusher! I am helpless (***poor in spirit***), and in my response (***mourn***), Jesus comes to embrace me with His resource. We become the Kingdom of Heaven. The Kingdom is not a location or a place to dwell; it is a relationship. This relationship is in the interaction and communication of the Living Word and His Written Word. I am helpless to keep His Word. But the Living Word does not communicate the Written Word as in the Old Covenant. He does not appear on Mt. Sinai with stone tablets to read but embraces the core of my being and whispers His word in my heart. He reveals the Scriptures until they become the fresh speaking of His heart and His voice to my heart. In the speaking and revelation of His Word, He energizes and elevates me to the high level of His Word. In embracing all He reveals, I become what He reveals! Not to embrace His heart's revelation would be not to embrace Him.

Does this mean there are no disagreements in interpretations of some passages? Of course not! Levels of maturity are among those in a relationship with Jesus. Jesus said, ***"Whoever therefore breaks*** (luo – annuls or makes void) ***one of the least of these commandments*** (entole – authoritative prescriptions), ***and teaches men so, shall be called least*** (elachistos – immature or little ones) ***in the kingdom of heaven"*** (Matthew 5:19). Does any person in the Kingdom relationship have full knowledge of the revelation of the Living Word about the Written Word? Of course not! However, all Kingdom people cling to the Living Word and grow in the revelation of the Written Word! I am a Jesus Pusher!

I am a Jesus Pusher! ***"For I say to you, that unless your righteousness exceeds the righteousness of the scribes and Pharisees, you will by no means enter the kingdom of heaven"*** (Matthew 5:20). This statement must have shocked those who heard it. In a previous verse, we saw the righteousness of the immature, little one, who is in oneness with Jesus, shall exceed (perisseuo) the righteousness of the scribes and Pharisees. Jesus was contrasting the righteousness **of the scribes and Pharisees** with individuals helpless and sourced by the Spirit. The scribes are professionals, and the Pharisees form a sect. The scribes were the acknowledged expounders and teachers of the Old Testament. The Pharisees were those who attempted to make everybody think they were adhering to the Old Testament.

We discover the strength of this statement in the use of ***shall exceed***. The actual statement in the Greek text is revealing: ***"I say*** (ego) ***For*** (gar) ***unto you*** (humin) ***that*** (hoti) ***except*** (ean me) ***shall exceed*** (perisseuo) ***your*** (humon) ***the*** (he) ***righteousness*** (dikaiosune) ***much more*** (pleion) ***of the*** (ton) ***scribes and Pharisees."*** "Perisseuo" and "pleion" emphasize the same focus. In the English translation, "pleion" is not translated. "Perisseuo" means "to overflow like a river out of its banks;" "pleion" means "more in number, quantity, or quality." Jesus said that His presence fills our lives, reveals the Scriptures, and produces righteousness within us on a level that cannot compare to the legalistic, self-sourced righteousness of the scribes and Pharisees. I will embrace Jesus through the Scriptures. I am a Jesus Pusher!

I am a Jesus Pusher! ***"For I say to you, that unless your righteousness exceeds the righteousness of the scribes and Pharisees, you will by no means enter the kingdom of heaven"*** (Matthew 5:20). Jesus called everyone, even the ordinary people, to a higher standard than the professional religious people practiced. The heart of the Scriptures tells us that we cannot live without Him. The Scriptures consistently make us conscious of our helplessness. This consciousness releases Jesus to source us to a new level of living. The scribes and Pharisees developed an oral tradition about the Scriptures. The Pharisees adjusted the impossible standard of the Scriptures, establishing laws they could accomplish. Jesus highlights this in the next section of this chapter (Matthew 5:21-48). The following section is a revelation of the inner content of the Kingdom of Heaven. In my helplessness (***poor in spirit***), the Living Word embraces me. The Living Word brings a revelation of the Written Word to the relationship. In this intimate communication, the strength of His nature flows through me, for when He communicates truth, He shares Himself! The Living Word calls me through the Written Word.

The issue always rests on my response to Jesus! Am I willing to merge with Him until He is my life? Serving Jesus by doing certain required things is the righteousness of the scribes and Pharisees. They accomplished keeping specific regulations but had no intimate relationship with God. Jesus calls us to a Living Word and Written Word intimate relationship that would reproduce His life in our world. I am a Jesus pusher!

I am a Jesus Pusher! The Sermon on the Mount is a manifesto of the Kingdom of Heaven. This Kingdom is not a location; you do not take a long journey to arrive at this place. The Kingdom of Heaven is a relationship with Jesus. As Jesus described it, the Kingdom is the helplessness of a person sourced by the Spirit of God! In the intertwining of God and man, God creates a new unit. This unit explodes with meekness, righteousness, mercy, purity, peace, and victory amid persecution (Matthew 5:3-10). A man filled with God influences the world; he becomes *"salt"* and *"light."* The Sermon on the Mount describes this intimate relationship, the Kingdom of Heaven.

However, when we carefully consider the Sermon on the Mount, it describes Jesus. If there is any question about the statements of the sermon, you view the life of Jesus for clarification. For example, the proposal of seeking the Kingdom of Heaven first is defined clearly in the Garden of Gethsemane (Matthew 6:33 and 26:39). Jesus forcibly demonstrates the content of *"love your enemies"* in the crucifixion (Matthew 5:44; Luke 23:34). Each fundamental principle or concept manifests itself throughout the ministry of Jesus. He is the Sermon on the Mount. If the secret to His life was the fullness of the Spirit, could the same Spirit source me? Indeed, He is that Spirit. I am a Jesus Pusher!

I am a Jesus Pusher! If the Sermon on the Mount describes the Kingdom of Heaven, we immediately know that Jesus is the Kingdom of Heaven. He unites a helpless man with God's Spirit. Jesus is the first member of the Kingdom; He introduces the New Covenant to humanity. Jesus demonstrated all the qualities of the Beatitudes, leaving no doubt about the function of His life. His life flowed with the influence of the Kingdom. He is the *"light of the world."* What was the tangible core of the relationship Jesus experienced with the Father? The Scriptures are the cores! Jesus continually highlighted the importance of the Scriptures throughout His ministry. The Scriptures were not just a tool for ministry, but they were the foundation for His life's experience. He based His existence as a man on the Scriptures. Amid temptation, He clung to the Scriptures to hear the voice of the Father (Matthew 4:1-11). When He desired to explain His life to the disciples, He took them to the Scriptures (Luke 24:44-45). Jesus used the reality of the Scriptures as the center of His conflict with the leaders of Israel. These leaders strayed from *"He who is of God hears God's words"* (John 8:47).

After Jesus established the "Formation of the Kingdom" (Matthew 5:3-12) and set forth the "Function of the Kingdom" (Matthew 5:13-16), He declared the relationship between the Kingdom person and the Scriptures, the "Fulfillment of the Kingdom, Acknowledged" (Matthew 5:17-20). Jesus glorifies the Scriptures. The Pharisees and scribes developed the "oral traditions" or "traditions of the elders." They were six hundred and thirteen applications of the Scriptures and were necessary to apply the principles of the Scriptures to everyday life.

However, these traditions became of more excellent value to them than the Scriptures. In accusing Jesus of breaking the Law of God, they referred to their oral traditions. Jesus never proposed breaking the Law of God (the Scriptures). He brought clarity to what God intended in the Scriptures. His perspective of the Scriptures must become ours. I am a Jesus Pusher!

Jesus PUSHER | 300

I am a Jesus Pusher! ***"Do not think that I came to destroy the Law or the Prophets. I did not come to destroy but to fulfill"*** (Matthew 5:17). Jesus is the completion of the Scriptures, and it is a reality as the heart of the statement in our verse (Matthew 5:17). He begins His statement with a focus on "thinking." However, the meaning is not a casual thought or a passing consideration but is a translation of the Greek word "nomizo." This Greek term comes from the Greek word "nomos," meaning "law." In fact, ***"Law"*** in our verse translates the Greek word "nomos." ***"Law"*** in our verse. Therefore, ***"do not think"*** means "to suppose, assume, to regard or acknowledge as custom, to have and hold as customary or as a law."

In other words, Jesus is concerned as to how we view Him as the Messiah, which was a valid concern. The difficulty He repeatedly faced with His disciples flowed from their misunderstanding of what He came to achieve. They saw Him as a military Messiah; He was ***"gentle and lowly in heart"*** (Matthew 11:29). They saw Him as a temporal Messiah ruling an earthly Kingdom (Acts 1:16). This viewpoint was the basis for their rebuke regarding His predictions about His death and resurrection (Matthew 16:22), not a momentary thought but was the customary perspective of their lives. They took the Scriptures and adjusted them to develop their view. Jesus did not come to demolish the Scriptures. However, in filling out the Scriptures, they would gain a new perspective and approach to the Kingdom of Heaven. He wants to do the same for us. Will we listen to Him through the Scriptures? I am a Jesus Pusher!

I am a Jesus Pusher! The Pharisees developed their "oral traditions," which became more important than the Scriptures. I see this truth consistently needing an application to my perspective. I know the influence of the traditions and cultures in which I was raised. We developed our "oral traditions" that became more important than the Scriptures. What we heard weekly from the pulpit was not the Scriptures but our traditions. People were condemned to eternal hell by a God delighted to send them there for wearing red ties, earrings, wedding rings, and makeup. We developed the Sabbath day rules as binding as those of the Jews. You could not go to the store, play ball, or take a newspaper on Sunday (not even the Sabbath day). These things became more important to us than the Scriptures.

But there is a danger! Those days are gone; we are free. The tendency is to establish the identical pattern to the other extreme. We develop "oral traditions" that frees us to do anything we desire. If there are no absolutes, we can embrace sexual impurities like homosexuality and adultery as acceptable. We can focus on materialism and use the Gospel to obtain it. Where are the Scriptures? How am I going to know the truth? We find the answer in Jesus! The answer is not just Jesus in His presence but Jesus in the Scriptures. I must know the living presence of the indwelling Spirit of Jesus, but I must know His presence as He speaks through His word. He did not come to demolish the Scriptures; He came to fulfill them in every way. The Scriptures become complete and arrive at a new level in Jesus. I must experience the mind of Christ, thinking as He does, have His perspective, and develop His pattern. I can do this only through the Scriptures as He fulfills them in me! I am a Jesus Pusher!

I am a Jesus Pusher! Jesus began this section (The Fulfillment of the Kingdom) with "me nomizo," translated as ***"do not think."*** This statement determines the strength of the section. How serious is Jesus in His statements? How much attention should I pay to them? These two Greek words establish it all! I investigated many translations of this verse, and there were four approaches used. Some used "do not suppose," "do not assume," or "do not misunderstand." The majority consistently used ***"do not think."*** Keep in mind; the emphasis is on custom or law. In other words, it is not a fleeting thought but an established way of viewing things.

Changing your traditional thought patterns is difficult. One of the difficulties with breaking habits is the established thought in the habit. Those who attempt to break the smoking habit express this. Breaking the habit is not just a chemical addiction but also a habit of the thought process. The pattern of thinking causes the smoker to reach out for a cigarette when there is none. Victory over temper is not focused on never being upset; it is the pattern that being upset expresses. The Pharisees and scribes destroyed or demolished the Scriptures through their "oral traditions." It was their consistent thought pattern. They did this by replacing the Scriptures with these traditions. Jesus makes this bold statement, "I have not come to do as they did. I came to fulfill, reestablish, and complete the Scriptures." In this statement, He distinctly asks us to join Him. I am a Jesus Pusher who commits Himself to the truth of the Scriptures!

Jesus PUSHER | 303

I am a Jesus Pusher! "***Do not think that I came to destroy the Law or the Prophets. I did not come to destroy but to fulfill***" (Matthew 5:17). Jesus begins this verse with the Greek word "me," translated ***"not."*** Being the first word of the Greek text highlights this as the emphasis of the passage. However, as we progress in the passage, the word "not" appears again but does not translate the same Greek word. The other Greek word is "ouk."

The Greek lexicon makes a vital distinction between the emphases of these two words. They are each negative particles. In Greek grammar, particles are words generally providing fine shades of modification to verbs and other words in the sentence, focusing on the verbs. There are some critical distinctions between these two negatives, "me" and "ouk." "Me" implies a dependent and conditional negative; thus, it is subjective. "Ouk" is, in a sense, objective expressing a direct and total negation independently. "Me" is the negative of will, wish, or doubt, while "ouk" denies the fact. "Me" implies the one speaking and writing conceives or supposes a thing not in existence but as the individual's opinion. "Ouk" says that it does not exist, the nonexistent reality. Jesus did not come to destroy the Scriptures but to fulfill them. Any undermining of the Scriptures, any addition to the Scriptures, and any adjustment of the truth for self-benefit violates who Jesus is. If I embrace Him, I must embrace the Scriptures. I am a Jesus Pusher!

I am a Jesus Pusher! "***Do not think that I came to destroy the Law or the Prophets. I did not come to destroy but to fulfill***" (Matthew 5:17). Jesus is the speaker of the passage. He begins with "***Not***" (Me). This beginning is His idea and intention and is an expression and conclusion of His opinion. In this statement, we see Jesus' view of why He came into the world. His purpose through His omniscience as the second member of the Trinity was clear. But as man, limited in His knowledge and thinking, what is His view? Involved in His perspective is NOT the destruction of the Scriptures. He is not saying, "The Scriptures are all right, but . . ." Nor His intent to change a thing about the Scriptures. As we move into the next verse, He gives details to exactly what He means. "***For assuredly, I say to you, till heaven and earth pass away, one jot or one tittle will by no means pass from the law till all is fulfilled***" (Matthew 5:18). A **"jot"** (iota) is the smallest letter of the Greek alphabet. A **"tittle"** (keraia) is a small mark helping distinguish one Hebrew letter from another.

Jesus expands this idea by using the word **"not"** (ouk). He did **"not come to destroy but to fulfill,"** an expression of His opinion; this is a biblical statement of reality. This expression is the way things are despite many opinions. Jesus confronted the perspective of the Pharisees and scribes with this reality. You and I must see our views against the truth of the Scriptures! BUT Jesus must also see His perspective compared to reality. When He does, they are the same! Jesus' opinion is the same as the Scriptures. Jesus equated His Words with the Words of the Scriptures (Matthew 24:35), not because He had authority over the Scriptures, but because He submitted to the Scriptures. To embrace Jesus is to embrace the Scriptures. I am a Jesus pusher!

I am a Jesus Pusher! The New Covenant is the infilling of the Spirit of Jesus in the believer, giving us the mind of Christ through the Scriptures. Any deviation from the Scriptures is a deviation from the mind of Christ, His indwelt presence. Any disagreement from the mind of Christ is a disagreement with the Scriptures. No one can divide them; they are the same! In this passage, Jesus calls us to share His mind. The Scriptures are an expression of the mind of Christ. Think of the wonder of being indwelt with the mind of Christ as you hold what He says in your hand, the Scriptures. He reveals His truth to you. His habits, pattern of thought, and "oral traditions" are now yours.

The last section of this chapter is powerful (Matthew 5:21-48). Our paragraph, "The Fulfillment of the Kingdom, Acknowledged" (Matthew 5:17-20), introduces this last section. In verse twenty and throughout the previous section, the resounding statement is, *"But I say to you."* Jesus gives us His opinion, but His opinion is the same as the Scriptures. He brings us back to the Scriptures. If we join the perspective of Jesus' mind, we will join the Scriptures. The Scriptures must be more important than what we have "made up" about the Scriptures. To push Jesus, the Person is to push the Scriptures, His Word! I am a Jesus Pusher!

I am a Jesus Pusher! The "Gospel" means "good news!" Although there is much bad news, this is never the message of Jesus. After expressing the tremendous love of God in giving His only begotten Son, Jesus said, ***"Do not think that I came to destroy the Law or the Prophets. I did not come to destroy but to fulfill"*** (Matthew 5:17). Although the statement of Jesus in our passage is negative, it is positive. The negative side of the statement's purpose is to emphasize the positive. The focus is not on destruction but fulfillment. Jesus did not come to demolish; He came to complete in every way!

However, let us focus on the negative side of Jesus' statement. The fulfillment of the Scriptures will, of necessity, eliminate the "oral traditions" of the Jews. Jesus plainly said, "The Fulfillment of the Kingdom, Application" (Matthew 5:21:48). He took each of their "oral traditions" and highlighted the biblical truth found in the Scriptures. This destruction of their "oral traditions" became difficult for them. It quickly brought them to the conclusion of eliminating Jesus. In other words, the proposition of Jesus was so strong that they must destroy Him. You must either destroy Jesus' influence in your life or allow the destruction of your preconceived "oral traditions." Destruction of your "oral traditions" requires a spirit of openness and seeking, always the heart of the spiritual experience. If you have narrow, opinionated, and rigid thoughts, you will never know the fullness of Jesus' Spirit in your life. If you are going to have the mind of Christ, you must openly embrace the Scriptures and whatever changes it will make in your life. Are you open to His leadership? Will you allow Him to change your mind? I am a Jesus Pusher!

I am a Jesus Pusher! ***"Do not think that I came to destroy the Law or the Prophets. I did not come to destroy but to fulfill"*** (Matthew 5:17). In our verse, Jesus distinctly speaks about "His coming." How is His coming related to the Scriptures? He was emphatic about this, saying it twice. His coming is the subject and verb of the two sentences in this verse. He does not want anyone to think, ***"I came"*** to destroy the Scriptures. He continues this emphasis by saying, ***"I did not come,"*** a translation of the Greek word "erchomai," to destroy but to fulfill. The verb "erchomai" is in the aorist tense, active voice, and indicative mood, meaning it is a simple statement of fact. The aorist tense is without emphasis when the verb happens, but the focus is on the verb's action. The active voice means the subject is participating and even responsible for the action of the verb.

Jesus gave this emphasis previously. His references are so numerous that they form "the coming statements" of Jesus. He instructed the disciples to go to the next towns saying, ***"that I may preach there also, because for this purpose I have come forth"*** (Mark 1:38). The Pharisees criticized Jesus for eating with tax collectors and sinners. His response was, ***"For I did not come to call the righteous, but sinners, to repentance"*** (Matthew 9:13). He instructed His disciples before sending them into ministry. ***"Do not think that I came to bring peace on earth. I did not come to bring peace but a sword"*** (Matthew 10:34). In our passage and the additional verses, Jesus' focus is on purpose. His relationship with the Scriptures defines the redemptive purpose of His coming. Redemption shapes His role and destiny. Would that not do the same for us? Do not live without your life discovered in the Scriptures. I am a Jesus Pusher!

I am a Jesus Pusher! ***"Do not think that I came to destroy the Law or the Prophets. I did not come to destroy but to fulfill"*** (Matthew 5:17). Jesus said, ***"I came"*** in a positive statement and also in the negative, ***"I did not come."*** "The Coming One," the Scriptures were given beforehand, give us insight and understanding of Jesus. Jesus preceded the Scriptures; He produced them! The statement in the Scriptures did not determine the actions of Jesus; instead, Jesus determined the Scriptures. "God is holy" not because the Scriptures say so, but the Scriptures declare He is holy because He is! Because He is "The Coming One," He gave us a document of what He will look like when He comes.

The Scriptures seem to shape the life of Jesus; the Scriptures produced Him. The resurrected Lord said to His disciples, ***"These are the words which I spoke to you while I was still with you. That all things must be fulfilled which were written in the Law of Moses and the Prophets and the Psalms concerning Me"*** (Luke 24:44). As he was hanging on the cross, Jesus cried, ***"I thirst!"*** John explains, ***"After this, Jesus knowing that all things were now accomplished that the Scriptures might be fulfilled said, "I thirst!"*** (John 19:28). He surrendered His life to the control of the Father and let the authority of the Written Word dictate His life. That is a privilege of the merger with Him. The inward Living Word and the outward Written Word come together to cause our lives. We are a product of His person speaking to us! I am a Jesus Person!

Jesus PUSHER | 309

I am a Jesus Pusher! Can you visualize the positive drive at the core of Jesus' life? He participated in the Trinity's plan for redeeming the world. He stretched into all the Father's desires. What a privilege to be a part of it? Listen to the words He spoke to His earthly parents. ***"Why did you seek Me? Did you not know that I must be about My Father's business?"*** (Luke 2:49). We can gain insight from Jesus' use of the Greek word "dei." The content of a sentence containing this verb is fundamental, unquestioned, often anonymous, and deterministic. It most often designates an unconditional necessity. At twelve, Jesus had this positive focus to participate with His Father.

Two important events in Jesus' ministry highlight the Fathers' approval. The launching of His ministry took place at the culmination of thirty years of living. As the fullness of the Spirit descended on Him, and God birthed the New Covenant (the Kingdom of God), the Father descended crying, ***"This is My beloved Son, in whom I am well pleased"*** (Matthew 3:17). While God transfigured Jesus in the presence of Moses and Elijah, the Father descended and cried, ***"This is My beloved Son, in whom I am well pleased. Hear Him!"*** (Matthew 17:5). Jesus fulfilled the heart's desire of the Father, which we see in the Scriptures. He came under the Scriptures' authority, the core of the intimate relationship with the Father, the Living Word, and the Written Word. I must live in harmony of the Word within and the Word without! I am a Jesus Pusher!

I am a Jesus Pusher! Jesus consistently expressed the positive relationship He had with His Father throughout His ministry. He said, ***"My Father has been working until now, and I have been working"*** (John 5:17). He proclaimed a partnership between the Father and Son, and it was so intimate that it consisted of sourcing! He said, ***"Most assuredly, I say to you, the Son can do nothing of Himself, but what He sees the Father do; for whatever He does, the Son also does in like manner"*** (John 5:19). In the unity between the Father and the Son, what the Son does is what the Father is doing; the Father is the source of the Son. Jesus came demonstrating the positive heart of the Father. To overstate the loving heart of the Father as revealed in Jesus is impossible. He has come to do this. God swallows the anger and judgment toward us in the vast depth of the loving, positive force of His passionate love. Let this truth smother you in its warmth!

If the coming of Jesus is positive, then Jesus' fulfillment of the Scriptures is positive. In other words, the Scriptures' Old Testament has not been a misrepresentation of God, the Father. Therefore, Jesus will not destroy the Law or the Prophets. They are true; thus, Jesus comes to fulfill them! He gives us a clear and concise picture of what the Father's heart has been throughout the Old Testament Scriptures. We are now seeing the positive, real heart of the Father. Perhaps our impressions of the Old Testament are wrong, and Jesus is correcting them. No wonder I am a Jesus pusher!

Jesus PUSHER | 311

I am a Jesus Pusher! The theme of Jesus' coming connects to the reality of Jesus being sent! "Pempo" means "to dispatch, to send," and it is a parallel word to the Greek word "apostello," translated apostle. Jesus consistently made statements such as, ***"Peace to you! As the Father has sent*** (apostello) ***Me, I also send*** (pempo) ***you"*** (John 20:21). Matthew uses prophecies in the first four chapters of his writing in nearly every paragraph. The prophecy is a message of the plan to send Jesus. God established the Scriptures; they carve out the boundaries of the movement of God for us. Jesus verifies this plan. Paul illuminated this truth. ***"But when the fullness of the time had come, God sent forth His Son, born of a woman, born under the law"*** (Galatians 4:4). Was this not the content of the first prophecy found in the Scriptures? He promised, "the Seed" (Genesis 3:15). Paul expounded this. ***"Now to Abraham and his Seed were the promises made. He does not say, 'And to seeds,' as of many, but as of one, 'And to your Seed, who is Christ"*** (Galatians 3:16).

God's plan is always positive! He has never planned against us. He is constantly for us! As the positive plan of God unfolds through the Scriptures, He sends Jesus. His presence comes; His presence is positive! In our helplessness, the Spirit of Jesus comes. He fills us and brings the formation of the Kingdom of God. Jesus pronounces the accomplishment of the New Covenant. He comes! He is the positive explosion of the heart of the Trinity into our world, fulfilling the plan of God! We must embrace Him! I am a Jesus pusher!

Jesus PUSHER | 312

I am a Jesus Pusher! God, the Father, did not send His Son for condemnation and judgment. Jesus said, *"For God did not send His Son into the world to condemn the world, but that the world through Him might be saved"* (John 3:17). That does not mean there is no condemnation; however, Jesus does not contain condemnation. Jesus continued, *"He who believes in Him is not condemned; but he who does not believe is condemned already, because he has not believed in the name of the only begotten Son of God. And this is the condemnation, that the light has come into the world, and men loved darkness rather than light, because their deeds were evil"* (John 3:18-19). Although condemnation is present, it is not the positive plan of God. Sin contains its own condemnation and brings about its own destruction. God sends us nothing but the positive!

Jesus did not come to judge the world. Listen to His words. *"And if anyone hears My words and does not believe, I do not judge him; for I did not come to judge the world but to save the world"* (John 12:47). However, His coming into the world means judgment. He said, *"He who rejects Me, and does not receive My words, has that which judges him — the word that I have spoken will judge him in the last day"* (John 12:48). With the coming of light, those who love darkness reject it. Jesus came to attest to the truth. *"Everyone who is of the truth hears My voice"* (John 18:37). Not to hear His voice is to reject the Word. If we reject the Word, we reject who He is! God judges us by such rejection. Embrace the positive heart of God, Jesus! I am a Jesus Pusher!

Jesus PUSHER | 313

I am a Jesus Pusher! Jesus states His intention twice, ***"Do not think that I came to destroy the Law or the Prophets. I did not come to destroy"*** (Matthew 5:17). Jesus coming intends no destruction. That is true in every area of life; however, the focus of our passage is on the Scriptures. Jesus did not come to hinder, eliminate, or destroy one small ***"tittle"*** of the Scriptures. He did not come to change directions or to start something not intended, meaning the Scriptures do not contain negative intent but positive salvation.

Jesus gives us the intent of God's heart even in the Old Testament. He does not say that He is the God of the New Testament, and the God of the Old Testament was wrong. Jesus is the visible image of the invisible God of the Old Testament (Colossians 1:15) without discrepancy between them. The Old Testament was the beginning of the complete revelation in Jesus. He came to fulfill the Scriptures. In Jesus, we have a complete understanding of what took place in the Old Testament. In Jesus, the plan of God is revealed and comes together. In Jesus, the heartbeat of God gives His real intent. Jesus did not come to destroy and contradict the Scriptures but to fulfill them! Jesus reveals that God is "safe." We can trust Jesus. I must surrender my life to Him as He surrendered His life to His Father. He wants to fulfill the Scriptures in me. I am a Jesus pusher!

I am a Jesus Pusher! ***"Do not think that I came to destroy the Law or the Prophets. I did not come to destroy but to fulfill"*** (Matthew 5:17). Some view "to fulfill" as "to fill out" or "fill full." They understand the rest of the chapter (Matthew 5:21-48) as Jesus canceling the moral law of the Old Testament. He canceled it and established a new interpretation of this moral law; in other words, He added to it. Jesus leaves no doubt about what He is saying. ***"For I say to you, that unless your righteousness exceeds the righteousness of the scribes and Pharisees, you will by no means enter the kingdom of heaven"*** (Matthew 5:20). Considering this statement, Jesus says the oral traditions of the scribes and Pharisees are over against the real intent and heart of the Scriptures. Jesus never intends to destroy, cancel, or add to the Scriptures. He reveals, clarifies, and focuses us on the truth of the Scriptures.

There is no place in the Scriptures where the idea of "filling out" can be applied to the law, even when the Scriptures express the spirit of the law. In each case, the statement uniformly means "to fulfill." Paul said, ***"Owe no one anything except to love one another, for he who loves another has fulfilled the law"*** (Romans 13:8). The use of the language demands ***"has fulfilled"*** must be understood as taking what is (the law) and completing it. Therefore, we must not think of "to fulfill" as "to fill out." we must understand that Jesus said He came not to fill out or to supplement the Law by additional elements, but "to fulfill" it, by obeying it and being made under it. His presence does this in my life! I am a Jesus pusher!

I am a Jesus pusher! The writer of the Book of Hebrews makes an interesting statement. *In that He says, "A new covenant," He has made the first obsolete. Now what is becoming obsolete and growing old is ready to vanish away* (Hebrews 8:13). On first consideration, you might think this writer is speaking of the Old Testament as *"obsolete," "growing old,"* and *"ready to vanish away."* However, the chapter and even this verse focus on the covenants, not the Scriptures. He distinctly refers *to the covenant that I made with their fathers in the day when I took them by the hand to lead them out of the land of Egypt* (Hebrews 8:9). The writer quotes God as saying, *"I will make a new covenant with the house of Israel and with the house of Judah"* (Hebrews 8:8). Although the Hebrew writer focuses on covenants, Jesus focuses on the Old Testament Scriptures (*Law or the Prophets*). The inadequacy of the Old Covenant is evident; the necessity of the New Covenant is absolute. But Jesus highlights the plan of God as seen in the Scriptures, of which these covenants are simply a part. Nothing is "obsolete," "growing old," or "ready to vanish away" about the plan of God as revealed in the Scriptures. He fully accomplished the Law and the Prophets. He fulfilled every symbol and ceremony in the temple structure regarding Himself. He was the only man who adequately kept the law (Hebrews 4:15). Now He wants to merge with me and do the same through me! I am a Jesus Pusher!

I am a Jesus Pusher! We interpret *"fulfill"* in light of *"the Prophets."* The Scriptures contain "the Law and the Prophets." The idea of *"fulfill"* suggesting "to fill out" as in complementing or adding is inadmissible considering the "Prophets." Jesus did not come to fill out or expound their predictions about the Messiah. Indeed, He did not add to the number of prophetic utterances. Jesus fulfilled all that the prophets proposed. The prophets spoke of verbal and predictive prophecies, and symbolic prophecies established symbols, feast days, and ceremonies. Hundreds of prophecies are in both categories, and Jesus fulfills everyone. Someone calculated the odds connected to one man fulfilling all three hundred and thirty-two verbal predictive prophecies. One chance out of eighty-four with one hundred zeros behind it is the odds! Many of them were detailed and not understood by the prophet. Jesus did not partially fulfill, nor did He complete most of them. Jesus finished and fulfilled all these prophecies.

Whenever the word *"fulfill"* is used about anything prophetical, it is in the sense of "to fulfill." In other words, we never use it with prophecy in the sense of complementing or adding to the prophecy. We discovered this in the Book of Matthew. In the first four chapters of his book, Matthew uses this word in almost every paragraph. He establishes the validity of Jesus as the Messiah who fulfills the prophetic requirements of the Scriptures. The Greek word "pleroo," translated *fulfill,* is used consistently in all these passages and our text (Matthew 5:17). It describes a container full of content. Matthew tells story after story involving Jesus. He plainly says these events fill up the container of the prophecies spoken by the prophets. Consider what the Trinity God has done through Jesus for you! I am a Jesus Pusher!

I am a Jesus Pusher! *"Do not think that I came to destroy the Law or the Prophets. I did not come to destroy but to fulfill"* (Matthew 5:17). A definition of the word "discharge" in the English dictionary is "to do all required to fulfill a responsibility or perform a duty." This definition comes within the parameter of *"fulfill."* Jesus came to fulfill, accomplish all the law required, and perform the duty of what was spoken by the prophets! He did not come to add to the law or to give additional prophecies. He came to fulfill the Scriptures.

After boldly saying His intentions not to destroy the Law or the Prophets, Jesus declares the eternal state of the Scriptures. He says, *"Till heaven and earth pass away, one jot or one tittle will by no means pass from the law till all is fulfilled"* (Matthew 5:18). This statement extends His intent not to destroy but to fulfill. He places His intent not to destroy the Scriptures in the context of their eternal state. But the key is found in the final statement, *"till all is fulfilled."* The New International Version translates this phrase, *"until everything is accomplished."* A different Greek word, "pleroo," translated *fulfill*, is in the previous verse. *"Is fulfilled"* is the Greek word "ginomai." It means "to come into being," "to cause to be," or "to become," giving us a clear focus of what Jesus intended in the word *fulfill*. He did not come to destroy the Scriptures but to accomplish all contained in them! He wants to do this in your life. I am a Jesus Pusher!

Jesus PUSHER | 318

I am a Jesus Pusher! We discover a wonder contained in the word *fulfill*. First, Jesus fulfilled the Scriptures in "revelation." We already discussed how perverted the Scriptures became with the beliefs of the Pharisees, Sadducees, and scribes. God reduced His intent to redeem a world to the nation of Israel. Their nationalistic view of Judaism isolated them. Isolation became prejudice. Their application of the Old Testament law became dominated by defilement laws and cleansing procedures. This application naturally gravitated into a militaristic view of the coming Messiah. They viewed the Kingdom of God as the Kingdom of Israel standing supreme against the Gentile world. The laws of the Scriptures applying directly to them were adjusted and reduced to fit their needs. External acts became the focus.; personal necessity became the motive; self-justification sets the standard. Jesus boldly discharged a new view of the Scriptures. He restored it to its proper meaning; He revealed its intent as seen from the heart of God.

If you have only the Scriptures, you will quickly adjust its truth to satisfy your self-sourcing. You must consistently see the Scriptures in light of Jesus. The Scriptures become clear when seen through the person of Jesus. To discover the Scriptures, give clarity to the person of Jesus while He gives clarity to the Scriptures is a marvel. No wonder the Scriptures call Him *"the Word"* (John 1:1). God fills me, and I allow Him to speak His word into my life. I am a Jesus Pusher!

I am a Jesus Pusher! ***"Do not think that I came to destroy the Law or the Prophets. I did not come to destroy but to fulfill"*** (Matthew 5:17). Jesus has fulfilled the Scriptures in "realization." Who has been obedient to the law of God? ***"For all have sinned and fall short of the glory of God"*** (Romans 3:23) is a haunting message. To find partial obedience to the law has no more value than disobedience to the law is distressing. ***"For whoever shall keep the whole law, and yet stumble in one point, he is guilty of all"*** (James 2:10). All generations of humanity stand guilty before the Scriptures. Then Jesus came! He came with the express design of meeting the holy demands of the Scriptures, to offer to God what is justly required. He magnified the law by rendering to it perfect obedience in thought, word, and deed. Concerning the prophets, His mission was to make good predictions about Himself. He performed the work the Scriptures announced He should do. Jesus fulfilled the Scriptures.

Jesus has fulfilled the Scriptures in "restoration." He gives us the true meaning and revelation of the Scriptures. He obeyed the Scriptures in aspects of law and prophecy. Although we applaud Him for these accomplishments, the greatest of all is that He restored us to Himself as found in the Scriptures. In accomplishing the whole duty of the law and paying the total penalty for failure regarding the law, God fully restores us in Jesus. Jesus imparts His Spirit to us; the Spirit of the One who completes the law is living through us. ***"Love does no harm to a neighbor; therefore love is the fulfillment of the law"*** (Romans 3:10). While Jesus continues with the Sermon on the

Mount, He says, ***"Therefore, whatever you want men to do to you, do also to them, for this is the Law and the Prophets"*** (Matthew 7:12). God fulfills Jesus in the Scriptures; God fulfills Jesus in me! I am a Jesus Pusher!

I am a Jesus Pusher! *"For assuredly, I say to you, till heaven and earth pass away, one jot or one tittle will by no means pass from the law till all is fulfilled"* (Matthew 5:18). The Greek word "gar," translated *"for,"* is the second word in the Greek text. Jesus uses it to form the boundaries and give the focus of our verse. He uses it to establish the connection between the preceding verse and the content of Jesus' continued statement. "Gar" is an explanatory conjunction. The Word provides a reason for the previous statement. His statement begins with *"assuredly."* The Greek word is "amen," often translated as "truly, assuredly, or amen," it is an emphatic particle used to express stress, either inclusion or intensity. "Amen" is regularly followed by, *"I say to you."* This phrase completes a solemn formula or truth and indicates that what is to follow is very important!

Jesus continues with a contrast between *"heaven and earth"* and *"one jot or tittle . . . from the law."* The phrase "heaven and earth" is used in the New Testament to refer to the totality of physical creation. In this context, "heaven" does not refer to the permanent dwelling place of the Christian but is a part of the physical universe. When connected with "earth," it forms a phrase highlighting our physical creation. In their culture and ours, "heaven and earth" is used as a reference to permanence. "The sun rising in the morning" is a certainty in our minds. However, what God says in Scripture is more permanent than this creation. In reality, "heaven and earth" will pass away, but not the Scriptures. Jesus fulfilled this permanent document of truth, the Written Word, and I will come under His authority in the Word. I am a Jesus Pusher!

I am a Jesus Pusher! *"For assuredly, I say to you, till heaven and earth pass away, one jot or one tittle will by no means pass from the law till all is fulfilled"* (Matthew 5:18). Peter wrote, *"But the heavens and the earth which are now preserved by the same word, are reserved for fire until the day of judgment and perdition of ungodly men"* (2 Peter 3:7). The phrase *"the same word"* refers to the words God spoke in creating the "heavens and the earth." The Word of God was before creation was responsible for the creation and will endure beyond creation! The psalmist saw the duration of creation compared to the nature of God. He wrote: *"Of old You laid the foundation of the earth, and the heavens are the work of Your hands. They will perish, but You will endure; Yes, they will all grow old like a garment; Like a cloak You will change them, and they will be changed. But You are the same, and Your years will have no end"* (Psalms 102:25-27).

Jesus equating His own words with the Word of God is significant to notice. He said, *"Heaven and earth will pass away, but My words will by no means pass away"* (Matthew 24:35). What is true of the Scriptures as referenced by the Law is also true of Jesus' teaching. They are timeless! He is the fulfillment of the Scriptures, the Word of God. It is not our understanding of the Scriptures that will never cease; what God said in the Scriptures is timeless. There is a depth of the Scriptures we have not reached! Jesus wants to fill you and share the depth of His Word with you. I am a Jesus pusher!

I am a Jesus Pusher! *"For assuredly, I say to you, till heaven and earth pass away, one jot or one tittle will by no means pass from the law till all is fulfilled"* (Matthew 5:18). Jesus contrasts this end of creation with the continuation of the Scriptures. He refers to *"one jot or tittle"* to illustrate this truth, a proverbial mode of expression among the Jews. The Greek word "iota," translated as *"jot,"* is the smallest letter of the Greek alphabet and expresses smallness or the minutest part of something. The Hebrew word "yodh" refers to the smallest letter of the Hebrew alphabet, which looks like an apostrophe. The Greek word "keraia," translated *"tittle,"* means "little horn." It refers to the small marks that help distinguish one Hebrew letter from another. An example is in the English language. We determine the letter "c" from the letter "e" by the "tittle inside the "e." Not only will the smallest letter not be erased, but even the smallest part of a letter will not be erased from the Scriptures. The tiniest, most insignificant part of the Scriptures will not be removed or modified!

How easily we translate the Scriptures and add our thoughts. We do not have the original manuscripts, which creates questions about our present Bible. The original language of the Scriptures is not our language, which demands translation. Scholars differ on word meanings based on the context of the passage. Personal theology shades our view and determines our translation. Even with all these difficulties, Jesus calls us to an openness to the indwelling Living Word revealing the Written Word. Will we bend our lives under the authority of the Word? I am a Jesus Pusher!

I am a Jesus Pusher! "***For assuredly, I say to you, till heaven and earth pass away, one jot or one tittle will by no means pass from the law till all is fulfilled***" (Matthew 5:18). Two statements beginning with the Greek word "heos," translated **"till,"** exist. The first statement is "***till*** (heos) (an)***pass*** (parelthe)." This statement relates to "heaven and earth." You can use the word "till" (heos) in two ways. First, it can indicate the continuity of an action or the finality of action. Second, we can use it for what is continuing or for what is concluded. Jesus uses "heos" inclusively in our passage regarding ***"heaven and earth."*** The Scriptures will continue until the creation ceases to be and will continue afterward as well! The second statement is "***till*** (heos) (an) ***all*** (panta) ***is fulfilled*** (ginomai)." Notice this is a different Greek word for ***"fulfilled"*** than in the previous verse (Matthew 5:17). "Ginomai" means "to become." The smallest detail of the Scriptures will not be destroyed or dissolved until it becomes and is accomplished, and then it will continue in its completed form! Jesus is NOT saying that the Scriptures will be dissolved after they are completed, accomplished, or at the end of creation. The Scriptures are eternal!

Jesus presents us with His perspective of the Scriptures. The Bible is not only a book of information and instruction. The Living Word indwells the believer and actively flows into the Scriptures as if He is speaking the words. The Written Word becomes a living organism as an extension of the Living Word. God speaks life into us through this unity. This speaking of God is eternal! Jesus wants to indwell you and speak to you through His Word. Will you listen? I am a Jesus Pusher!

I am a Jesus Pusher! "***For assuredly, I say to you, till heaven and earth pass away, one jot or one tittle will by no means pass from the law till all is fulfilled***" (Matthew 5:18). Jesus presents the reality of "consistency." God and His Word are the same revelation! There is no inconsistency between Scriptural revelation about God and God Himself! The Scriptures correctly understood give an inerrant revelation of God, adequately embraced and seen, offers a duplication of the Scriptures. Do the Scriptures contain everything there is to know about God? This question remains to be answered. As an illustration, we can compare the Scriptures to an onion with its layers. When one reveals a passage of the Scriptures, then he discovers another layer. It does not contradict the previous revelation but gives additional insight and expands the truth of the revelation, usually so powerful in its impact that it can be called new. There does not seem to be an end to the depth of the Scriptures. God and His Word are the same revelation!

We do not worship a book. The Scriptures are not our God but a revelation of our God and His Word! The Scriptures are what He speaks in a revelation of who He is, describing a fundamental principle; the authority of a person's word is the basis of the person's authority; therefore, to come under the authority of the person, I must come under the authority of his word. To be under the authority of God, I must come under the authority of His Word. I am listening because I am a Jesus pusher!

I am a Jesus Pusher! *"**For assuredly, I say to you, till heaven and earth pass away, one jot or one tittle will by no means pass from the law till all is fulfilled"** (Matthew 5:18). Jesus presents the "composition" of the Scriptures. The part and the whole of the Scriptures are integrated. Jesus described this in the phrase **"one jot or one tittle."** This emphasis establishes the integration of the Scriptures. From the hook of one letter to the complete letter to the word containing the letter to the sentence in which the word abides, to the paragraph, to the chapter, to the book, and the whole Scriptures, the truth is fulfilled! Jesus did not place eternal weight on the meaning of one little mark but the combined truth of the Scriptures. A progressive revelation is given to us throughout the Old Testament Scriptures, climaxing in Jesus.

Jesus is the fulfillment, completion, and full accomplishment of all Scriptures. No wonder He is called *"the Word"* (John 1:1). All God spoke in the Scriptures is lived and revealed in the life of Jesus. Jesus is the visible image of the invisible God (Colossians 1:15). Therefore, Jesus is the "composite" of the Scriptures and the Trinity God. If you desire to be intimate with Jesus, His word reveals Him; if you want intimacy with God, He is Jesus revealed and speaking through the Scriptures. No one can know Jesus without the Written Word, the Bible, or the Living Word, His indwelling Spirit. The Written Word and the Living Word must both be active, or the truth is perverted. Jesus wants to share my mind to reveal Himself to me through the Scriptures. It is as if His lips part and He speaks the Scriptures to me. I know Jesus through the Scriptures. I am a Jesus Pusher!

Jesus PUSHER | 326

I am a Jesus Pusher! *"For assuredly, I say to you, till heaven and earth pass away, one jot or one tittle will by no means pass from the law till all is fulfilled"* (Matthew 5:18). In the "Fulfilled Scriptures" (Matthew 5:17), the "Final Scriptures" (Matthew 5:18) are found. The "interaction" of these two realities creates one revelation. This revelation is Jesus! That means Jesus is of great "consequence!" The impact of the "Fulfilled Scriptures" is found in this Person. He is the "Coming One" (I came) who does not desire or purpose to eliminate the Scriptures (*Do not think I came to destroy – I did not come to destroy*) but to complete in every way the Scriptures (*but to fulfill*). Jesus expands this reality or gives it content in the "Final Scriptures." The Scriptures are eternal; everything they indicate and speak will appear (*all is fulfilled*).), meaning Jesus is the end, goal, and purpose of the Scriptures. Without Him, the Scriptures consist of a dream unfulfilled. Because everything it proposes is incomplete, it is unsuccessful. We find the authority and strength of Jesus in the Scriptures.

Jesus' authority in the Scriptures is the basis of every *"one jot or one tittle"* proclaiming Him. The flow of the letter's smallest mark, the word in every sentence, and every paragraph forming the chapters that constitute the books shout the revelation of Jesus. If we preach the Bible, we must reveal Jesus. Any suggestion that a verse highlights a subject other than Jesus is a misinterpretation of the verse. The Scriptures push nothing but Jesus. If you are in tune with the revelation of the Scriptures, you are a Jesus pusher!

I am a Jesus Pusher! *"For assuredly, I say to you, till heaven and earth pass away, one jot or one tittle will by no means pass from the law till all is fulfilled"* (Matthew 5:18). Jesus is of great "consequence" in the Scriptures because He is the "completion" of the Scriptures. Note the final statement of the "Final Scriptures," *"till* (heos) (an) *all* (panta) *is fulfilled* (ginomai) (Matthew 5:18). "Ginomai," translated *"is fulfilled,"* and meaning, "to become," is a different Greek word translated *"fulfilled"* in the previous verse (Matthew 5:17). All the pieces of the Scriptures from *"one jot or one tittle"* are coming together. The Scriptures are pieces of a puzzle uniquely fitting together; they form one picture, Jesus. They do not form Jesus to cause Jesus! The Scriptures flow from the heart of God in a progressive revelation, bringing us to a completed picture; it is Jesus. God described Jesus for us in the Scriptures. Jesus is now completing the Scriptures. The Scriptures are not a road map to heaven, an instructional manual for life, or a book of rules for living; they are about Jesus.

The "construction" of the Scriptures is Jesus. The Scriptures describe everything God desires for you. The peace, joy, power, strength, wisdom, and life described are in Jesus. Therefore, the focus of your life should be Jesus. If everything God desires for you is in the content of the Scriptures, and the content of the Scriptures, and it is in Jesus, you must embrace Him, and then you will embrace the Scriptures. The Scriptures will be "in" Jesus for all eternity. Therefore, we are not simply referring to the Written Word but also the living Word. They are interacting! Will there be a written form of the Scriptures in heaven that we will study and investigate together? I do not know. But it is not a point of concern. Jesus is *the Word*. I am a Jesus Pusher!

Jesus PUSHER | 328

I am a Jesus Pusher! *"Whoever therefore breaks one of the least of these commandments, and teaches men so, shall be called least in the kingdom of heaven; but whoever does and teaches them, he shall be called great in the kingdom of heaven"* (Matthew 5:19). We must carefully consider this verse in light of the premise of the Sermon on the Mount. The Kingdom is not a location or place to dwell but a relationship with Jesus to embrace! The requirement of this relationship is not in achievement or activities but helplessness (*poor in spirit*), or *"least."* About status, helplessness is the only level in the Kingdom of Heaven. Everyone is *"least."* The moment we elevate ourselves to a position of accomplishment, we are no longer in the Kingdom. James wrote, *"For whoever shall keep the whole law, and yet stumble in one point, he is guilty of all"* (James 2:10). If so, no one *"shall be called great in the kingdom of heaven."* We have all broken *"one of the least of these commandments, and by our very actions taught men so."* We should *"be called least in the kingdom of heaven."*

However, we are not worthless or insignificant. When we unite with the person of Jesus, we become the Kingdom of God, the new creature of the New Covenant, the new creature of the New Covenant. Who He is merges with who I am (helpless). I become one with the One who fulfilled the Scriptures, bringing me into His greatness. As he fulfilled the law in His authority, He now fills the law in my humanity. He accomplishes this on the platform of my helplessness. No wonder I am a Jesus Pusher!

I am a Jesus Pusher! *"Whoever therefore breaks one of the least of these commandments, and teaches men so, shall be called least in the kingdom of heaven; but whoever does and teaches them, he shall be called great in the kingdom of heaven"* (Matthew 5:19). Jesus "fulfilled the Scriptures (Matthew 5:17). His fulfillment of the Scriptures is based on the eternal existence of the "final Scriptures" (Matthew 5:18). Now Jesus presents the "frame of the Scriptures" (Matthew 5:19). Jesus spoke to His culture in their language. They developed so many oral traditions that it was impossible to observe them all. One law contradicted another. Debates arose over *"which is the great commandment in the law"* (Matthew 22:36). The language became *"least"* and *"great."* However, this does not apply to the Scriptures, where every *"jot"* and *"tittle"* is significant. Since the Scriptural law is far beyond us, we are all "least in the kingdom of heaven."

But Jesus is beyond us; He achieved another level! Because Jesus became *"least"* and fulfilled the law and established a new category, "kingdom of heaven." He became "great" because He embraced "least." He opened the door for us to join him in the merger! I will embrace "least" in my life as He did, and He will fill me with His "great." His filling me does not rest on what I accomplish, for I am helpless; it is who I am in Him! No wonder I am a Jesus pusher!

I am a Jesus Pusher! ***"Whoever therefore breaks one of the least of these commandments, and teaches men so, shall be called least in the kingdom of heaven; but whoever does and teaches them, he shall be called great in the kingdom of heaven"*** (Matthew 5:19). There is a correlation between your view of the Scriptures and what you teach. . If you regard parts of the Scriptures as ***"least"*** and unimportant, you will reveal that in what you do and teach. If you choose the parts of the Scriptures you want to focus on, it will shape your expression of truth. Your relationship with the Scriptures will determine the level and presentation of your life.

Jesus uses the word ***"teaches"*** twice in this passage. The Greek word "didasko" is used ninety-seven times as a verb and fifty-nine times as a noun in the New Testament. It expresses the idea of "to instruct" or "to place something in someone's mind." In our passage, the idea of ***"does"*** is connected with the word ***"teaches."*** In describing the individual who embraces only part of the Scriptures as valuable, Jesus uses the word "luo," translated ***"breaks,"*** meaning "to loosen." The word means "to loosen" something fastened, such as a prisoner. It means "to dissolve," as in sever or break. The Book of Acts describes the stern of a ship broken by the violence of the waves (Acts 27:41). In our passage, ***"one of the least of these commandments"*** would be dissolved, annulled, or made void. In other words, it is not necessary to "do." In describing a person who embraces the Scriptures thoroughly, Jesus uses the Greek word "poieo" for ***"does."*** This word expresses what is in the individual expressing more than mere activity or accomplishing a deed. The word means "trees bearing (poieo) fruit."

Jesus came to fulfill the Scriptures. In this accomplishment, He set aside, dissolved, or annulled no part of it. It was not what Jesus did, but what was in Him bearing fruit through Him. That is what He wants to be in us! I am a Jesus Pusher!

Jesus PUSHER | 331

I am a Jesus Pusher! ***"Whoever therefore breaks one of the least of these commandments, and teaches men so, shall be called least in the kingdom of heaven; but whoever does and teaches them, he shall be called great in the kingdom of heaven"*** (Matthew 5:19). The subject of ***"the kingdom of heaven,"*** is mentioned twice in our passage, and is directly connected to each possible situation suggested by Jesus. This subject is not mentioned from the last Beatitude (Matthew 5:10) to our passage (Matthew 5:19). Jesus began the Beatitudes with the subject of the Kingdom (Matthew 5:3), and He ended the Beatitudes with the same subject (Matthew 5:10). Now He ties it directly to our relationship with the Scriptures. As He discusses the Scriptures, Jesus reflects on ***"the kingdom of heaven"*** formed in the Beatitudes. Could it be that the Scriptures are the heart of the Kingdom?

The Kingdom of Heaven is not a location but a relationship. Heaven is a real place, and eternity will find us living there. The Kingdom of Heaven is a spiritual intimacy between God and man. In the Kingdom language, Jesus is the King. He is not the kind of King as seen in our world. Jesus is King in the style of the Kingdom, a bleeding, suffering, and dying King. Jesus is the Servant King! He wants to provide, source, and supply every need in our lives. His plan is always for our best; He has no selfish angle. Everything promised in the Scriptures is in Jesus, and Jesus is in us! The new creature, the Kingdom person, experiences the fulfillment of the Scriptures. I am a Jesus Pusher!

I am a Jesus Pusher! ***"For I say to you, that unless your righteousness exceeds the righteousness of the scribes and Pharisees, you will by no means enter the kingdom of heaven"*** (Matthew 5:20). Jesus presents a significant contrast between ***"the righteousness of the scribes and the Pharisees"*** and the righteousness required to ***"enter the kingdom of heaven."*** The scribes were scholars and teachers of the Scriptures and custodians of the Jewish traditions. The Pharisees advocated precision in the interpretation and performance of the Mosaic code. Theologically and philosophically, they seemed miles apart. The central problem of differences was "righteousness." The Pharisees and scribes criticized Jesus for His liberal views of the oral traditions. Jesus consistently revealed the liberal position of the Pharisees and scribes concerning the law. Jesus established the standard of the Kingdom of Heaven as righteousness that ***"exceeds the righteousness of the scribes and Pharisees."*** This standard is not a goal to which we should aspire; it is the beginning standard for entrance into the Kingdom of Heaven.

The Father filled Jesus, and Jesus viewed the Scriptures through the eyes of His Spirit. The scribes and Pharisees viewed the Scriptures from their self-centered perspective. In fulfilling the Scriptures through the fullness of the Spirit, Jesus moved into a new level of righteousness that the scribes and the Pharisees could not even consider. Jesus calls us to a new level. That new level is not one of "doing" but of intimacy with Him in "being." What an opportunity we have! I am a Jesus Pusher!

Jesus PUSHER | 333

I am a Jesus Pusher! ***"For I say to you, that unless your righteousness exceeds the righteousness of the scribes and Pharisees, you will by no means enter the kingdom of heaven"*** (Matthew 5:20). The Jews could not comprehend how anyone could be more righteous than the scribes and Pharisees. The typical Jewish home had a small patio at the back of its house. Along the edge of the deck, they would grow small herb plants. The fruit of these plants consisted of herbs the size of a pea. The scribes and Pharisees would slice off one-tenth of this small herb to properly tithe. How could anyone tithe more than the scribes and Pharisees? The scribes and Pharisees were in attendance and observed all Jewish feast days. How could anyone be more righteous than compliance to all Jewish feast days? The scribes and Pharisees religiously maintained the necessary sacrifices required by God. How could anyone make more sacrifices or attend more rituals?

The difference in approach between Jesus and the scribes and Pharisees is in focus. The scribes and Pharisees focused on the cosmetic aspect of religion, the external. Jesus always seemed concerned about the inner heart and nature of an individual. The oral traditions of the Pharisees regarded external activities. Although these applications came from the Scriptures, the Pharisees only saw the Scriptures as instructions and laws. Jesus embraced the Scriptures as an expression of the Father's heart. The Kingdom of Heaven is a relationship of intimacy between a helpless person and the Father. Through the activity of the Father's nature, on the platform of my helplessness, He fulfills the Scriptures in spirit and deed. I dwell in the Kingdom relationship. I am a Jesus Pusher!

I am a Jesus Pusher! *"For I say to you, that unless your righteousness exceeds the righteousness of the scribes and Pharisees, you will by no means enter the kingdom of heaven"* (Matthew 5:20). Jesus spent three years of ministry calling the scribes and Pharisees to an inward embracing of the reality of God. They so resisted His teaching that it ended in His crucifixion. A few days before this event, Jesus preached His final public message to a large crowd (Matthew 23). It consisted of a warning against the external emphasis of the scribes and Pharisees. He appealed to His disciples and the crowd not to be like them (Matthew 23:1). In describing this damning religious approach, He said, *"For you cleanse the outside of the cup and dish, but inside they are full of extortion and self-indulgence"* (Matthew 23:25). He continued by explaining what He meant to have no misunderstanding. *"Even so you also outwardly appear righteous to men, but inside you are full of hypocrisy and lawlessness"* (Matthew 23:28). The consequence of such a state became evident. *"Serpents, brood of vipers! How can you escape the condemnation of hell?"* (Matthew 23:33).

The Old Testament prophets often highlighted the shift from the external law to the internal reality of His presence. Jeremiah expressed the words of God in crying, *"I will put My law in their minds, and write it on their hearts; and I will be their God, and they shall be My people"* (Jeremiah 31:33). Ezekiel cried to his people with the words of God. *"I will give you a new heart and put a new spirit within you; I will take the heart of stone out of your flesh and give you a heart of flesh. I will put My Spirit within you and cause you to walk in My statutes, and you will keep My judgments and do them"* (Ezekiel 36:26-27). Although the scribes and Pharisees lived in the time of the Old Covenant, they lived in expectation of the fullness of the Spirit. Living in the external observance, they were to long for the coming of the Messiah and the transition of the internal reality. Yes, the righteousness of the Kingdom of Heaven would far exceed the righteousness of the Old Covenant! I am a Jesus Pusher!

I am a Jesus Pusher! "***For I say to you, that unless your righteousness exceeds the righteousness of the scribes and Pharisees, you will by no means enter the kingdom of heaven***" (Matthew 5:20). How do you calibrate or measure "***righteousness.***" To determine that our righteousness exceeds the righteousness of the scribes and Pharisees, we must discover this, highlighting one of the major pitfalls of legalism. When we measure "***righteousness***" by the letter of the law, the spirit of the law is quickly lost, meaning our measurement becomes inadequate and partial. Immediately we begin to focus on what we can easily accomplish and disregard or excuse those things more difficult.

Jesus clearly said this in His final preached message. "***For you pay tithe of mint and anise and cummin, and have neglected the weightier matters of the law: justice and mercy and faith. These you ought to have done, without leaving the others undone***" (Matthew 23:23). Indeed, they were meticulous concerning tithing, even in more significant measure than the Old Testament Scriptures stated. Yet, those issues of concern to the heart of God, they ignored. The concerns of God's heart are not issues we can discipline ourselves to do. They must flow from a changed nature, the Kingdom person. Jesus must fill me. I am a Jesus Pusher!

Jesus PUSHER | 336

I am a Jesus Pusher! *"For I say to you, that unless your righteousness exceeds the righteousness of the scribes and Pharisees, you will by no means enter the kingdom of heaven"* (Matthew 5:20). The Pharisees were extremely upset because the disciples picked and ate grain from the grainfields on the Sabbath day (Matthew 12:2). Thus, they broke the Sabbath rules punishable by stoning. Jesus gave them Old Testament illustrations where similar acts occurred, and God approved. His final statement to them was a quotation, *"I desire mercy and not sacrifice"* (Matthew 12:7; Hosea 6:6). The Old Testament commanded sacrifices, so this was not wrong. But there is a higher priority in the heart of God. They set aside the deep things of the heart, the more complicated, and focused on the offerings and sacrifices.

A careful examination of our lives may reveal this pattern. An individual forty pounds overweight criticizes the individual who smokes. The Christian who will not speak to his neighbor condemns the murderer. The Christian who refuses to tithe judges the thief. Who can know the depths of their own heart? Jesus calls for openness! Will He not speak to us? He calls us to the new righteousness of His indwelling nature. I am a Jesus pusher!

Jesus PUSHER | 337

I am a Jesus Pusher! *"**For I say to you, that unless your righteousness exceeds the righteousness of the scribes and Pharisees, you will by no means enter the kingdom of heaven**"* (Matthew 5:20). The approach of the scribes and the Pharisees regarding righteousness was self-sourcing. Their righteousness was utterly self-centered. Self for self-glory sourced their righteousness. They became self-satisfied in a religious status of superiority based on their self-sourced activities. They developed a religious system designed to maintain and enhance this self-satisfaction. Their religious activities focused on external, showy things about which they could boast. Jesus confronted them on this issue; He said, *"**How can you believe, who receive honor from one another, and do not seek the honor that comes from the only God?**"* (John 5:44). The Greek word "doxa," translated as *"**honor,**"* refers to opinion and perspective. They received approval and commendation from each other. In this closed system of self-approval, they developed their righteousness. They were never open to the opinion of God.

This approach appeared in their charitable deeds. As they did a charitable deed, the blowing of a trumpet announced their generous gift (Matthew 6:2). In their prayer life, *"**they love to pray standing in the synagogues and on the corners of the streets, that they may be seen by men**"* (Matthew 6:5). When they fasted, *"**they disfigure their faces that they may appear to men to be fasting**"* (Matthew 6:16). With all the instruction and warning Jesus gave to them, their self-sourcing did not change. In His last public sermon, Jesus proclaimed,

"But all their works they do to be seen by men" (Matthew 23:5). Coming to a spiritual death to self-sourcing would mean the Spirit of Jesus would live through them. Not to experience death to self-sourcing meant crucifying Jesus. It is not different for us. I am a Jesus Pusher!

I am a Jesus Pusher! "***For I say to you, that unless your righteousness exceeds the righteousness of the scribes and Pharisees, you will by no means enter the kingdom of heaven***" (Matthew 5:20). Self-sourced righteousness was all the scribes and Pharisees could claim. "***For they being ignorant of God's righteousness, and seeking to establish their own righteousness, have not submitted to the righteousness of God***" (Romans 10:3). Our self-centered will is a supreme trap. We continually fight for ourselves, defend ourselves, and promote ourselves. We base our value and worth on the achievement of self. The only answer to this dilemma is in the message of the Sermon on the Mount. We must "***mourn***" over our helplessness. When we fully embrace our state of destitution, Jesus becomes our source. No wonder Paul exclaimed, "***For Christ is the end of the law for righteousness to everyone who believes***" (Romans 10:4). The Greek word "telos," translated as "***end,***" means "completion" or "fulfillment." Jesus fulfills the Scriptures in us. There is nothing I can achieve that will bring me to this level. The Kingdom's righteousness is not in "doing" but in "relationship." I must be His! I am a Jesus Pusher!

Jesus PUSHER | **339**

I am a Jesus pusher! "For I say to you, that unless your righteousness exceeds the righteousness of the scribes and Pharisees, you will by no means enter the kingdom of heaven" (Matthew 5:20). "Lego," translated *"I say,"* is the first Greek word in our verse. This beginning is a parallel to verse eighteen with the same statement. These words highlight and emphasize the rest of the sentence. What He says becomes emphatic and significant. All the wisdom and knowledge of God indwelling Jesus produces His proposition. We must not treat it lightly.

The second word in the Greek text in our verse is "gar," translated *for.* It assigns a reason for an argument. Jesus is definite about "The Fulfilled Scriptures" (Matthew 5:17). No annulling or addition is in Jesus' relationship with the Scriptures. The reason for this reality is "The Final Scriptures" (Matthew 5:18). The Scriptures are eternal, providing "The Frame of the Scriptures" (Matthew 5:19). It is the boundary within which a Kingdom person lives. Because this is true, Jesus is compelled to communicate this climactic statement (Matthew 5:20). In a sense, it is truth flowing forth from His argument about the Scriptures. On the other hand, it is the reason He proposes this position of the Scriptures. The fulfillment of the Scriptures in Jesus restores humanity to a new level of righteousness required for a person in the Kingdom of Heaven. The Scriptures fulfilled in Jesus open a new door for merging with God in such intimacy that we give expression to His nature, righteousness. That is our destiny! No wonder I am a Jesus Pusher!

I am a Jesus pusher! *"For I say to you, that unless your righteousness exceeds the righteousness of the scribes and Pharisees, you will by no means enter the kingdom of heaven"* (Matthew 5:20). The strong words used in this conclusion are *"you"* and *"yours"* (Matthew 5:20). The opening statement of our passage focuses on the crowd to whom He is speaking, *"For I say to you (humin)."* That places the passage's meaning in that day's cultural setting. We must carefully investigate and understand the Scriptures and righteousness considering the context of Jesus' day. However, He is even more forceful in linking them directly to the righteousness required by saying, *"your righteousness."* No hint of "imputed righteousness" is in His statement. Jesus speaks directly to the individual; He refers to the righteousness they possess. Additional ceremonies or activities are not required to produce a shell or image of righteousness. Finally, Jesus uses *"you"* as the subject contained in the main verb, *enter* (eiserchomai), at the end of the verse as a warning and encouragement placed on each person listening to His message. Each one must have a personal righteousness to enter the relationship known as the "Kingdom of Heaven." This approach promotes questions about "how." "What should I do?" "How can I improve?" But Jesus has already dismissed all those questions as unimportant and irrelevant. We discover our helplessness in "The Formation of the Kingdom" (Matthew 5:3-12). Any attempt to self-source righteousness places us equal to the scribes and Pharisees whose righteousness is beneath the requirement. Jesus proposes personal righteousness, the fulfillment of the Scriptures in our lives.

I am a Jesus pusher! *"**For I say to you, that unless your righteousness exceeds the righteousness of the scribes and Pharisees, you will by no means enter the kingdom of heaven**"* (Matthew 5:20). At first glance, you might consider Jesus changed subjects. He moves from *"**the Law or the Prophets,**"* the Old Testament Scriptures, to *"**righteousness.**"* However, further thought reveals that this is a result of the previous verse (Matthew 5:19). The Scriptures are the boundaries of the righteousness. Jesus compels us to act within the limits of the Scriptures. The Scriptures are the standard by which I can be righteous.

The Greek word "dikaiosune," translated ***righteousness,*** is a noun that is the subject of the sentence. In the Hebrew language, the "tsadaq" word group focuses on "being right." This concept was consistently connected to the covenant God had with His people. We forcibly see a unilateral covenant in the first third of Israelite history. God was their King. We forcibly see a unilateral covenant in the first third of Israelite history. God was their King; they did not have a man king. God provided deliverance from slavery, water from a rock, quail in the bush, manna from the sky, clothing that lasted, and deliverance from their enemies. Although the Israelites were involved in all events, God was their Source! Because God provided everything in the covenant, Israel needed only one thing. They must live within the boundary of the covenant. The boundary was the Law (Scriptures). Living within this boundary was *"**righteousness.**"* However, Israel found it impossible to keep the law! Jesus came to fulfill the Law, Scriptures! We find righteousness only in Him! In merging with Jesus, He fulfills the Scriptures in us. I am a Jesus pusher!!

I am a Jesus pusher! *"**For I say to you, that unless your righteousness exceeds the righteousness of the scribes and Pharisees, you will by no means enter the kingdom of heaven**"* (Matthew 5:20). The meaning was a reference to a life in conformity to a known standard or law. The Pharisees developed their oral traditions. Thus *"righteousness"* was understood in the adherence to the "oral traditions" based upon the Scriptures. Jesus takes us before the "oral traditions" to the Scriptures themselves. The Scriptures are the boundary within which the Kingdom person lives. Any deviation from the Scriptures eliminates the status of "righteousness." Therefore, the standard of righteousness is the Scriptures. The righteousness of a Kingdom person must exceed that of the scribes and Pharisees. The six hundred and thirteen oral traditions became their standard of righteousness. Although the oral traditions may have been initially an application of the Scriptures, they became more important than the Scriptures. In effect, the oral traditions substituted stale, rigid activities for living relationship in the covenant.

The Pharisees and scribes found they could not achieve the standard of righteousness in the Scriptures. Why? No doubt, they felt the problem was the law, the commandments. If they could adjust the commandments, all would be well. They did not realize the problem was with the "source," not the Scriptures. They lived through self-sourcing in all areas; thus, their righteousness was self-sourced. Jesus is the new Source for fulfilling the Scriptures and being righteous! I am a Jesus pusher!!

I am a Jesus pusher! *"For I say to you, that unless your righteousness exceeds the righteousness of the scribes and Pharisees, you will by no means enter the kingdom of heaven"* (Matthew 5:20). The oral traditions were their attempt to simplify the commandments. This simplification placed them in reach with self-sourcing. However, this did not work despite self-justification and all endeavors. The next step was to select the most important laws and focus on keeping them. But what is the most important commandment? Lengthy debates began to arise. A *"lawyer"* confronted Jesus. Here is the question he wanted to debate with Jesus. *"Teacher, which is the great commandment in the law?"* (Matthew 22:36). *"Jesus said to him, 'You shall love the Lord your God with all your heart, with all your soul, and with all your mind.' This is the first and great commandment. And the second is like it: 'You shall love your neighbor as yourself.' On these two commandments hang all the Law and the Prophets"* (Matthew 22:37-40).

The Greek word "krematai," translated *hang*, is a metaphor. A custom was hanging the laws in a public place for all to see, meaning that the Scriptures contained love and relationship. These were by far the most familiar, most quoted, and most copied Scripture passages in Judaism. Jesus acclaimed these verses as the great commandment; they are the heart of the Scriptures. We can only know righteousness within the boundaries of the Scriptures. Jesus fulfills the Scriptures, and He wants to merge with us, expressing the heart of the Scriptures through us! In Him, we are righteous, loving God and each other! I am a Jesus Pusher!!

I am a Jesus pusher! *"For I say to you, that unless your righteousness exceeds the righteousness of the scribes and Pharisees, you will by no means enter the kingdom of heaven"* (Matthew 5:20). In our passage, Jesus strongly calls everyone to a new level of righteousness, because there is a new sourcing. Jesus sets the standard above the highest they could imagine for their day, the righteousness of the scribes and Pharisees. He said, *"For I say to you, that unless your righteousness exceeds* (perisseuo) *. . ."* (Matthew 5:20). *"Exceeds"* is the main verb; it expresses the idea of abundance, to be in excess, or to exceed in number of measure. However, there is a Greek adverb, "pleion," not translated into English translations. It modifies the verb *"exceeds"* and is a superlative. A superlative expresses the highest or a high degree of quality. It means "many, much, or utmost," increasing the emphasis of the verb *"exceeds."*

This standard would seem impossible unless everyone fully understood "The Formation of the Kingdom." The Beatitudes express God's nature flowing through the new creation of the Kingdom of Heaven. We are revealed in our helplessness now experiencing the flow of His Spirit. In embracing oneness with Him, we become the Kingdom of God. The scribes and Pharisees sourced their righteousness from their helplessness, and they experienced nothing but failure and defeat. No comparison is between the self-sourcing of the Old Covenant and the Spirit-sourcing of the New Covenant. The merger between God and man produces a life that *"exceeds"* in righteousness, the righteousness of God! Jesus wants to live in and through me! I am a Jesus Pusher!!

I am a Jesus pusher!! ***"For I say to you, that unless your righteousness exceeds the righteousness of the scribes and Pharisees, you will by no means enter the kingdom of heaven"*** (Matthew 5:20). The response to Jesus' message was astonishment (Matthew 7:28).). The Greek word "explesso," translated ***astonished***, means "to knock out of one's senses." The impact of Jesus' message from the beginning was beyond anything they heard from the scribes (Matthew 7:29). Who could think there was righteousness more excellent than the scribes and Pharisees? But the most startling is "when" we must experience this righteousness. If it is a goal to be achieved eventually, we might find it challenging to engage in meriting such righteousness. However, Jesus again presents this righteousness as a gift of oneness in Him. We do not receive this at the end of the journey. We have this righteousness at the beginning. You do not progress slowly toward such righteousness; you experience it at the entrance to the Kingdom. This righteousness is the result of becoming the Kingdom!

The phrase "by no means" is a translation of two Greek words, "ou me." These are two negatives side by side. "Ou" is an independent negative. It states the reality of the case. "Me" is a dependent negative expressing a personal opinion and belief. The reality of truth and Jesus' opinion are the same! ***"You . . . enter"*** is a translation of the Greek word "eiserchomai." The prefix of the main word is "eis," which means "into." The main word "erchomai" means "to come." You do not develop into righteousness after dwelling in the Kingdom for a time; instead, you start with it. In our helplessness, we experience His person; in this combination, the Kingdom becomes a reality. He expresses His nature through us, the nature of meekness, fulfillment, mercy, holiness, peace, and joy amid persecution (Matthew 5:3-12). I am a Jesus pusher!!!

I am a Jesus pusher! As we progress through the Sermon on the Mount, we must always return to the overall view. We began with the ingredients of the Kingdom, "The Formation of the Kingdom" (Matthew 5:3-12). We are *"poor in spirit"* (Matthew 5:3). We are destitute in all resource, and we dwell in a state of helplessness, which causes our "mourning" (Matthew 5:4). We must have a consistent consciousness of our condition. The One who comforts unites with us! God forms the Kingdom in this unity between Himself and man. We are comforted, meek, filled, merciful, pure in heart, peacemakers, and victorious in persecution (Matthew 5:4-12).

We can see the imagery of salt and light in "The Function of the Kingdom" (Matthew 5:13-16), a state of being! The world "sees" because we "are" in the merger with Him. God presented this dream in the Old Covenant and now fulfills it in the New Covenant. Jesus proposes a beautiful picture, "The Fulfillment of the Kingdom, Acknowledged" (Matthew 5:17-20), every law, proposal, and intent of the Scriptures. The Living Word and the Written Word are united in one presentation.

What does this look like for us? The final section of this chapter is "The Fulfillment of the Kingdom, The Application" (Matthew 5:21-48). As we step into this section, beware of the jolt. Jesus compares man's best effort with the best effort of God and man united in the Kingdom. There are six major areas of comparison. Merger with Jesus causes Him to live out His life in every relationship! I am a Jesus pusher!

I am a Jesus pusher! The premise of the Sermon on the Mount is my helplessness merged with His greatness! Jesus illustrates this reality in six significant areas of our lives. MURDER/hate and forgiveness (Matthew 5:21-25)

>MORALITY/adultery and lust (Matthew 5:26-30)
>
>MARRIAGE/divorce and concern (Matthew 5:31-32)
>
>MORALS/swearing and honesty (Matthew 5:33-37)
>
>MALICE/revenge and forgiveness (Matthew 5:38-42)
>
>MOTIVE/hate and love (Matthew 5:43-48)

As we view these six areas of application, two things are happening. One is INTENSIFICATION. Jesus introduced this with the call to righteousness that *"exceeds the righteousness of the scribes and Pharisees"* (Matthew 5:20). The call of each application is an impossibility. We are to move from not murdering to eliminating anger, refraining from adultery to destroying lust, causing division to causing godliness, forced honesty to always being honest, receiving justice to generous forgiving, and from hating to perfect love.

Jesus does a second interesting thing in this application, the fulfillment of the Kingdom INTERNATIONALIZATION. Each illustration moves from an exterior behavior to an internal motive. No wonder Jesus cried out at the end of this chapter, *"Therefore you shall be perfect, just as your Father in heaven is perfect"* (Matthew 5:48). What else could we be? His nature indwells our poverty-stricken hearts and sources us with His being. We live an impossible life and dwell in an impossible state. What we desperately try to achieve in the outward and fail is superseded by the inward reality through union with Him. He eliminates the effort and replaces struggling with resting. The Kingdom of God becomes who we are. Our lives reveal His heart. Rejoice in this hour. Union with Him is the Kingdom. I am a Jesus pusher!!!

I am a Jesus pusher!!! In the Sermon on the Mount, Jesus launches into the proclamation of six illustrations giving explanation and validity to His proposition. Jesus spiritually weaves the illustrations to form one message, the message of the "perfect nature of the Father" (Matthew 5:48). Jesus addresses every area of living in these six illustrations. He gives us three sets with two illustrations each. The first addresses the "Cardinal Truth" about life, containing the illustrations of "Murder" (Matthew 5:21-26) and "Morality" (Matthew 5:27-30). Here we investigate our view of relationships within the context of life. If righteousness is not present in this realm, there is no possibility for purity in the remaining areas. The following two illustrations consider "Covenant Truth." "Marriage (Matthew 5:31-32) and "Morals" (Matthew 5:33-37) expand God's nature into our commitment to each other. Without His nature, we fail in all our covenant interactions with others. The last two illustrations address "Core Truth." "Malice" (Matthew 5:38-42) and "Motive" (Matthew 5:43-48) demand a heart filled with God's nature. He calls us to be like Him!

In each illustration, Jesus discusses the sermon's premise. He does not give detailed teaching on the subject of the illustration but applies the New Covenant, the filling of the Holy Spirit, to the subject! It appears that it is impossible to achieve each illustration supporting the premise of the message. We are helpless and can do nothing without the intimacy and enhancement of Jesus' presence. He does not aid us but merges with us to form a new creature, the Kingdom person. This new person lives on a level the Old Testament people only dreamed about. Life is in Jesus! I am a Jesus pusher!!!

I am a Jesus pusher!!! ***"You have heard it said to those of old . . . But I say to you"*** (Matthew 5:21, 22). Truth has an essential, core, and fundamental understanding. Guilt is proof of this statement displayed in your life. Each time you go against "present knowledge," you experience guilt. God planned distinct avenues for the communication of truth. One of those avenues is "Artistic Speaking." All true artistic works are a product of the individual; they constitute how the artist feels, thinks, and cares. All creation, flowing from His inner being, carries the touch of His Person. Are you not made in His image (Genesis 1:26)? Another avenue is "Audio Speaking." God is not silent. The author of Hebrews writes, ***"has in these last days spoken to us by His Son"*** (Hebrews 1:2). God spoke in the Old Testament through a cloud by day, a pillar of fire by night, a burning bush, and a snake on a pole. God also gave us writings on tablets of stone. The list is endless! In our previous study (Matthew 5:17-20), Jesus declared God's proclamation through the Scriptures. He has not left us without instruction. God also uses "Atmospheric Speaking." God consistently bombards the atmosphere of our living with His presence and speaking. Jesus did not say, "You have read." Many in the crowd Jesus spoke to could not read. Even if they could read, the Old Testament scrolls were unavailable. He referred to what their teachers had taught them. God permeated the atmosphere of their culture. Jesus uses all of these methods to speak the heart of God to us! Will we listen to Him? I am a Jesus pusher!!!

I am a Jesus pusher!! "***You have heard it said to those of old . . . But I say to you***" (Matthew 5:21-22). A mission statement of the past generation was, "You and I have no right to hear the Gospel message again until every man in the world has heard it at least once. We have heard it more than our share compared to those who have never heard it. But God is so gracious and merciful to us. To all spoken in the past, Jesus added, ***"But I say to you!"*** Jesus has "Authoritative Speaking." The Greek word (lego) translated as ***"I say"*** is one word. However, Jesus added the Greek word "ego," translated as ***"I,"*** giving a double emphasis on the word ***"I."***

Jesus now gives the proper explanation of the Scriptures. The "Fulfillment of the Kingdom, Acknowledged" (Matthew 5:17-20) provides the significance of this statement. Jesus does not discard the Scriptures. He fulfills and explains what God intended in the Scriptures. This explanation is true of the inner witness He placed in you. Jesus gives content to the design of your being, His image. If there were any misunderstandings or wrong focus regarding what God intended, Jesus clarified it. No one has the right to do this equal to Jesus. He is the fulfillment of the Scriptures. Not one jot or tittle passed away until Jesus completed the Scriptures. In this fulfillment is the authority to speak to us. The issue is not whether He is speaking or has the authority to speak; the problem is whether we are listening. Listening means to come under the authority of what He says. The Living and Written Word are united in presenting the truth to our lives. He is not only speaking but empowering obedience in our abandonment to Him. He becomes both the truth to be obeyed and the obedience of the truth. I am a Jesus pusher!!!

I am a Jesus pusher!!! ***"You have heard it said to those of old . . . But I say to you"*** (Matthew 5:21-22). Jesus equates His words with God's words because they are God's words. He said, ***"You have heard that it was said to them of old"*** (Matthew 5:21). The undercurrent of this statement is that God spoke to them in the past. The foundation of this truth is God Himself. The truth about ***"murder"*** was not first spoken in the law but was spoken by God before the law (Genesis 9:6). God spoke this from the beginning. Now Jesus fulfilled this, speaking with clarification! The section (Matthew 5:17-20) introduced our passage and declared the speaking of God. Jesus revealed His relationship with the Scriptures, hearing the voice of the Father through the Scriptures. God placed His nature on the table of our world in written form. Jesus, the Second Member of the Trinity, came to our world to submit His life to the formation of this nature. He fulfills everything God spoke in the Scriptures. Jesus is the speaking of God to us! No wonder the Scriptures call Him "the Word." All the Scriptures say about murder is clarified and made seeable in Jesus.

You cannot understand the Scriptures without intimacy with Jesus. You cannot believe the Scriptures without believing in Jesus. The Living Word expresses the Written Word; they are the same. Now Jesus speaks the Word to us! He is "Accusative Speaking." The standard of not committing the physical act of murder is considered a compromise to the truth of God's nature. What was once a great accomplishment is now regarded as subnormal for even the beginner in the Kingdom of Heaven. This standard is a call for the intimacy Jesus has with the Father to become present in us.

I am a Jesus pusher!!! *"But I say to you that whoever
is angry with his brother shall be in danger of the
judgement"* (Matthew 5:22). Jesus never participates in
"Argument Speaking" of the Scriptures. In previous studies,
we discovered a fallacy that gripped the Jewish nation. They
operated under the assumption that the Scriptures' study was
more valuable than doing the Scriptures. This fallacy caused
debates, arguments, and discussions of the law but put little
emphasis on practical living. The disobedience of the Scriptures
had little consequence in their minds. Although the Pharisees
were continually upset with Jesus because He and His disciples
broke their laws, they were more upset about His teachings
about the Scriptures. Jesus calling His disciples to live beyond the
righteousness of the Pharisees irritated them.

Now Jesus gives His disciples His "Application Speaking."
Everything Jesus lived and said about *"You shall not murder"*
is now going to be applied to our lives. He equates anger with
murder (Matthew 5:22). While the outside deed of murder is
a product of anger, the presence of anger is the same as murder.
This revelation becomes even more disturbing as He applies it
to our relationship with God (Matthew 5:23-24). I feel content
and secure in my relationship with God. I am one of the "people
of God," but this relationship with God is suddenly questioned.
It is not because I have murdered but because I am not in the
right relationship with my fellow man. The focus is not on how
my fellowman feels about me but how I feel about him. The two
categories of relationship with God and relationship with man
now overlap (Matthew 22:37-39). I want to be an expression of
Jesus to my fellow man! I am a Jesus pusher!!!

I am a Jesus pusher!!! ***But I say to you that whoever is angry with his brother shall be in danger of the judgement"*** (Matthew 5:22). This passage is a part of the "Application Speaking" of Jesus (Matthew 5:21-26). Jesus applies the premise of the Sermon on the Mount, linking our relationship with God to our relationship with our fellowmen. His application is not about how we outwardly treat them but how we inwardly feel about them.

Jesus continued to illustrate this truth in an "Adornment Speaking." He placed the truth in the middle of their daily hour of prayer and sacrificial offerings (Matthew 5:23-24). The implication is that our religious activities supersede our relationship with others. Our relationship with others overrides the importance of our duty to God. In other words, our commitment to God is to express His heart to our fellowmen. He plants this truth in the middle of an argument over practical matters, which might take you to court (Matthew 5:25, 26). Live in inner peace and let this peace flow to your circumstances. Jesus is not proposing that we must never have an adversary but that we must never be one! These would be impossible and frightening proposals except for the reality of the "Formation of the Kingdom" (Matthew 5:3-12). God fills our helplessness with His resource. As the fullness of the Spirit produced this through Jesus, He will do this through us. We become one with the Spirit of Jesus, forming a new creature, the Kingdom person! I am a Jesus pusher!!!

I am a Jesus pusher!!! ***"You have heard that it was said to those of old, 'You shall not murder'"*** (Matthew 5:21). Why does Jesus begin with "murder?" Murder is a violent act that tries to destroy the image of God. God spoke all creation into being, but ***"formed man of the dust of the ground and breathed into his nostrils the breath of life; and man became a living being"*** (Genesis 2:7). Our structure has the fingerprints of God upon it. ***"So God created man in His own image; in the image of God He created him; male and female He created them"*** (Genesis 1:27). After the flood, God spoke to Noah the first Biblical law concerning murder. ***"Whoever sheds man's blood, by man his blood shall be shed; for in the image of God He made man"*** (Genesis 9:6). As Jesus expands this in our passage, "anger," "Raca" (treating your brother as worthless), and calling him a "fool" (a stupid one) expresses contempt for the image of God in which He created man (Matthew 5:22).

What is the image of God? It is not the physical shape of our being. The biblical account highlights the essence of relationship. We are created beings capable of relationship with God's nature; the rest of creation does not have this. The indication is that all creation has a connection with God through our relationship with Him. We are the critical element that links all creation to God. The Kingdom of Heaven is the fulfillment of the image of God! We are helpless. He comes in His resource, His nature, and with God, we become the Kingdom of Heaven. The capacity of this relationship is the heart of the image of God in our creation. Jesus wants to indwell me! I am a Jesus pusher!!!

Jesus PUSHER | 355

I am a Jesus pusher!!! *"You have heard that it was said to those of old, 'You shall not murder'"* (Matthew 5:21). Jesus starts His six illustrations with murder because it is rebellion against the image of God. Murder is an attempt to abolish the physical expression of the relationship between God and man. For this reason, Jesus quickly moves into the spiritual application of this physical act. Anger has the same result as murder; therefore, anger equals murder. It abolishes relationships. This result is and has always been the demonic desire. Jesus said, *"You are of your father the devil, and the desires of your father you want to do. He was a murderer* (manslayer) *from the beginning, and does not stand in the truth"* (John 8:44). It seems the devil's single desire is to destroy the image of God that continually confronts him in every human being. In our fallen nature (carnal mind), we share the nature Satan personifies. Murder, anger, and hate flow from our heart's center, attempting to abolish all evidence of the image of God around us.

Jesus calls us to the merge Adam had with God. That is our destiny! God wants to fill us with Himself, so we might express His invisible image to our world. While murdering another may eliminate that person's expression, anger and hate in me eliminates His image through me! We do not express His attributes such as omnipresence or omniscience. We express who God is, His image! His holy nature merges with us to form a new creature. The Spirit of Jesus and I become one! I am a Jesus pusher!!!

I am a Jesus pusher!!! ***"You have heard that it was said to those of old, 'You shall not murder'"*** (Matthew 5:21). Jesus proceeds to highlight the division between your brother (created in the image of God) and you (created in the image of God). He offers the picture of the amazing daily sacrifice on the altar (Matthew 5:23). This daily sacrifice illustrates all truth about the relationship between God and man. This relationship is the image of God fulfilled in every person offering sacrifice. God has a specific plan for my life! My fingerprints differ from all others who have ever been or will ever be. My DNA is distinctive to me! My personality is unique in all its expressions of ideas and thoughts. Therefore, the image of God is not a focus on all humanity but on every person.

If God fills my helplessness with His Person, I do not become like you! God's image expresses itself through me, uniquely and specifically planned and determined by God! The division between us murders the plan of God's image in each of us. How may I be in oneness with God's image in my life if I will not embrace the image of God in your life? How I feel about you affects how I feel about God! His plan for you and me comes together to express God's large plan for everyone, the redemptive plan. Murder, anger, treating you as worthless, and viewing you as stupid destroys the plan of God. Reconciliation restores the plan! A person cannot propose to embrace the plan of God for their life while destroying the plan of God for another. No wonder Jesus said that we must ***"leave your gift there before the altar, and go your way. First be reconciled to your brother, and then come and offer your gift"*** (Matthew 5:24). I am a Jesus pusher!!!

I am a Jesus pusher!!! ***"You have heard that it was said to those of old, 'You shall not murder'"*** (Matthew 5:21). Murder, anger, and hate are attempts to destroy the image of God in another. Jesus does not address the resistance issue from the one with whom you want reconciliation. Why? In our passage, this seems to be a non-issue! I cannot do anything about what is in my brother. His response is never an excuse for my resistance to being reconciled. In other words, reconciliation must take place in me towards my brother. It must express and offer reconciliation; His response is not the issue. My response to reconciliation is an expression of God's nature possessing me. Therefore, "murder" (resisting reconciliation with my brother) not only destroys my brother, but it also destroys me.

Our righteousness must exceed the righteousness of the person who justifies his disdain and contempt for his brother. The spiritual realm of our individual lives cannot maintain the nature of God and the nature of Satan within the same realm. Jesus will state this again and again. At the close of the Lord's Prayer, Jesus said, ***"For if you forgive men their trespasses, your heavenly Father will also forgive you. But if you do not forgive men their trespasses, neither will your Father forgive your trespasses"*** (Matthew 6:14-15). The provision of God's heart through Jesus is the forgiveness of every individual. God forgives everyone! Every person decides if they will accept such forgiveness and live in reconciliation with God. My heart should never cause a lack of relationship through reconciliation! I want the heart of Jesus. I am a Jesus pusher!!!

I am a Jesus pusher!!! ***"You have heard that it was said to those of old, 'You shall not murder'"*** (Matthew 5:21). Jesus calls us to exceed the righteousness of the scribes and Pharisees by moving from not committing physical murder to not having an attitude of murder. Considering my brother stupid and viewing him as worthless is an attitude of anger. We can only experience this high level of righteousness in the Kingdom of Heaven. The Kingdom of Heaven is your helplessness filled with His nature. If you are the Kingdom, there is no need to offer sacrifices at the altar of God unless you go to your brother with the attitude of God. Oneness with the Father cannot be known except in the flow of His nature through us to others. Whether your brother accepts reconciliation with you is not the issue. The issue is the flow of God's nature through you; anything less than this flow is murder.

The further Jesus proceeds in the passage (Matthew 5:21-26), the farther He gets from the subject of "physical murder." He insists that we must render everything necessary to our brother, who becomes our adversary, to keep our differences from coming to the public court. My brother may refuse reconciliation and become my enemy. Does that nullify any requirement to cater to his desires or demands? Can I not shake the dust off my feet and depart? Have I not done my part to reconcile and need to go no further? Jesus is practical in His approach to the materialistic world and our relationship with His Father. We must render to our brother, who becomes our adversary, everything necessary to restore him, even paying ***"the last penny"*** (Matthew 5:26). It is the heart of Jesus. I am a Jesus pusher!!!

I am a Jesus pusher!! *"You have heard that it was said to those of old"* (Matthew 5:21). Bible scholars are divided about the introductory statement of this verse. Jesus said, *"You have heard that it was said,"* then He added the phrase, *"those* (tois) *of old."* The Bible translators are divided on using the words *"to"* or *"by"* to connect the two phrases. If *"to"* is used, it assumes Moses spoke, *"You shall not kill,"* to the fathers of Israel. Now Jesus overruled the Scriptures by adding superior instructions. However, if *"by"* is used, Jesus' reference is to the interpretation of the scribes of the Scriptures. Jesus restated the true meaning of the Old Testament to correct the adjustment the scribes and Pharisees imposed on the Scriptures.

Jesus just said, *"Do not think that I came to destroy the Law or the Prophets. I did not come to destroy but to fulfill"* (Matthew 5:17). Jesus continued without variance regarding His relationship with the Scriptures, the nature and heart of God given to us in written form. Embracing the Scriptures is embracing the nature of God. Jesus became man and allowed the Scriptures to shape His life. The Scriptures express the nature of God, and Jesus reveals the nature of God. He wants to bring us back to the truth of the Scriptures. Nothing beyond or above this exists! Jesus is the Living Word who speaks the Written Word to our lives. Will we be listening? I am a Jesus pusher!!!

I am a Jesus pusher!!! *"You have heard that it was said to those of old, 'You shall not murder,'. . . But I say to you"* (Matthew 5:21-22). The truth of the Scriptures is not about a physical ACTION but a spiritual ATTITUDE (Matthew 5:22). Perhaps we should begin with a disclaimer. We are not among those who advocate that physical actions do not matter, nor do we propose that physical activities do not exist or are random. The attitude of the heart will, of necessity, declare itself in a person's actions. Thus, physical activity becomes a symptom of the person's core. Jesus expressed this in His first statement about murder. Murder is a physical act that expresses the attitude of anger and the need to demean and belittle another person (Matthew 5:22).

Every generation battles to keep this concept in proper perspective. When we do not hold this perspective, it is called antinomianism. Antinomianism is the view that Christians are exempt from the demands of moral law because of the abundance of divine grace, the only source of salvation. Many accused the Apostle Paul of holding this false doctrine. He wrote, *"And why not say, 'Let us do evil that good may come'? − as we are slanderously reported and as some affirm that we say"* (Romans 3:8). Paul heartily denied the accusation that proper conduct is irrelevant in the Christian experience. He also wrote, *"What shall we say then? Shall we continue in sin that grace may abound? Certainly not! How shall we who died to sin live any longer in it?"* (Romans 6:1-2). He continued, *"What then? Shall we sin because we are not under law but under grace? Certainly not!*

Do you not know that to whom you present yourselves slaves to obey, you are that one's slaves whom you obey, whether of sin leading to death, or of obedience leading to righteousness?" (Romans 6:15-16). Jesus must fill us! I am a Jesus pusher!!!

I am a Jesus pusher!!! "***You have heard that it was said to those of old, 'You shall not murder,'... But I say to you***" (Matthew 5:21-22). Jesus does not dismiss the importance of the physical. He highlights the source of such action. John, in his first epistle, exposed the Gnostics of his hour. They were antinomian in their teaching. This thought produced an unscriptural dualism that divorced matter from spirit. Irredeemably corrupted was the state of all matter or physical. The obvious conclusion of this thought is a dualistic world. The Gnostics believed it does not matter what you do in the physical because it is only the spirit of man that matters. They practiced their body passions without inhibition so their soul might shine brighter in comparison. The Gnostics proposed, "Give to the flesh the things of the flesh and to the spirit the things of the spirit."

Jesus brings us back to the Scriptural view! In human life, we cannot separate the physical and spiritual, and we must maintain the inner action of these two vital areas. What goes on in one area deeply affects what happens in another area. Our spiritual attitude affects our physical activity, as our physical activity affects our spiritual attitude. However, do not be tricked into the perspective that physical activity is the only measure of the spiritual attitude. We must not judge murder by its physical action. The attitude of the heart births the physical actions. The Kingdom person merges with the nature of God and gives expression to the holiness of God. Jesus and the believer have formed a new creature! I am a Jesus pusher!!!

Jesus PUSHER | 362

I am a Jesus pusher!!! ***"You have heard that it was said to those of old, 'You shall not murder,'... But I say to you"*** (Matthew 5:21-22). The New Covenant focuses on the inner spiritual attitude demonstrated in physical action, changing our approach to "correction!" If I want a life change, where do I start? I have to get off of these drugs; I must go to some meetings and quit drinking; I must stop killing people. I will buy a punching bag, put a picture of the person I hate on it, vent all my murderous thoughts on that picture and beat it to death. This therapy may eliminate the physical act of murder, but it only temporarily calms my murderous desire. That may be better than no correction at all, especially if I am the one you want to murder. However, this approach does not solve the problem. The problem is in the spiritual attitude. We need a nature change in the depth of our being. All other corrections are a bandage, not a correction. We go to counseling, take anger management classes, and attend twelve-step programs. These only help us if they bring us a nature change in our spiritual attitude.

Jesus proposes we embrace our helplessness so the Spirit of Jesus can merge with us. His nature fused with our nature will radically change the source of our outward actions. That is not the management of our anger but the elimination of it. One might protest, "This is impossible." That merely proves the premise of Jesus' sermon. We are helpless. He must come and saturate our lives with Himself. His heart and my heart must become one. We have moved from rules to a relationship, from law to loyalty to a Person. Jesus is the answer! I am a Jesus pusher!!!

I am a Jesus pusher!!! ***"You have heard that it was said to those of old, 'You shall not murder,'...But I say to you"*** (Matthew 5:21, 22). The New Covenant focuses on the inner spiritual attitude demonstrated in physical action. This truth will also change our approach to "conviction." How easy it is to justify my physical "action." Yes, I did kill him; but he deserved to die after what he did to me! The scribes, Sadducees, and Pharisees were firmly in this category. They could justify their actions against Jesus and the disciples because of their law. The law told them they were right. But legalism measures only outward physical activity. Are we guilty in our spiritual attitude? The measure of right and wrong is the spiritual attitude, not the physical action.

This truth will change our approach to "communication." What causes ministry? What do we want to achieve as a church ministering to our community? Is it to get bad people to do good things? Is it to take homeless people and bring them back into society as productive people? Is it to take those in prison and establish lives according to the laws of the land? Does not every person need a nature change in their relationship with Jesus?

Can we begin with who we are? Will you and I examine every physical act of our lives in light of the spiritual attitude that produces it? Oh, I want the mind of Christ! I am a Jesus pusher!

Jesus PUSHER | **364**

I am a Jesus pusher!!! Jesus proposed that the truth of the Scriptures would move us from a physical ASSOCIATION to a spiritual ATTACHMENT (Matthew 5:23-24). Jesus addressed His disciples and many common Jews. They participated daily in an animal sacrifice to God. The significance of this sacrifice contains the spiritual type or symbol it represented. It was not the physical act of killing an animal that brought them into the presence of God. The attitude of acceptance, belief, and the embrace of the spiritual value symbolized in the act is the heart of the matter!

This attitude is why Jesus interrupted our physical association (whatever it may be) and pointed us to our attitude toward each other. God is not interested in a physical routine of worship. Is He thrilled with how high we raise our hands in praise? Is the issue how loud you sing or shout His name? If you and I do not embrace His heart as we sing His name on Sunday, we are the same as the one cursing His name on Monday. Moreover, if we have the right spiritual attitude in bringing our sacrifice to Him, He will convict us of any wrong attitude toward our brother. In other words, there is no way to have a proper attitude toward God in worship and maintain a bad attitude toward each other. We cannot overlook this conflict. God will continually remind us of how He feels about our brother.

Can we begin with ourselves? Do I have the mind of Christ? Is my attitude towards those around me the attitude of Christ? I must merge with Him. I am a Jesus pusher!!!

Jesus PUSHER | 365

I am a Jesus pusher!! In the illustration of "murder," Jesus concludes by moving from a physical ADVERSARY to spiritual ACCOUNTING (5:2-26). There is a definite progression in the overall passage. Jesus moves from highlighting an inner attitude of murder (Matthew 5:22) to a conflict between brothers (Matthew 5:23) to an adversary (Matthew 5:25). If I do not have the nature or attitude of God, my relationship with others progresses downward. Jesus moves from an inner spiritual condition (Matthew 5:22) to an encounter with my brother (Matthew 5:23), to an officer, to the judge, to prison (Matthew 5:25).

In other words, do not allow anyone to become your adversary. Where do we begin? It starts with your attitude, the attitude of Jesus! The focus of this passage is on my spiritual attitude. I cannot control what others may do. How they feel or what they express is beyond my jurisdiction. However, this is not true of my state. I must know the mind of Christ! Those who might be my adversaries cannot because God reconciles me with them. The adversarial attitude will be cleansed in my heart by the mind of Christ. I may be their adversary in their mind, but in my heart, they are not.

The plea of Jesus from the first words of the Sermon on the Mount is that we are the helpless ones who embrace our poverty (Matthew 5:3, 4). God fills us with His nature, forming the Kingdom of God. Flowing through and from this new creation is meekness, filling, mercy, and peace, and in the experience of persecution, we can fully see these elements (Matthew 5:10). I want my life to push Jesus!

www.ingramcontent.com/pod-product-compliance
Lightning Source LLC
Chambersburg PA
CBHW020148090426
42734CB00008B/737